Into No Man's Land

Into
No Man's Land

A HISTORICAL MEMOIR

Irene Miller

Voice/Vision Holocaust Survivor Oral History Archive
University of Michigan-Dearborn

University of Michigan-Dearborn
4901 Evergreen Rd.
Dearborn, MI 48128

All images are from the author's personal collection, except as noted in the captions. Images not from the author's personal collection are reprinted with permission of their respective copyright holders.

ISBN 13: 978-0-933691-18-6

Library of Congress Control Number: 2012942103

*Dedicated to my sons Avner and Dan and
to my daughter Naomi who lives in my heart.*

CONTENTS

ACKNOWLEDGEMENTS

They say that it takes a village to raise a child; I found out that it takes almost a village to publish a memoir.

I am grateful to everyone who was a part of that village.

Specifically my gratitude goes to Barbara Kriigel, representing the University of Michigan-Dearborn, for her help in many phases of publishing this book. Her diverse knowledge and willingness to assist made working with her a pleasure.

My thanks to Tish O'Dowd for inviting me to her class "Advanced Fiction Writing" at the University of Michigan, and for editing the first draft of my manuscript. The "No Man's Land" chapter I wrote in her class as a free-standing story. My fellow students, each younger than my children, said that it was an interesting story, but unreal. I did not tell them it was a chapter of my life.

Thanks to Judith Glass for the generosity of her time and for her skills in editing the memoir.

I am grateful to Katherine McCracken for her close, critical reading of the manuscript.

I thank Sandy Kashdan-Werner for copy editing.

My gratitude goes to Miriam Brysk for the cover of my book and for editing the photographs.

Thanks to Harriet Saperstein and Loraine Stear for their constructive feedback and support.

Foreword

In 1998, Dr. Sidney Bolkosky, Director of the Voice/Vision Holocaust Survivor Oral History Archive, conducted an oral history interview with Irene Miller. During her interview, Irene is asked if she considers herself a survivor and she quickly replies, "No, no." When queried further, however, she more cautiously answers, "It has become part of my identity. It's not something I carry in my head or in my pocket on a daily basis. But it is part of my identity. How active of an identity, in day in and day out life, I don't think about it." For many Holocaust survivors, questions of identity are closely tied to their experiences during the war. As interviews like Irene's show, there were many paths to survival, and not all of them led through the camps and ghettos of what David Rousset called the "concentrationary universe."

Irene Miller's *Into No Man's Land: A Historical Memoir* is a chronicle of one of these many paths; one not travelled by the majority of those who survived the Holocaust. As such, it is an important contribution to Holocaust literature not only because it chronicles a different type of survival, but also because it is the story of a world lost and of a child forced to endure the pain of separation and the deaths of loved ones. Furthermore, it is important because it invokes broader questions about the Holocaust and how we, as observers of the past, view it now. How is the Holocaust defined and who defines it? Do different types of Holocaust survival exist? If so, can they be compared with each other?

As curator of the Voice/Vision Holocaust Survivor Oral History Archive, I often receive inquiries from Holocaust survivors or their family members about conducting an interview for the archive. In most instances, these survivors share what could be considered a "common" Holocaust experience. Nazi occupation was followed by increased repression, ghettoization, and transport via cattle car to either a concentration camp, forced labor camp or to a death camp like Auschwitz-Birkenau. This experience was usually followed either by liberation by the Red Army or transport back to other camps in Germany, where most were then liberated by British or American forces. Time in a displaced persons camp represents a pause in this journey that usually ends with immigration to the United States, Canada or Israel.

This trajectory has been well documented not only by historians, but by the survivors themselves. In addition to the oral history interviews and testimonies that thousands of survivors have given since the end of the Second World War, there exists an equally large body of memoirs written by Holocaust survivors. When these are combined with other modes of memory, they form the body of Holocaust survivor narratives.

This is not to say, or even to imply that what they endured resembles anything close to what one might consider common. What it does allude to is the idea that when one thinks of Holocaust survivors, one immediately associates their experience with the physical manifestation of the Holocaust; the camps and ghettos established by the Nazi regime during the Second World War. For the most part, this identification is true. Their recollections form the closest connections that we, as observers of the past, can make with the Holocaust.

I am also approached about interviewing Jews who, one way or another, were able to escape the Holocaust, or at least a full physical confrontation with it. Some escaped overseas by emigrating from what would become Nazi occupied Europe prior to 1939. Others went into hiding and spent the war years either concealed in physical hiding places or living openly under assumed names and identities. Some fled to the dense forests of eastern Poland (now Belarus) where they helped wage partisan warfare against the Nazi occupiers, while others escaped across the border into the Soviet Union.

For this group, questions of survival, or more precisely, whether or not they are considered survivors, sometime arise. By escaping or hiding, they avoided the harshest confrontation with the concentrationary universe. This is not to say, however, that their experiences, whether in hiding, as partisans or as émigrés, are less harrowing, emotional, or traumatic than those who endured the camps and ghettos. They are, however, and must be considered, Holocaust survivors too. For if one measures the Holocaust in terms that go beyond the loss of human life, if one takes into account the separation of families, the loss of community, and the destruction of a culture, *all who were targeted by the Nazis are survivors.* Their recollections, whether presented as written memoirs or as recorded interviews and testimonies, help form a more complete picture of survival.

Of those who fled the Holocaust by leaving Nazi occupied Europe, perhaps the most harrowing experiences belong to the approximately 300,000 Polish Jews who escaped across the Nazi-Soviet frontier between 1939 and 1941. From the time they left their homes until the moment they reached the line of demarcation, these fugitives faced constant peril; either from capture by the Germans or betrayal by the Poles. Many arrived at the border only to find it closed and rather than turning back, they endured the cold of an early winter, living in the open in a kind of no man's land, in hopes of crossing the border before they starved or froze to death.

Those who got through traded an almost certain confrontation with the concentrationary universe created by one totalitarian regime for a different type of encounter with another. Although Stalinist Russia lacked the destructive imperatives of Hitler's Germany, it had, since the 1930s, undertaken genocidal measures of its own against people it identified as "enemies" of the state. In the Soviet Union, foreigners of any religious, political or economic stripe were unwelcome and distrusted. This resulted in the separation, transportation and relocation of those deemed untrustworthy by the Soviet state. This relocation often ended far into the interior of the Soviet Union, sometimes to Soviet work camps, where many lost their lives through illness or overwork. This experience, while less brutal than under the Nazis, took its own physical and mental toll on those who suffered through it.

As future generations contend with the Holocaust and its implications for society, the interviews and memoirs of Holocaust survivors, no matter what their experience, will serve as valuable resources in their quest for understanding. *Into No Man's Land*, as a chronicle of a different Holocaust experience, is sure to be included among these resources.

Jamie L. Wraight, Ph.D.
Curator and Historian,
The Voice/Vision Holocaust Survivor Oral History Archive
The University of Michigan-Dearborn
July 2012

1

Before the War

Sunday after dinner I eased myself into the corner of the family room's brown leather couch — a spot where the contours of my body are imprinted from many evening hours of reading.

Naomi reached for "A Vanished World" by Vishniak on the gray marble table. She opened to a page showing a shopping street in the heart of the Jewish quarter in Warsaw, in 1938.

In jeans and a black turtleneck, resting her hand on the page, Naomi stood silently for a moment.

"Mom, you never talk about your childhood, about your parents and your family. There is so much of your life marked as 'PAST' that I hardly know about. You promised you'd tell me."

"Naomi, it was so long ago, I wouldn't even know where to begin."

"Start with the earliest experience from childhood you can remember. Please."

"I will try."

Naomi rolled the brown ottoman under my feet.

Kicking off her sneakers, she curled up next to me on the couch. Looking at my daughter's oval face, her dark-brown hair, hazel eyes, and full lips, I saw myself in a photograph when I was four years old, standing in front of our rented summer cottage, in a sleeveless,

*flowered calico dress with two big pockets, a rubber ball in hand,
long braids resting on my shoulders.*

*Suddenly, I had an urge to braid Naomi's hair, but instead, I laid
my hand on her head and felt the soft, smooth texture of her hair. I
pulled the gray afghan off the back of the couch and covered Naomi's
bare feet.*

"I don't know where we were coming from, but it was very
dark and my parents and I were riding in a *droszka*, a horse-
drawn carriage. The four- and five-story apartment buildings
stood solidly one beside the other, forming a row without the
slightest gap between them, as if *ulica* Niska, the street I lived
on, was one long building. Electric streetlights brightly illuminated the area. Stillness hung all around us; the buildings,
the pavement, the cables stretched across the street were all
soundly asleep. Even the leaves on the lilac and acacia trees
in the park we passed appeared suspended, motionless, their
powerful aroma filling the air. In this silence, the clip-clop of
the horse carrying us though the Jewish section of Warsaw
sounded thunderous. The doors to Pani Bernstinowa's grocery were closed, the butcher shop was dark, but the sidewalk-
level window of the cobbler's apartment had a dim light
burning.

The entrance to our five-story apartment building at
Niska 16 looked like the gates of a fortress: two big, dark
brown metal doors, ajar in the daytime, locked at night, led
to a square courtyard surrounded by buildings with separate
entrances to each section. Tata rang the doorbell and after a
few minutes, the doorman shuffled out with his feet in slippers, a white nightshirt reaching his ankles, a cotton cap tilted
to the left, and a lantern in his hand.

'Good evening, Pan Miller,' the doorman bowed. To compensate the man for his trouble, Tata gave him a few coins.

Tata carried me up the stairs; we lived on the fifth floor, and there was no elevator. The entrance to our home was on the right of the hall, across from the Kowalski family. On the hallway ceiling, between the two apartments, was a pull-down hatch leading into an attic. This was the mystery door I was not allowed to enter or inquire much about. From time to time, I noticed one of my parents pull up a ladder, climb into the attic, and disappear for a while. Visits to the attic were always accompanied by tension and whispers between my parents. Not until I was old enough for my sister Halina to trust me with secrets did I learn something about the nature of the attic and the source of the tension.

Our apartment door opened into a big room that served as a kitchen, dining room, play room, political assembly place, and, at times, Tata's work room. To the right of the entrance stood a black metal four-burner coal stove and oven. A few inches off the floor was a small door where Mama periodically threw in coal with a small shovel stored in a metal bucket next to the stove. I loved watching the flames forming different shapes when Mama shoveled in the coal.

'Don't sit too close,' Mama warned me, but I inched closer and closer to peek into the belly of the stove. Across from the stove, against the wall, stood a long wooden table with four chairs and a few stools. The table looked like a butcher's block with straight legs. There was always room for my parents' friends who dropped in unexpectedly during mealtimes. Some, having been out of work, or for some other reason empty-pocketed, timed their visit to have a meal with us. There had hardly been a time in our home when we sat down to dinner without the company of some friend who dropped in; as we had no telephone, their visits were unannounced. I grew up believing that a home was a place where friends come whenever they are so inclined, that you share your food with them, or your bed, if need be.

Next to the table was a big kitchen sink that served not only for washing dishes but for washing us as well—we had no bathroom. In winter, the outside ledge of the window served as our cooling storage for butter and other perishable food.

A small table and a cupboard were at the far end of this all-purpose room. This table often served as a base for a big board on which my parents composed designs in veneer to be placed on armoires and other furniture that my father was making. I loved watching my parents experiment with forming a design by placing the veneer one way or another.

Our apartment included one other big room that served as the family's bedroom. A drape separated our parents' bed from the bed that my sister and I shared. Against one wall stood an armoire the length of the room. In the center of the bedroom was a pot-bellied, coal-burning heating stove with an exhaust pipe extending through the ceiling.

I have two vivid images of the armoire: my mother keeping polished yellow apples, *złote renaty*, among the neatly folded linen to give our bedding a fresh smell, and seeing the whole armoire covered with a bloody red liquid. Mama, with the help of a friend, bottled cherries and plums to make wine. Carafes and bottles were lined up along the top of the armoire. Early one morning we were awakened by an enormous explosion. Corks were flying through the air, the overly fermented contents of the bottles splattering all over the ceiling and the armoire. I believe this was my mother's last attempt at wine-making.

Mietek, a single man and a frequent visitor, showed up occasionally with a bag of great finds. 'This new store on Zamenhofa is selling salami ends — take a look at all this good stuff.' He emptied his bag into a dish standing on the kitchen table. One day Mietek arrived with a bag of ends from a variety of cakes: cheesecake, torte, French pastry, and others. The patisserie baked these in sheets and sliced them into squares as individual pastries, leaving the narrow strips along the edges for bargain hunters.

I have memories of aromas coming out of Pani Kowalska's kitchen before Christmas. She would bring a plate of butter cookies for Halina and me, two of them in the shape of a lamb. For some time I believed that Pani Kowalskowa had been baking the cookies in honor of Halina's birthday, December 24, until one day I asked Mama why our neighbor wasn't baking cookies for my birthday in April. Mama explained that this was Pani Kowalskowa's holiday, just as some of our neighbors baked *homantashen* for Purim. My mother baked neither butter cookies for Christmas nor *homantashen* for Purim.

My parents were born into religious families, but independently, sometime in their teens, they became politically active and turned away from religion. Their Jewish cultural identity, however, remained a strong force throughout their lives. They read Yiddish literature and newspapers, attended the Yiddish theater, belonged to Jewish labor unions and other organizations. As I was learning Yiddish during the war years, I realized what a beautiful literary Yiddish my mother spoke and wrote. I heard admiring comments about my mother's Yiddish from many who knew the language well.

While no religion had been practiced in our home, my parents must have been ambivalent about bringing up their children without any. For some Jewish holidays they would send Halina and me to *Ciocia* Fela. I remember the long festive table covered with a white linen tablecloth, elegant tableware, candles, and the aroma of the wonderful *cholent Ciocia* Fela served for dinner."

"Ciocia? *Aunt. And what is* cholent, *Mom?*"

"A casserole made of meat, potatoes, and a variety of beans, stuffed chicken necks or kishke. *Because observant Jews aren't al-*

*lowed to light a fire on the Sabbath, this dish was placed in a fireplace
or some low-heat oven Friday evening before sundown. It cooked
very slowly until the next day when the family was ready for mid-
day dinner. The slow cooking blended the flavors and turned all the
ingredients brown; it was delicious."*

*"This dish sounds like a killer with all the calories and fatty
stuff."*

*"In those days, Naomi, no one counted calories or was concerned
about cholesterol."*

"Of my mother's twelve siblings, eight lived in Warsaw, all
but one married with children. Among them were a poor tailor, a poorer cobbler, a painter, a well-to-do builder, and a lot
of cousins. Everyone in the family except my parents adhered
to the Jewish religion and traditions to one degree or another.

My mother's other four brothers and sister lived in France
and Belgium. Father had only one sibling—a younger brother
Moshe, married with one child. I have a photo of Moshe in
the uniform of the Polish army. His mother gave birth to
eleven, but only the oldest and youngest survived.

My paternal grandmother Syma Lea, a big, strong woman,
her feet solidly planted on the ground in flat shoes, lived in a
small town or maybe a *shtetl*. Periodically she visited us, arriving loaded with a variety of cakes, *grievene* in a jar (melted
chicken fat with dried-out pieces of the original *shmaltz*), and
other dishes of her making. She shouted from the courtyard
for one of us to come help her carry up her bundles. My ma-
ternal grandmother I vaguely remember as a plump woman
with dangling pearl earrings, sitting in a chair looking stern.

The women in my family must have been hardier than the
men, both my grandfathers having died before I was born.

When my mother was alive I never thought of asking her
about our extended family—they all seemed so remote and
unreal, and I was so busy living in the present and planning

the future, always planning the future. All my Polish relatives perished in the Holocaust, nearly one hundred of them. Now I have no one to ask; Halina knows only a little more than I do about our family.

My parents were members of the Communist Party, illegal in Poland. Their lives had been driven by the mission to achieve fair treatment for workers within a political system that respects labor and compensates it in accordance with its contribution to society. To my parents and their friends, communism represented freedom from oppression and exploitation, an idea shared by many progressive, liberal people.

My father was the missionary. Mother believed in the communist principles, but her passion did not equal my father's, and she followed selectively the many expectations of a comrade. Mother had been criticized by other party members for using cosmetics and for dressing stylishly: a black tailored suit for the theater, high heels and a knitted dress for walking in town, a fox collar tossed over her winter coat, and other such unproletarian attire. These were considered bourgeois frivolities that a comrade should not indulge in.

I assume other women comrades felt similarly conflicted about the unfeminine expectations of the party. Under my parents' bed I once discovered a suitcase and, being a curious little girl, opened it, knowing that I shouldn't. It was full of mysterious items I had never before seen—women's silk and chiffon undergarments in the most unusual styles: underpants that looked like a short flowing skirt made of almost transparent fabric, bras of lace, little somethings with two spaghetti straps. In secret, I asked Halina if she knew of this suitcase—I didn't dare ask Mama. Halina didn't even know the suitcase existed, let alone what these things were and who they belonged to.

Many years later I asked my mother about the mystery suitcase. My parents' friend Esther, a devout communist, had lived in France for a few years before her Communist Party days. When she joined the Party, she considered it decadent to wear these delicate feminine items but was unwilling to part with them, so she asked my mother to store them for her. I had a tough time imagining Esther, her hair cut into a short pageboy, with her dark cotton skirt and sensible shoes, wearing these dainties.

Some years after the war I visited Esther in Israel. She told me she had been married for a year but threw the guy out of her house. 'He was not a good comrade; he was an exploiter of my labor.'

I never asked Esther about the fancy underwear. Our world having collapsed, all our loved ones gone, it was not a time to reminisce about frilly things.

Father, a labor union leader, believed that only within the communist system can workers get fair treatment. Before I understood what the concepts meant, I heard about 'Ownership of the means of production,' 'Exploitation of labor,' and 'From each according to his ability, and to each according to his needs.' Mama often told her friends that all they had to do to learn my father's political secrets was to sleep with him. 'All workers unite under the red flag!' my father often shouted in his sleep. I didn't understand what all that meant.

Our attic was the hiding place of pamphlets, fliers, and various other forbidden recruitment materials. 'They searched at Zygmund's,' someone ran into the house to announce. Though most of our parents' friends had no telephones, they clearly had a well-developed messenger system. Whenever police searched one of the houses, in no time all comrades were informed. Almost the instant the message reached my parents, they rushed to the attic to hide the material stored there and reorganize some other nooks in the house. I was told that if a stranger came to the house, I was to remain quiet and ask no questions—I was known for asking many questions of adults.

Announcements of police raids on apartments of comrades happened often; my parents lived in constant dread of their communist identity becoming known to the police. They talked about their imprisoned friends with concern and respect. I came to believe that being incarcerated was a sign of bravery, a badge of honor. Mama reinforced this notion of mine when she summoned my sister and me one afternoon.

'Halina and Irka, I want to talk to you.'

Her words sounded strange—Mama never made such declarations, she just talked.

'You are going to have a new friend.'

'A friend for Halina, or me?' I asked, puzzled.

'For both of you, like a new sister.'

'A baby sister?' I got excited.

'No, a seven-year-old girl. Magda will live with us for some time. We have to be very nice to her, Magda's parents are in jail.'

Magda must be a special person because her parents were in jail, I reflected. For a long time thereafter, not fully understanding what jail meant, I wondered who would be very nice to Halina and me if our parents go to jail.

Both of Magda's parents, communist comrades, had been arrested and sentenced to a year in jail. Magda's father was a Jew, her mother a Catholic, but religion played as minor a role in their home as it did in ours. Magda and I became good friends. She slept on my side of the bed. Between Halina and me in age, Magda preferred to play with me. Halina was a cautious, obedient, responsible girl, and a bit of a worrier. I was curious, eager to explore, often got in trouble without knowing how, and was always losing things. Our friend Mietek teased me that, if I could just stop losing things, I'd make a brave comrade or a smart general.

Magda, a shy, quiet girl, readily followed me in my search for new games. I don't remember having any toys, but our vivid imaginations turned many household items into play objects. Empty bottles filled with water became musical instruments, chairs turned over were trains or buses.

'Today, you girls get a special treat,' Mama told Magda and me.

'What kind of treat?' I jumped up excitedly.

'We are going to the Shalom Aleichem exhibit for children.'

'Who is Shalom Aleichem?' I wanted to know.

'He was a man who wrote beautiful stories in Yiddish about Jews and how they lived. People all over the world read Shalom Aleichem's books.'

'But I don't know how to read, Mama.'

'You will not have to read. We will see pictures, dolls and doll houses that tell the stories.'

Halina didn't want to come with us. The exhibit was for kids — she was too grown-up for it.

Outfitted in our going-out dresses, as all proper girls would have been, we walked a few blocks to the *tramwaj* (trolley).

'Girls, walk, don't jump,' Mama kept telling us, but I liked to hop and to jump. It was fun to watch how Magda's blue dress and my gray skirt twirled and moved with us. Mama, in her beige knit dress and high heels, walked behind us. I don't know how she could see with the brim of her hat falling over her eyes.

All the seats on the trolley were taken, but a gentleman rose to offer Mama his seat. Magda and I held hands with Mama to keep from falling when the *tramwaj* took a sharp turn.

The Shalom Aleichem exhibit was set in a vast hall. An overpowering mural glared at us as we entered. On it, an enormous woman in a dark peasant dress with a flowered apron, her head wrapped in a black kerchief, was chasing a tiny man who hardly reached her waist. She swung a cast-iron frying pan over his head. The title was *"Złate mit di patelnie,"* Złate with the frying pan. Many big paintings hung on the walls, but that particular image stays with me. Scattered throughout the hall were miniature models of villages, and model interiors of homes with people seated around a Sabbath dinner or in other domestic situations. Mama explained to me and Magda what all these objects signified, and she told us some of the Shalom Aleichem stories these images were drawn from.

My parents' political ideology also incorporated the ideals of the Spanish Revolution. General Franco was a household name, and news of the war's developments was a frequent subject of discussion among my parents and their friends.

One evening, as we were sitting down to dinner, someone knocked on the door. Tata welcomed the visitor with unusual exuberance, 'Motl, we weren't sure whether you would be getting here today or tomorrow. You must be hungry and tired!'

The visitor, a young man in his early twenties, was even taller than my six-foot father. He must have traveled some distance; my parents kept asking him about his journey to Warsaw. Hungry he certainly was. Mama set an additional plate for Motl, and I watched him devour whatever was put before him.

'Are you going to stay with us?' I asked the visitor.

'Irka, don't bother Motl—he is exhausted,' Mama reprimanded me.

'I'll stay for a little while, if I have your permission,' Motl answered, giving me a big smile. Shrugging, I smiled back. Our visitor came with a sleeping bag, and right after supper he turned in for the night in the corner of our sleeping room. For the remainder of his two weeks with us, Motl slept in the kitchen.

When I awakened the next morning, Motl was standing barefoot in pajama bottoms with his arms stretched over his head, holding the ends of a broomstick. With his bare chest and disheveled black hair, Motl looked like a skinny, tall boy.

'Motl, what are you doing?' I wanted to know.

'I am exercising to be strong.'

'How strong do you want to get?'

'Strong enough to be a good fighter.'

No one I knew exercised to be strong, or to prepare to be a fighter. No one I knew exercised at all. It seemed a curious business.

'Who are you going to fight?'

'The Spanish fascist.'

'Oh! Franco?'

'What do you know about Franco?'

'He is a bad man. He hates the workers.' I recited a Polish poem:

Ojceić Pedra był dynamitardem
I tak mówił gdy wyruszał w bój
Kraj obronię dynamitem twardym
Jak nie ja to syn obroni mój

Długo bronił się zacięty Madryt,
Długo wróg Madrytu nie mógł zgnieść
Bo w nim ludzi bochaterskie kadry
Własną krwią pisały swoją pieśń

In translation:

Pedro's father was a dynamite expert.
"I will defend my country with my dynamite,

and, if I fail, my son will carry on."
So he declared before each battle.

Madrid defended itself for very long;
For very long the enemy had been unable to conquer it,
For its brave people
With their own blood had written their song.

Motl lifted me into the air laughing, 'Where did you learn this, Ireczka?'

'I don't remember, I just know it,' I told him.

Motl found a stick in our attic; he smoothed it with sand-paper. And I exercised with Motl every morning; we had agreed that he would wake me before starting his workout. I could ask Motl any question that popped into my head, and he patiently answered them all. He was the first adult who answered all my questions. I kept asking him if he was already strong enough to fight the fascists. But I didn't want him to leave us.

My parents' friends visited often during the two weeks Motl was with us. Mietek arrived with bigger bags of the salami stubs and the cake edges. Mama sliced more bread and filled more bowls with home-made sauerkraut, and the aroma of coffee made with chicory permeated the apartment. Listening to the talk of the adults, I was getting quite an education on the Spanish Civil War and the International Brigade that Motl planned to join. Discussions were animated, and when I was alone with him, I asked him to explain why some people were helping Franco if he was such a cruel person—why weren't they helping the good side?

I was saddened when Motl left for Spain, but consoled that he was going to free the workers, as Mama told me. With Motl's departure, the Spanish war became a personal matter to me, and General Franco my personal enemy. I kept asking my mother whether Motl was winning and what he wrote.

'He's too busy fighting to write,' Mama told me.

"I believe it was Ernest Hemingway who wrote, 'No man ever entered the earth more honorably than those who died in Spain.' Well, Naomi, our friend Motl entered the earth honorably a few weeks after joining the Brigade. I didn't learn about Motl's death until many years later."

"Mom, what was the Spanish Civil War about?"

"For a few years, Spain was a republic. Then the military, under the leadership of Francisco Franco, staged a coup that started the bloody Revolution or Civil War that raged from 1936 until 1939. The fascist leader of Italy, Benito Mussolini, as well as the German Nazis, supported Franco with arms and soldiers, but no government aided the fighters for democracy."

"Why didn't any country help the revolutionaries?"

"Politics, Naomi, politics. The threat of fascism, however, motivated many liberals throughout the world to volunteer and fight side by side with the Spanish republicans."

"They don't teach us much in school about this kind of history."

"Some of it, Naomi, I learned by living it."

"We children were not officially indoctrinated into our parents' politics, but being a part of their life, we naturally absorbed it. Zuć Falangę do smietnika, kupój Tydzień Robotnika"—Throw Falanga *into the trash and buy the* Worker's Weekly. *Magda and I repeated this injunction to each other, not understanding what Falanga was and why we should trash it."*

"Mom, what was Falanga?*"*

*"*Falanga *was one of the most extremist and most violently anti-Semitic political parties in pre-war Poland; I assume it put out a publication by this same name."*

"While anti-Semitism was deeply rooted in Polish culture and I experienced it after the war, as a young child I had no awareness of it. Not only did we have Christian neighbors a few feet from our

door, but my parents had Christian friends who were a part of our lives. When I was old enough to differentiate between the Yiddish and Polish print, I looked on puzzled as my mother would read in Polish from a Yiddish newspaper to her non-Jewish friends. When I questioned her, she explained that the Yiddish newspaper had something important she wanted her friends to know and thus she was translating the article."

"By the mid- and late-thirties, anti-Semitism had greatly intensified in Poland and was not only sanctioned but instigated by the government."

"Why did the Poles hate Jews, Mom?"

"I don't have the answer, Naomi. There is no logic to this hate, but there is rarely logic to any hate. Historically, Jews had been the scapegoat for all that ailed Poland: poverty, the absence of democracy, political turmoil, and so on."

"My father, a trained accountant, was unable to find work, so he made furniture, a trade he learned as a boy helping his father. Furniture-making supported the family. We did not live in luxury, but neither were we deprived of any necessities.

The last three summers before the war, Mama, together with a friend, rented a small cottage about thirty miles from Warsaw. Halina, Lusia, the daughter of Mama's friend, and I enjoyed the woods and beach and the space to run around in and explore nature—things we didn't have in Warsaw. Climbing trees, chasing butterflies, picking wild flowers and braiding them into garlands, watching a local farmer milk a goat into my cup were exciting experiences. I wanted to milk the goat myself, but the farmer wouldn't let me, fearing it might kick me.

Jan, a young man of the landed gentry, came to visit us often and brought me chocolates and other sweets. He had a huge dog, the size of a small pony. I was afraid of dogs, but when Jan took my hand and gently stroked the dog, the dog's fur felt soft and warm. Little by little Jan and the dog became my friends. Jan showed up one morning asking Mama if he could take me to visit his mother. He promised I could ride on the dog. Mama hesitated, but I pestered her until she gave in.

Part of the way I walked, or rather should say hopped, as had been my habit all my childhood, and part of the way the dog obediently carried me on his back. Jan had a pocketful of chocolates and indulged me. Before we reached his parents' home, he led me to a well, pulled out his white handkerchief, and washed my face and hands, sticky from chocolate. I don't remember what Jan's mother looked like, or their house, other than its being large. I only remember Jan as a tall, muscular kind man, who liked to laugh, but I recall my great joy and excitement over this expedition.

Summer at the cottage was also when I first experienced an almost paralyzing fear that for a while changed my perception of the friendliness of nature and the world around me. Mama took Halina, Lusia, and me for a long walk. I am unsure whether we had a specific destination; we passed farmhouses, grassy fields, empty dirt roads that appeared to lead nowhere. After a while our road brought us into a lush green field with a variety of flowers: bluebonnets, cornflowers, Icelandic poppies and others. It was a sunny, beautiful day, and I challenged Lusia to see who could hop faster. Exhausted after a long competition, we both slowed down, Halina and Mama out ahead of us. With my last spurt of energy, I ran to catch up with Mama, Lusia following at a slower pace. Abruptly Lusia turned away and ran into the field to pick flowers. Suddenly, we heard a terrifying scream and saw Lusia getting shorter and shorter. '*Boże mój, Boże mój!*' (my God), Mama's roaring voice came out from the bottom of her belly as she kicked off her sandals and ran towards Lusia with Halina and me following, not understanding what was happening. All I could see was my friend sinking into the ground, hands outstretched over her head, screaming in terror.

"Stay, don't move!" Mama yelled back to Halina and me as she was running towards Lusia. We hesitated a moment, but continued to follow our mother. When she got close to Lusia, Mama stretched herself flat on her stomach, reaching for Lusia's hand—the girl was waist deep in the ground.

Halina and I lay in back of Mama, each grabbing one of her ankles. Realizing we were behind her, Mama shouted, 'Pull my legs, pull them hard, move back as you pull them, slowly, slowly!'

Now Mama was holding both of Lusia's hands, but the girl, as though she weighed a ton, wasn't budging.

'Pull me harder—harder, with all your strength!' Mama called to us.

Halina and I pulling Mama, and Mama pulling Lusia, we groaned and labored and little by little drew her out of the quicksand. Lusia, covered with mud up to her armpits, was shaking and could not stop crying. Mama told us to turn around and follow her, as she tried to retrace the path by which we reached Lusia. When we got to the road, muddy and dirty, I stood stunned, unable to move, looking at the earth beneath my feet, fearing it might cave in. Halina and Lusia were crying, Mama was yelling, and I was too petrified to move. Mama grabbed my hand, yanking me hard and screaming at all of us, 'I told you to walk and not to run! I told you to stay next to me! See what happens when you don't mind me!'

Holding Lusia's hand, Mama kept walking so fast that Halina and I had to run to keep up with her. She complained angrily all the way home. Being behind her, however, and unable to see her face, I paid little attention to what she was saying.

We didn't discuss this terrifying experience with Mama or with any other grown-up. Even Halina and I didn't talk much about it between us; it's as though the incident never occurred. We were safe and that's all that mattered. Likewise, later in life, Mama would never discuss with Halina and me how we felt about our many frightening experiences during the war. I presume that my mother believed that silence nullified traumatic incidents, or perhaps that children were blissfully forgetful.

Coming back to our cottage, without washing up or changing my muddy dress, I ran into the nearby woods, not wanting to hear Mama's shouting. I felt like crying. I was scared to move away from my favorite tree. I never thought that someone could drown in the ground. How will I know where it is safe to walk? Lusia almost died, she almost died. Sitting quietly, I suddenly thought of Stella.

Stella, my sister's best friend, the daughter of our friends the Farbers, died a few months before we left for the cottage. She was hit by a car while riding a bicycle to a ballet class. She survived the accident but developed gangrene, and died within a few days. Stella's parents turned into stones. They sat on a burgundy velour sofa for weeks, silent, almost motionless. Only occasionally the grieving mother would sway in a slow, rhythmic motion, tears flowing down her face, repeating, 'Shifrale, my Shifrale,' Stella's Yiddish name, in a whisper.

The Farbers' apartment was so dark you had to find your way by touch. I came in daily with Mama and Halina and helped carry the food Mama made for the Farbers, food that no one ate. From time to time other friends walked in to pay their respects and to comfort the grieving parents who could not be consoled—their only child, the beautiful, gifted, and gentle daughter had died. There being no way to give comfort, the visitors sat in silence, touching the parents' hands and swaying with them.

I dreaded the visits, yet was drawn to this cavernous place of sorrow. On the third or fourth day, as I sat next to Pani Farberowa on the velour sofa, she placed her hand on my head and stroked it over and over. On all subsequent visits, I took the same spot on the sofa, and Pani Farberowa either stroked my head or pulled me closer to her. I was the youngest visitor and the only person to whom she responded.

I didn't fully understand the finality of death, but I clearly perceived how it altered the lives of loved ones left behind. During the war, when I saw people killed, people dying, and no one bringing food or sitting silently on sofas, my understanding of grief behavior had to adjust rapidly.

We still were in the summer cottage when our father got wind of the forthcoming German attack on Poland. Tata showed up in the middle of the week—something he had never done before—and without the cream-filled pastries or any of the other goodies he usually brought us when visiting. That same day, we packed and returned to Warsaw on the evening train. I didn't understand what was going on, but the silence and tension were so heavy I knew not to ask.

My parents' constant whispers made me anxious. I wished they would tell us exactly what was happening. Mama shopped frantically for whatever she could get in the grocery stores: flour, sugar, oil, bread—lots of bread, soap, candles, toilet paper—anything of household use.

My parents had never considered it their role to play with their children or to worry how we spent time at home. Now, however, Mama was so preoccupied with preparation for the war that Halina and I seemed remote from her thoughts. One morning when I got up, I found a barrel of sliced dried bread. Apparently Mama was making toast late into the night. That afternoon Tata came home with three heads of cabbage—Mama's project that evening was making sauerkraut. Anticipation of the war was by now widespread, and the rush on

the blood with the hem of her nightgown. She pulled closer to the dim kerosene lamp.

'Try not to wiggle, I can't see well.'

'It hurts, it hurts,' I cried.

'Hush, Irka. I know it hurts, but we have to take it out.'

We stayed in the shelter until the sirens informed us that this attack was over.

Most of the food we had been eating during this month of constant bombardment came from our pantry. Often it was dry toast and slightly pickled cabbage (not yet sauerkraut). Mama had heard that someone was selling horsemeat; she went to inquire as soon as the bombardment was over. The next day we ate meat; it was a little tough, but delicious.

The last bombing attack severed the water pipes, leaving us without water. A few streets over from us, emergency water had been piped in; we had to line up with containers and carry the water home—all of us walked for the water.

Two days later the Germans entered Warsaw. Terrified, I watched out of a neighbor's window as the German soldiers, their faces shut and emotionless, pounded the pavement with their rhythmic marching: one two, one two, one two; the sound drilling itself into my head. Their boots polished and shiny, kicking high in the air, the soldiers were goose-stepping down our street, a few abreast. There were thousands of them, marching and marching, pounding and pounding the pavement. I could hardly see their faces, or maybe I was afraid to look, but their boots haunted me in my sleep. Then came soldiers pulling zeppelins floating in the air. I was too frightened to appreciate the sight of something I had never seen before—a zeppelin. They were the size of a building, yet they glided with ease, secured only by ropes held by a few soldiers."

"Mom, what scary experiences for a little girl! You must have been so frightened. Why didn't you ever tell us about it?"

My parents Bella
and Israel Miller

My sister Halina
(right) age 8 and I
(left) age 3

Mama, Halina and I
at the summer cottage

Mama in center with siblings

Mama sitting
with sisters

Father in 1939

Uncle Moshe Miller in Polish Army

2

No Man's Land

"Mom, you have to tell me about the war years."

"Someday, Naomi, I will."

"No, no, I'm twenty-two. In a few months I'll be done with my master's degree and out of Ann Arbor. When is that 'someday' gonna come?"

"It is hard for me to talk about it."

"I understand, but I am your daughter—I have to know."

She was right, it is in a way my children's past. Without telling them about my experiences, I must have passed on to them some of my feelings and values generated by them.

I sat quietly for a few minutes, closing my eyes tightly, blocking out the image of the room and all its familiar objects, until the sounds, the smells, and the sights started coming to life: Warsaw, the no man's land, trains to Siberia, still more trains— Uzbekistan, Czelek, orphanages.

"Come, Naomi, sit next to me," and I began to relive my Holocaust years.

"It is 1939, and winter has come early. It's only November and the frost is savagely biting. Dressed in five layers of clothing underneath my coat, surrounded by thick walls of hay and roofed in by a heavy brown horse blanket, I am sweating. In the front of the wagon, hidden in the hay, are my father and my older sister Halina; in the rear, my mother and I.

It is quiet, so quiet I can hear my mother's breathing. Soft snow on the unpaved one-lane country road cushions the old mare's hooves. From time to time, a ditch or a rock interrupts the horse's slow swaying rhythm. The wagon, piled high with hay and covered with blankets, is indistinguishable from all the others on the country roads in Poland. Pan (Mr.) Maciej— unshaved, in old gray pants, with the collar of a tartan shirt sticking out of his black coat, and with a hole in his shoe exposing a black heavy sock—looks like many other farmers in the region. The wagon and Pan Maciej are intended to be inconspicuous, but at two in the morning, as the only moving object on this road, we can't be overlooked.

Should a German soldier stop the wagon to question Pan Maciej, he would hear that Pan Maciej is on his way to Nowagóra to help out his cousin who has lost all his hay in a barn fire.

Standing on tiptoes, straining my eyes, I peek through the holes in the blanket over my head, but I can see only black sky. A blade of hay tickles my nostrils, and I sneeze. With a quick firm hand Mama covers my mouth, pushes my head deeper into the wagon and whispers, 'Shh, shh.'

Lulled by the swaying of the wagon, I'm getting drowsy, but I have to watch for the German soldiers. 'I must watch for Germans,' I keep repeating to myself. What if I breathe too loud? What if I have to sneeze again? The Germans will murder us if they find us. I've seen dead people in the streets and in our courtyard, and I wonder whether it hurts very much when they kill you. I'm terrified, but I know better than to ask my mother. By now I've learned that some questions upset Mama, and I shouldn't ask them. I no longer believe in the omnipotence of my parents. They couldn't stop the bombs and fires, and they couldn't prevent my friend Zosia's leg from being torn off by an explosion. There are many questions for which my parents have no answers: Why are the German soldiers so mean? How far away are we going? When will we go back home?

The distant barking of a dog brings a smile to my face. I'm afraid of dogs, but dogs mean summers in the country, running in the woods, climbing trees, chasing butterflies, picking wild flowers and braiding them into garlands. Will we go to the country again? How will Zosia climb trees with only one leg?

It is dark, stuffy, and smelly under the blanket. Breathing is difficult, and seeing impossible. Pretending to be a hibernating bear or a brave cavewoman doesn't help; I'm scared and want Mama to hold my hand, but she doesn't.

After a very long ride without a word spoken, Pan Maciej stops the wagon, pulls off the blankets, and declares, 'You can all get off. We are now on the Russian side—you're safe.'

'When did we cross the border?' Tata asks.

'A kilometer and a half back,' Pan Maciej replies.

Tata is the first to jump off the wagon, brushing the hay off his clothing. He pulls Halina out of the hay, then Mama and me.

Not trusting that we're safe, not remembering how it feels to be safe, I hesitantly look around, but it's dark; all I can see are tall pines forming a secluded courtyard around us.

Pan Maciej unloads our belongings: two brown suitcases, two big black bags with bedding and clothing. Then he hands Mama a gray package with our valuables. Most of the money my parents have with them has been sewn into the linings of Halina's and my winter coats. There is not a lot of money—my parents are working people; they have a furniture workshop with equipment and materials, all left behind in Warsaw. Whatever money is in our coats came from selling our apartment lease to a Jewish family from the country who figured it would be safer to live in the capital than in their small village.

Pan Maciej reasoned that, should the Germans stop us, they would search us thoroughly and take everything away. 'Everybody can see you're city folks, and, pardon me, but Pani Millerowa looks very Jewish. The Germans won't bother with a poor farmer.' Thus, he carried our valuables.

My mother, with her big dark eyes, full lips, shiny black hair pulled back, and somewhat olive complexion, appeared to be of Spanish lineage. My father on the other hand — six-feet tall and slim, with reddish-blond hair and blue eyes, would have looked like the perfect Aryan type were it not for his generous nose.

Tata paid Pan Maciej the rest of his fee for our safe transit across the Polish border into Soviet territory.

'This is a nice spot to sleep; it isn't so cold with the trees around. In the morning, take a train to Białystok.'

'How do we get to the train?' Mama asks.

'Go straight in that direction,' he says, pointing to the tallest pine tree. 'It's about half a kilometer.'

Pan Maciej turns his wagon around, and whipping the mare, takes off at a gallop.

Mama pulls two heavy blankets out of a black bag, spreading one on the dry snow.

'We'll snuggle up to keep warm till morning,' she says. Halina and I in the center, our parents on the outside, we use the other blanket to cover us all. I lean my face against Tata's forearm, sticking out of his coat-sleeve. The little reddish-blond fuzz on his arm feels soft against my skin.

It seems that I've just fallen asleep when Mama's loud, panicky voice wakes me up. *'Bóze mój, Bóze mój.'* With her hands covering her face, she doesn't notice that I've awakened.

'Srulik, look, look, what is this? Where are we?' Mama is shaking my father, a sound sleeper.

Inching closer to the pines, I stick my head out between the branches. It's daylight. Before me lies a field with thousands and thousands of people crowded together like a colony of ants. Most still sleep, but some are moving around aimlessly. A few feet from me stands a boy of two or three, clutching a dirty stuffed doll with straw sticking out where its hands once were. He looks at the trees, then straight at me, staring curiously for a few seconds before running back to a cluster of sleeping people. He is fully dressed in a wrinkled gray winter coat, a woolen hat pulled over his ears, but he has no gloves. All the sleeping people are wearing coats. Has someone dropped them all off to go to Białystok in the morning?

I turn around to find my mother and father talking in Yiddish. Lips tight, hands gesturing in all directions, they look angry. I know it's something Halina and I aren't supposed to know. Our parents' secrets are always in Yiddish. I wake my sister. 'Halina, Halina, look at all the people.'

'Don't bother me. Go to sleep.' She hides under the blanket.

I pull the blanket off. 'It's morning. Get up!'

'We will wait here. Tata will find out who all these people are. There's some mistake,' Mama tells us.

I don't understand what mistake Mama is talking about, but I know better than to ask. Tata isn't long in coming back.

'Bella, we're in no man's land. This *złodziej, drań* didn't take us across the border.'

'Mama, what is a no man's land?' I ask.

'Not now. ' Mama brushes me off impatiently.

'Halina, what is a no man's land?'

'I don't know.'

45

'Is it a place just for girls and women, but not for men?'

'Don't ask dumb questions,' Halina snaps, her short auburn hair disheveled, and her blue eyes appearing dusty gray.

'How come you don't know?' I ask, thinking it's stupid of her not to know; she is five years older than I am.

'Irka, leave me alone.'

No one wants to talk to me. I am going to find out for myself, but Mama grabs me by my arm. Now, in the daylight, I see all around us are dried human feces. Disgusted, I want to get out of this place fast.

'Srulik, how long have the people been here?'

'Some for a few weeks.' And again the conversation between my parents turns Yiddish.

'I'll go out and find a spot for us. Stay here with Tata,' Mama instructs us. Peeking between the branches of the pines, I can see Mama looking around, stopping to talk to people, gesturing. I wonder what they are talking about.

Mama returns with instructions. 'Srulik, take the suitcases. Halina and Irka, carry the black bag by the ends, and I'll take the rest.' We follow Mama, placing our feet carefully to avoid stepping on the sitting people. Mama lays her bags on the snow in a spot big enough to hold our belongings, but not much more. On one side of us is a family of three with a girl my age. Her eyes are blue like Halina's and my Tata's.

'Did someone paint her hair with a crayon?' I whisper to Halina, holding back the giggles.

'No, silly. Some people just have red hair.'

'Red like that?'

'Yeah.'

On the other side of us an older couple sits close together under a blanket. When Mama says good morning, they just nod. There are people everywhere, but they pay us little attention. Later we learn that people have been arriving daily, some coming on their own, intending to seek safety in the Soviet territory, unaware that the borders have been closed and are now rigorously guarded by Soviet soldiers. Others, like my family, have hired a Polish guide only to be left stranded in the no man's land.

Mama stacks the suitcases one on top of the other, then adds one of the black bags. Spreading a blanket down on the snow, the gray package with our valuables right next to her, she tells us to sit. From a tapestry bag she pulls a loaf of bread and a slab of cheese, setting them on a small white tablecloth. People around us stare. Behind me, I hear a woman's sneering voice, 'A tablecloth? How about the Rosenthal china? Give them a week or two, and they won't remember these things ever existed.'

The girl next to us peers intently at our spread.

'What is your name?' Mama inquires.

'Marysia'

'Would you like some bread and cheese, Marysia?' Mama asks.

Hesitantly, Marysia moves closer. I take her hand and pull her down next to me. I'm hungry. The dark, crusty bread and cheese that Mama bought from Pan Maciej are delicious. Marysia eats slowly, taking tiny bites. Her family has been in no man's land for five weeks.

'How do you get food here?' Mama asks Pani Goldbergowa, Marysia's mother.

'The peasants in the area bring in food to sell, and they charge exorbitant prices.'

'How do you find them?'

'Don't worry, they'll find you. They come at sundown. These *goyim*, the anti-Semites, are getting fat on our misery, sucking our blood.'

Marysia follows me as I stand up. 'Don't go very far,' Mama calls. In the distance, I see a fire and smoke rising; Marysia and I head in that direction. People are pushing towards the flames, trying to warm their hands, some with metal cups or enamel bowls full of snow they want to melt. I can't see the people's faces. A fat man is in front of me, the scratchy belt of his coat scraping my nose. Marysia and I move to another spot.

'I made the fire. Don't push. You want a fire, make it yourself!' a bearded man shouts.

'There's enough room for you—don't be such a hog,' someone says.

'You're a nasty old Jew,' says a woman pointing at the man, her finger in his face. Some step back a little, but no one walks away.

When I return to our spot, I find Mama sitting on the blanket surrounded by rusted metal bars, a few rocks, and some other odds and ends. Arms spread and palms up, she looks bewildered. On the blanket is the gray cloth that had wrapped our valuables. Facing each other, she and Tata sit motionless.

'What happened, Mama?' She doesn't answer. I repeat my question, but she continues ignoring me. She doesn't even see me.

'We were robbed, totally robbed! Not only did this son of a bitch dump us here to die, he also robbed us of everything,' my mother is telling Pani Goldbergowa.

'Bella, we aren't going to die. Don't say that,' my father interrupts.

'How are we going to get out of here? These people have been here for weeks!'

'I don't know yet how, but we will get out.'

'Back to the Germans?'

'No, Bella, not to Warsaw, not to the Germans. To the Soviet Union, they're our friends.'

'Friends? A strange way to treat friends, letting them starve and freeze to death in the fields. You call them friends?'

'Bella, there must be some good reason for all this, or some mistake. They are our comrades.'

'I don't understand, Srulik. Not giving a damn what happens to us is comradely? A mistake?'

My parents stop talking, averting their eyes from each other. Mama looks at the contents of the gray bundle. 'Everything we had of value is gone, the silver candelabra from my brother Hershel, the silver trays and flatware, the beautiful string of pearls from my sister Fela—everything. Everything we could sell to eat is gone. If not the frost, then hunger will get us. Everything, everything gone!'

'Bella, these are just things, we are alive.'

'For how long?'

Frightened by what Mama is saying, I want her to notice me and talk to me, but she still doesn't see me. My father turns to my mother and says something in Yiddish, and the conversation ends abruptly. Mama never again speaks about dying in no man's land. Scooping up the scattered rocks and metal pieces, Tata walks away to get rid of them. Mama busies herself pulling out bedding, some enamel cups, and a few spoons. Removing the tablecloth, she spreads the *pierzyna*, a very thick down comforter. Back home, I loved diving into the *pierzyna* when Mama wasn't around. With the poof came a slow descending into a warm, soft cloud.

'Come, Irka, I will take some of the clothes off you.' Covering us both with the comforter, Mama instructs me to take off my coat and all the dresses I'm wearing under it.

'Keep just your long underwear, the pants, and the sweater.'

'I will be cold, Mama.'

'You can always put on another sweater. You don't need all that stuff you have on.'

Next comes Halina's turn to remove some of her layers. We've worn as much as we could fit under our coats to minimize luggage. After I've removed all the dresses, my coat feels huge, sleeves covering my fingertips. The coat is a gift from Ciocia (aunt) Fela, my mother's oldest sister and the family matriarch. The oldest of twelve siblings, Fela was a nurturing, generous woman. A few days before our departure from Warsaw, she came over, loaded with clothing for Halina and me.

'Who knows, Bella, when next you can buy clothes for your girls, and they grow so fast.' Ciocia Fela brought us winter coats, two sizes too big, and sweaters. For each of us she had two pairs of shoes from 'Geller Shoes,' her store on Zamenhofa Street. One pair was a size bigger than I needed and the other still bigger.

People in the no man's land are now moving about, blowing into their palms, and rubbing their hands. Around us, talk, talk, talk, buzz, buzz, like a beehive. Fires are lit in a few spots.

Towards the end of the day, peasant women dressed in dark clothes and kerchiefs, carrying buckets and bundles under their arms, appear seemingly from nowhere. The woman who approaches us has warm cooked potatoes in their skins.

'*Czy pani ma masło?*' Mama asks.

No butter, just farmer's cheese

We eat potatoes and cheese for supper. Tata melts snow in a bowl and we each sip, taking turns.

Darkness sets in. The few fires still burning throw flickering light on the mass of people. With the diminished visibility, people are getting up and heading towards trees and bushes.

Coming back from the bushes, Pani Goldbergowa turns to my mother, 'Frozen human shit, scattered under the trees like pine cones, and bones sticking out from shallow graves will be the only trace of this multitude of homeless and unwanted people. Who will ever know of our misery in this no man's land?'

'Pani Goldbergowa, we must have hope.'

'Hope, Pani Millerowa? Who will save us?

'The world will soon find out what's happening here.'

'The world? The world doesn't give a damn what happens to the Jews.'

Mama falls silent as she slips her arm around my shoulder. It feels strange, I am not used to it. Mama isn't a hugger or toucher, but I like the feeling of her arm around me. After a while my family huddles under the *pierzyna*.

Days go by without much change. I am cold and hungry most of the time, but I don't complain. My mother's face shows clearly when she is worried and upset. Seeing her with folded arms and eyes downcast, I recall her comments to Pani Goldbergowa, and I fear dying.

Marysia and I try to make a snowman, but the snow, trampled by thousands of feet, is mushy and dirty. We are free to roam the area with little restriction from our mothers.

Mama keeps reminding us, 'Walk. Move. Don't sit for very long. You will be warmer if you move around. Keep your scarf over your face. Don't take off your mittens.' Some days the scarf over my face has a frozen patch around my mouth and nose, and now and then I turn it around so as to feel no wetness against my skin. Those days I crawl in under the *pierzyna* periodically to warm up.

Marysia and I know where we can find other kids and who has which toy or knows a good game. We ignore the motionless people slumped on suitcases or bundles, we ignore the ones who shout angrily. We head out to find other children to play with. Too big to play, Halina spends most of her time with Mama. Back home, she liked to read books, talk with her friends, and sometimes go to movies. I don't know what kind of movies she saw; she refused to take me along.

Those who have been out in this field for weeks appear frozen in space and distant in their thought, not reacting when stepped on, not complaining when pushed or shoved, not washing their hands and faces with snow as others do. People grow accustomed to hearing screams without bothering to inquire what is happening.

One morning a loud shriek rises from the group next to a fire not far from us. Mama runs in that direction, and I follow her.

'My baby, my baby, let me warm my baby!' a woman screams, pushing a small bundle wrapped in a blue baby blanket towards the fire.

'Let her get closer. Move a little, move a little, people,' pleads an old woman with a gray hat pulled over her face.

'You'll burn the baby!'

'Don't get so close!' another yells.

The mother, silent now, her blank eyes staring into the distance, pushes towards the fire, not hearing anyone. In a gray wrinkled coat, her dark tangled hair sticking out from under a kerchief, the mother is no taller than a ten-year-old.

'You're tired. Let me warm your baby by the fire,' Mama says, stretching out her arms to receive the bundle. With a quick motion, the woman clutches the baby to her bosom. Having gotten closer to the baby, Mama asks, 'How long has your little one been asleep, lady?' The mother doesn't answer.

Some people inch closer, and a burly man in a fur-collared coat turns to the mother, 'Woman, your baby is dead! It needs no warming.' Holding the baby tight against her chest, the mother stands motionless. People in the group come up to peek, to see if indeed the baby is dead. By now most are experts at recognizing suffocated babies, dehydrated babies, and just dead babies. A big man, his face hardly visible behind a woolen scarf, takes the baby out of the mother's arms. The mother doesn't resist, just stays there with her arms folded over her chest as if still cuddling her baby. Two older women come up. 'Come, little mother, you need some rest.' She moves with them like a sleepwalker on wooden legs.

The man holding the baby turns resolutely and heads towards the Soviet border where every few feet a soldier stands with a rifle. The group that was around the fire follows the man, and others join them, forming a procession.

Facing the soldiers, the burly man with the baby shouts, 'Another innocent life gone! You don't give a damn whether we live or die. You are barbarians!'

'Let us in. Let us in.'

'You are no better than the Nazis.'

'Can you watch us die one by one? You are brutes.'

'We want to talk to your leaders. We demand to talk to your leaders,' voices scream and plead. The soldiers, like stone statues, stand motionless, and silent. Slowly the people are inching forward, their breath, like steam, clouding their faces.

The soldiers come to life, pointing their rifles at the moving crowd. The crowd steps back, but not the man cradling the dead baby. Stretching his arms and leaning forward without moving his planted feet, the man lays the bundle in front of one of the soldiers. 'Now, you look at death. Live with it the way we do. We will pile all the dead at your feet.'

His double-breasted, dark green coat tightly buttoned, his red face wrinkled around the eyes, body rigid, the soldier kicks the bundle with his heavy black boot, rolling it back into the crowd.

The baby is later buried in a shallow grave. It is so tiny only a few shovelsful of earth are needed to make the grave in the frozen ground.

Daily, the old and young—men, women, and children— are dying, and the shovels are brought out. The Polish peasant women, in addition to their bundles and buckets, now carry shovels tucked under their arms.

'Look, they are selling death. When we no longer can eat bread, they sell us shovels,' Pani Goldbergowa observes.

The last few days have been extremely cold. Halina and I wear extra sweaters. My feet have been hurting for many days, but I say nothing. I don't want to make Mama sad. Halina notices me loosening the shoelaces and rubbing my feet.

'What is it?' she asks.

'It hurts, my feet hurt.'

'Did you tell Mama?'

'No.'

Halina takes my hand and walks me to where our mother is talking to a man. Mama takes me under the *pierzyna* and unlaces my shoes. My feet are swollen, and from one toe a sticky discharge is seeping through the sock.

'Don't touch it, Mama. It hurts.' My mother looks silently at my feet as a tear rolls down her cheek; she wipes it away with the sleeve of her coat. She applies Vaseline to soften the sock, waits a little, and pulls off my socks. She dabs a little of the Vaseline on my toes, then wraps my feet in Tata's wool socks.

Mama sits with me under the *pierzyna* until I fall asleep, my head under the canopy she's made out of a blanket and a few sticks. That night, I awake feeling someone pushing me. I jab him with my elbow but fall right back to sleep. In the morning, I wake up and, on my right, lies a man clutching a corner of the *pierzyna*.

'Get away, get away!' I shout. The stranger, curled up on his side, doesn't budge. Tata wakes up.

'Tata, there is a man, and he won't go away.'

'Get away from my child!' my father yells at the man.

I move closer to Mama.

The man continues to ignore us. Tata jumps up and grabs the man's arm but immediately drops it. The man's stiff white face looks as if it's covered with a coat of dried-up glue. His eyes, like balls of ice, stare at me, making me chilly all over.

People around us are now awake.

'The man is frozen. The man is dead,' voices say.

'Mama, is the man in my bed dead? Frozen?' I cry.

Mama pulls me under the *pierzyna*. 'Sh...sh. It's okay, it's okay. He was very cold and wanted to warm up.'

'But he was under the *pierzyna*, so why did he die?'

'He was old.'

'Are you and Tata old?'

'No, we are not old.' (My mother was thirty, my father thirty-eight.)

A few men help my father carry the dead man away. Again the shovels appear.

During the day, Tata moves around and talks with people; I don't know where he goes, but it is okay—Mama is with us. The last few evenings, Tata has been wandering around in the dark and sometimes isn't around when I go to sleep.

'Mama, it's dark. Where is Tata?'

'He likes to walk a little before going to sleep.'

'But it's so dark, he won't find us.'

'I'm sure he will. He knows exactly where we are.'

Two nights after the incident with the dead man, my father and mother are sitting in the dark on the *pierzyna* and talking Yiddish. Mama, arms folded over her chest, is stroking her shoulders. Tata continues talking and Mama nods. Puzzled, I watch Tata put on his brown sweater, then the blue cardigan, and over it a heavy navy sweater with white deer.

'Tata, are you that cold?' I inquire.

'Halina and Irka, Tata will have to take a long walk tonight,' Mama says.

'Tata, are you going to be back when we get up?' I ask.

'No, but I will be back in a little while.'

'Where are you going?'

'I'm going to see cousin Ślamek.'

'Ślamek? Oh, Tata, I want to go with you,' I jump up.

'No, Irka. Not tonight.'

'Please, Tata, please, I want to see Ślamek.' Ślamek was my favorite cousin.

Squatting, Tata puts his arms around Halina and me.

'I need to go alone. Stay here with Mama. I'll be back as soon as I can.'

Mama takes my hand as we watch Tata walk away.

'I want so much to see Ślamek. Why didn't Tata take me?'

'He couldn't.'

I watch my father's back as he grows smaller and smaller until I can see him no longer. We crawl in under the *pierzyna* and pretend to be sleeping, but I know Mama and Halina are also awake.

The next morning, people around us are whispering, 'I think Pan Miller got through; he must've gotten through.'

'He told me how he was going to do it,' Marysia's father says. My father becomes a hero, but I don't understand what it's all about. I want my Tata back with us. One morning, a week later, when I wake up, my father is sitting and talking with my mother.

'Tata, you're back!' I yell out. 'Did you see Ślamek?'

'Yes, I did.'

My father, crawling and pulling his body like a snake, smuggled himself through the Soviet border and got to Białystok, twenty kilometers from the no man's land. With my eighteen-year-old cousin's help, he bribed a petty official to get a letter permitting his family to cross the border. When Tata shows the sealed letter to the soldier on border patrol, it turns out that in Russian, it states, 'The man and his two children can cross into the Soviet Union.' Trying to bribe the young soldier doesn't help. He is vehement. 'Not the woman.'

'Bella, I can't leave you alone.'

'Srulik, you must take the children out of here.'

'That son of a bitch. How he fooled me. He told me it was for my wife and children. I couldn't even ask to read the letter, I don't read Russian.'

My parents switch to Yiddish briefly.

57

'Halina and Irka, you will go with Tata, and I will come later.'

'Bella, I won't leave you here for long. I'll come back to get you.'

'I know you will.'

'Mama, I don't want to go without you, I don't want to go without you,' I keep repeating.

'Go, Irka, go with Tata. The soldiers won't let me leave now, but soon I'll come.'

Halina starts crying.

Mama repacks our suitcase, pulling out her things. 'Keep the *pierzyna*,' Tata insists. My lips tight, eyes closed, I try to hold back tears, but they are flowing. Mama hugs us. Halina tugs me by the hand and we go. I turn back to see whether Mama is crying, but I can't tell—she stands with her hands covering her eyes. Halina and I walk side by side, she sobbing, I quietly choking on my tears. Will another dead man creep under Mama's *pierzyna*, will she have food? Why didn't the soldiers let her come with us? When will I see Mama? The questions are racing in my head, making me very sad. Even the idea of seeing Slamek doesn't help. I want Mama with us.

The Soviet soldiers make us wait until four in the afternoon, when the guards change.

I wonder how Tata will find his way in the forest without any roads and scarcely any light, but I try not to worry about it. Maybe tall people see better. My feet are wrapped in strips of linen my mother has made by tearing a sheet. Wearing my father's old shoes, I am looking to avoid rocks and hard branches. Every time my foot hits a hard surface, the pain is terrible. By now my feet are swollen beyond fitting into any of my own shoes. 'Lean on me,' Halina says, but that doesn't help. My six-foot-tall father with his long legs is forgetting that we can't keep up with him.

58

'Tata, don't walk so fast, my legs are short,' I remind him.

'We must hurry before it gets very dark.'

It is dark already, but I say nothing.

I step on a small rock and scream, 'Oh, my foot, my foot!'

'Halina, do you think that you could carry the black bag for a little bit?' Tata asks.

'I can.'

Handing the bag to my sister, my father picks me up with his free arm. A big suitcase in hand on one side, and me on his arm on the other, he walks on. It feels wonderful to be carried by my strong father. After about ten minutes I look at Halina and see the bag falling out of her arms.

'Tata, I feel better. I can walk now.'

Night descends upon us quickly. The forest is dark and scary. The reflection of the snow is our only illumination. It is the beginning of January; the frost is stinging and biting my hands and feet. Seeing me rub my hands, my father takes off his mittens and tells me to put them over mine.

'No, Tata, your hands will freeze.'

'Take them, take them. I'll pull down the sleeves of my sweater.'

I warm my hands and then pass the big mittens to Halina. My sister's coat hangs loosely on her thin frame, her blue eyes seem deeper in her face than I remember, her short hair hangs limp on her forehead. She seems smaller than in Warsaw.

After a while Halina gives the mittens back to our father whose hands have turned beet-red.

Holding Halina's hand, I look around, scared of what might leap out of the woods. Behind every tree I see a lion, a bear, or a wolf. Petrified, I hardly breathe. 'Come on,' Halina says and yanks my hand.

The snow, crunchy under our feet, sounds like the roar of a wild animal. I want to drown out these sounds with human voices, but Tata and Halina are walking in silence.

'Are there a lot of animals in the woods, Tata?'

'Don't be afraid. They are all asleep in the winter.'

'Tata, do we have far to go?'

'Not far. Are you very tired?'

'No,' I lie.

Eventually we find ourselves in an open area on a narrow road. We pass a few farmhouses with dim light in the windows, a barn, another barn.

'Tata, are we going to take a train to Białystok now?' I ask, remembering Pan Maciej's instructions.

'There is no train to Białystok from here. Maciej lied to us.'

I am puzzled, I have never heard of adults lying. I don't speak, but from time to time grab my sister's hand to steady myself.

'Halina, are you tired?' I ask.

'A little, just a little,' she says, and she cries.

'We will be there soon, very soon,' Tata tells us.

I don't know what the 'there' is, but I don't ask. Tata looks very serious. It's no time to talk to him.

'See that house straight ahead, with a light in the window?' Tata asks. 'Not far from there is the cabin Ślamek rented for us for two days.'

We pick up our pace. I can't wait to see my cousin. I forget about being tired, forget about my hurting feet. We soon will be in a cabin with Ślamek. A few minutes later, we arrive.

I run fast, knock on the door, and within seconds, right there in front of me is my beloved cousin.

'Ślamek, Ślamek!' I scream, not believing that it really is he, my Ciocia Fela's youngest son. Ślamek picks me up in his arms. 'Oh, my little dumpling,' he says, hugging me tightly. In the past, he used to pat my pudgy cheeks and teasingly call me 'little dumpling.' I adore this cousin of mine: kind, handsome, six-feet-tall, with dark wavy hair, big hazel eyes, and a smile that leaves all the girls swooning, who tells me funny stories, and feeds me chocolates. As he puts me down, he looks at my feet in my father's black, muddy shoes.

'Does it hurt you, little dumpling?'

'Yes.'

Ślamek hugs Halina and my father.

It is warm in this one-room cabin. In a potbelly stove, logs are burning. A single lightbulb hangs above a wooden table surrounded by five chairs made of branches. Against one wall lean a few military cots, the khaki canvas still new.

'Take off your coat,' Halina tells me, but I hesitate. For the last five weeks, while in the no man's land, I had my coat on day and night. It feels like a part of my body.

'I will be cold.'

'Don't be silly,' Halina tells me, grabbing my sleeve and pulling off the coat. I feel strange without my coat, but say nothing.

Ślamek brings a plate of fresh-buttered Kaiser rolls. Some are filled with chocolate chips, my favorite food. We each get a yellow apple, *złote renaty*, and mugs of hot, sweet tea. It has been a very long time since I've had either an apple or a Kaiser roll with chocolate chips. Back home, Mama used to put a few *złote renaty* in the linen closet to give the sheets a nice aroma.

We are all famished, and each bite feels heavenly. I pull my shoes off, and Ślamek winces at the bandage, encrusted with dry pus, over my toes, but says nothing. A few minutes later he returns with a basin of warm water, puts it on the floor next to my feet, and shakes in some powder from a metal box.

'Little dumpling, put your feet in the basin. They'll feel better.'

'Ouch!' I yell.

'I know it hurts, but the water will help you, it will soon stop hurting.'

I gorge on the Kaiser rolls while keeping my feet in the basin. After a while the rags wrapped around my feet soften, and my cousin carefully peels them off, exposing my swollen red feet. He dumps the water outdoors and returns with a big wooden tub.

Filling the tub half full with warm water, Ślamek undresses me.

'We need to scrub you to see your pretty little face.'

My father looks on, relieved that someone else is taking care of me. He has never bathed me, never fed me — this was my mother's job. It feels warm and soft in the tub; I want to stay in it forever.

Ślamek lifts me out of the tub into a warm towel. 'We will have to fatten up your cheeks, or I won't be able to call you my dumpling.' My cousin wraps me in the flannel top of his pajamas and tucks me into bed.

'Sleep with me, Ślamek.'

'Just for a little while. I need to help Halina and your Tata.'

Fully dressed, my cousin lies on top of the blanket, cradling my head on his chest. 'Ślamek, my Mama is alone in the no man's land. She is very sad. She is trying not to cry, she is trying so hard not to cry. When is my Mama gonna come?'

'Soon, Irka, very soon. Your Tata will go and fetch her.'

He wipes the tears from my face with his thumb, and I fall asleep in his arms."

"Mom, what happened to your mother?" Naomi asked.

"No, I can't anymore. Not tonight. Next Sunday," I tell her, my voice cracking.

3

Mama's Journey

The following Sunday, at nine in the morning, Naomi arrived in her brother's Honda.

It was a crisp morning, the snowy lawn sparkled, and outside the kitchen window icicles hung from the magnolia tree, but Naomi ran into the house coatless, brown cotton shirt hanging over her jeans, a purple scarf flung around her neck.

"Hi, Mom."

"My God, Naomi, you must be freezing," *I said, putting my arms around her.*

"I'm fine."

Plopping herself into a kitchen chair, stretching her legs under the table, half-reclining like a pious Jew at the Seder table, Naomi laced her fingers and stretched her arms, yawning.

"Did you have breakfast, Naomi?"

"Who can eat so early in the morning? I grabbed a Starbucks on the way."

"Eat something with me, I've been up for a while."

"Mom, you get up with the chickens. Did you work out already?"

"I don't know about the chickens, but I jogged earlier."

*I set out two brown plates — Arabia pottery, Naomi's favorite —
and out of the fridge took multigrain bread, Black Diamond sharp
cheddar, and cherry tomatoes, their green stems still on them.*

"Some orange juice, Naomi?"

"Yeah, thanks."

*We sat at the kitchen table facing each other, Naomi holding a
tall glass of juice, and I with hot water in a colorful earthenware
mug my son Danny made for me. Watching me tear off a small piece
of bread and a snippet of cheese, Naomi burst out laughing.*

*"Mom, you always take a dainty piece and then keep chipping
away at the rest. Just take a good chunk to begin with."*

"I like eating this way. I can have many helpings."

We both kept nibbling until the food was all gone.

*"Mom, I told my friends about the no man's land, and they could-
n't believe you really lived through it."*

*"Naomi, even now it seems unbelievable to me, but all I have to
do is close my eyes and think about that time, and I can bring it all
back: the pain in my frost-bitten feet, the growling hunger in my belly,
and the screams of mothers whose babies died. But I also remember
how, despite all that, I found ways to play with other children."*

*Naomi sat quietly looking at the cheese plate. Spotting a few
crumbs, she scooped them with her finger, then licked it.*

"Tell me what happened to your mother."

"Did Ślamek stay with you?"

*"No Naomi. My beloved cousin went back to Warsaw to be with
his parents, and perished like all my other relatives in Poland."*

"Mom, this must have made you very sad."

*"I can't find words to describe how sad it made me, I cry even
now thinking about it. At times I still fantasize that he is alive and
that unexpectedly I will meet him."*

"Oh. mom, mom." Naomi put her arms around me.

"I didn't hear the full story of my mother's experiences after we left her in the no man's land until I was almost grown up. Since I wasn't there, I will tell you as I heard it from my mother. Let's go into the den."

I sat in my corner of the couch, pulled the afghan over my feet—the den, being on the lower level, was much colder than the rest of the house.

"Come, we'll share the blanket."

"Thanks, Mom, I'll sit in the lounge-chair."

With Naomi facing me, I shut my eyes, and sat motionless a few moments.

"It is a few weeks since we left the no man's land. We now live in Ignatki, a camp for immigrant Jews, outside of Białystok. This densely wooded area, with cabins scattered like giant mushrooms sprouting out of the ground, had been part of an estate of a Polish prince before the Soviets confiscated it. The cabins must have at one time housed the workers.

Tata is gone most of the time. Sometimes neighbors in adjacent cabins offer us cooked food. 'Poor Miller girls, their father has to find a way to get their mother from the no man's land. The little Miller girl is a serious child. Kids grow up fast during a war, and without a mother,' I hear a neighbor say.

Halina, already twelve, is hovering over me like a little Mama. When Tata is gone for a few days, she worries all the time. In the daytime I don't think much about Tata, or Mama. I'm busy with other kids, sometimes playing in the snow, making up games, or just talking and talking. At night, though, I am scared that Tata might not come back. What will Halina and I do if he doesn't come back? When Halina helps me change the bandages and dabs on the ointment that Tata bought for my still-draining and aching feet, I think of Mama and miss her terribly. Nights on my cot, with the blanket over my head, I weep quietly. I dream about Mama and wake up startled, looking for her.

With no money for a train ticket, my father, under the cover of night, climbs to the roofs of trains headed towards the no man's land. Russian soldiers spot him and drag him off to jail. Five days later Tata is released and shows up in our camp.

'Where is Mama? Why didn't she come back with you?' Halina and I ask. Our father explains what happened. Two days later he leaves again, headed toward the border. This time Tata succeeds in reaching the no man's land.

Walking through the wooded area towards the trees where Pan Maciej originally dropped us off, my father is startled. He looks at the fields, a few weeks earlier crowded with people, now silent and empty. A child's muddy hat, a woman's shoe, a water-logged pillow, an open empty suitcase held together by one hinge, a dented metal cup, and a spoon lie before him, like corpses after a slaughter. In the distance he can see more strewn-about small objects. We had left Mama straight ahead, about ten yards from the trees. That spot is empty now. What happened to Bella? Where are all the people? Walking farther, Tata sees a peasant woman bending, scooping up some things from the ground, putting them in a bucket.

'Excuse me, weren't there once a lot of people here?'

'Yes. Jews. *Niemcy* (Germans) took them all back.'

'When did the Germans take them?'

'Two Sundays since, maybe three.'

Tata walks away and goes back behind the trees. He keeps looking and waiting, as if expecting Mama to jump down from a tree or pop up out of the snow-covered ground. He stays there waiting and waiting, unable to leave, unable to question the soldiers because it is illegal to be on the border without a travel permit. At nightfall Tata leaves the no man's land. Nothing to do, and no one to ask, he returns to the camp the same way he left—on the tops of trains.

It is evening when our father returns. The wood Halina and I gathered is burning in the stove. I am sitting on the cabin floor getting ready to change my bandages. My sister is after me with the tube in her hand; she is getting quite bossy. The door opens, Tata walks in. Seeing his drawn face, his downcast eyes, how slowly he is walking, almost dragging his feet, I know things aren't good. I don't ask. Neither does Halina, but we both look at Tata expectantly. What happened to my Mama? Did she freeze like the man under the *pierzyna*?

'The Germans took Mama back to Poland. She wasn't there,' Tata explains apologetically. I can no longer hold back my tears.

'Tata, will Mama come to us?'

'Yes, Irka, I'm sure she'll come.'

'How?' Halina asks.

'Your Mama will find a way.'

***

'*Achtung! Achtung!*' A blasting voice startles the sleeping people in the fields of the no man's land. Bella opens her eyes, but shuts them again to keep out the blinding rays of the powerful flashlight pointed at her face. 'Don't move!' a German command roars through a loudspeaker. Hesitatingly, Bella opens her eyes only to see a pair of black shiny boots two feet away. The nightmarish reality hits her—the Germans, the Germans are here! All around is a total stillness, the mass of people not stirring, not breathing—only the boots, the thud of marching boots piercing the silence.

Four columns of soldiers march east to west, dividing the field into four sections. They pause. One more roaring command in German, and five other columns of soldiers march south to north. With utmost precision and efficiency the people on the no man's land are split into twenty groups, each encircled by Nazi soldiers with cocked rifles.

Afraid to lift her head and find out who is in those boots, Bella closes her eyes to delay facing the monsters in marching boots. 'Is this the end? Will I ever see my girls? God, if you exist, please deliver me safely to my children,' Bella prays.

Dawn is creeping in and Bella can now see the movement of people in the distance, but no one around her dares to change position. After what feels like hours, but is no more than fifteen minutes or so, she hears 'Get up, get up! Grab your things and line up. *Schnell, schnell!*' the German soldiers are yelling, jabbing the people with rifles. The old man at Bella's side is slow in gathering his bags. A German soldier pushes the man with his rifle, rips the suitcase from his hand, and kicks it into the crowd. The man's wife reaches for her husband's hand, whispering, 'Forget the bags, Heniek. Come.'

In one hand Bella carries her suitcase, and with the other she drags the black bag with the *pierzyna* in it. At the blast of a whistle, people advance, following the soldiers. They hurry, hoping the fast pace will save them from the Nazi soldiers' fury. A woman turns to speak to her husband, a soldier hits her with the butt of his rifle, knocking her to the ground. 'Silence!' he yells. The husband pulls her to her feet.

Laden with whatever they could grab in a hurry, the procession of Jews walks in silence, trampling the snow. They walk and walk — for an hour, for two hours, clinging to one another, fearing empty spaces between them. Bella's heart is filled with terror, but she keeps pace with the others. The suitcase in her right hand feels terribly heavy, growing heavier and heavier with each step, as if to pull off her arm. The black bag is big and clumsy. Bella slows down to switch her load. Realizing that she has fallen a step behind, she picks up speed, dragging the bag on the ground. Suddenly, she feels a hard kick on her backside and hears a swoosh behind her. She loses her balance. A woman's arm grabs her, breaking her fall. With a swing of his bayonet, the soldier chops off Bella's bag, leaving only the cord in her hand. The bag with the *pierzyna* falls to the ground. The *pierzyna* is gone. It is gone. Like a severed limb, it lies there useless. People are stepping on it, kicking it, trampling it beneath their dirty shoes, but Bella doesn't turn to look. She keeps her head high and walks still holding the cord, feeling the fibers with the tips of her fingers, rolling the knot in the palm of her hand. A few minutes later she opens her hand, letting the cord drop to the ground.

The crowd walks. Thousands of people walking on and on, each step tougher to take. The first to abandon a suitcase or a bag are those with children; the little ones must be carried. But for many others the load has simply become too heavy to bear. Soon the road is strewn with abandoned possessions.

Most children, but not all, sensing the adults' terror, cling to their parents without crying. A tall young woman, a few people ahead of Bella, walks holding the hand of a five-year-old boy and a baby in her arms; her husband carries the luggage. The baby, wrapped in a man's dark jacket, can hardly be seen. It looks like another bundle of clothing grabbed up at the last minute. But suddenly the baby gives out a load shriek, piercing the silence like the edge of a sharp blade. '*Shh...shh,*' the mother rocks the baby girl, swaying with each step. The baby keeps screaming. The mother puts her thumb in the baby's mouth, the little one sucks for a few seconds, spits the thumb out, and screams again. Tension mounts in the crowd. Fear hangs in the air; you can almost touch it. It clings to the skin underneath the many layers of clothing. Clutching the baby to her bosom, the mother now frantically rocks the little one, repeating, 'Shh–shh, my angel,' but the baby girl doesn't stop crying. A woman behind the mother finds a crust of dry bread in her coat pocket and stretches her arm to pass it on to the mother. A German soldier, with two quick steps, is at the mother's side, yanking the baby from her arms and tossing it into the air like a flying football. Cocking his rifle, he shoots the baby while it is still airborne. The infant falls to the ground. A tiny leg, thin as a twig, sticks out from beneath the gray jacket now covering the baby's back and head. The baby's arms, like the wings of an injured bird, lie folded on the snow. Screaming, the mother runs to her child. The soldier, his rifle still cocked, watches the mother and, as she kneels next to her baby, her arms stretched and ready to embrace it, fires a single bullet into her head; her body falls on the body of her baby. A pool of blood forms around her head, a red crown on the fresh snow. The husband collapses. Someone props him up. The son cries. A man picks him up and carries him in his arms, pulling the father by the sleeve. The husband, his suitcases abandoned on the ground behind him, keeps walking, staring into the distance, as if detached from what has just happened to his baby and wife. People try to whisper to him, but he does not hear, does not react. He is elsewhere, somewhere removed from the death of his wife and child.

Bella expels a whistling sigh, gasping for air. Her chest heaving, she feels a vacuum in her lungs, the air sucked out of her. Momentarily she is flooded with heat, then shaking with chills. Tears flow down her face, but she continues walking.

No one looks back at the fallen mother and child. People move on, stunned by what they have just seen, horror mixed with fear reflected in their faces.

After hours of silently walking through fields, the people come to railroad tracks and a line of boxcars. No station, no conductor visible, just a train in a field. The Germans stop. No matter where the trains take them, the people feel relieved, no longer having to walk. When the soldiers move away, the woman who broke Bella's fall asks, 'How are you doing?'

'I can't shake off the mother and the baby. It's barbaric, unbelievable.'

'There are no words for it.'

'Thanks for helping me. I'm Bella Miller.'

'I am Greta Burger.'

Light brown hair cropped short in a stylish way, deep blue-gray eyes and a bouncy light walk make this tall twenty-four-year-old woman appear out of place among the tired, haggard-looking people. Greta had been in the no man's land only a week.

The soldiers return. All whispers cease.

Exhausted, some people sit on their suitcases, but a jab with a rifle or a blow with the butt brings them back to their feet. 'Where are we going? What will they do with us?' are the questions on everyone's mind as the crowd stands and waits, not knowing for what. It is snowing again. Bella is extremely thirsty, not having drunk or eaten since the previous day. She opens her mouth to catch a few snowflakes to wet her tongue. Suddenly a German command—'*Scheisse*'—and the soldiers shove the people under the train, pushing them with their boots and guns.

'What did they say?' a woman asks Greta.

'They want us to relieve ourselves under the train.'

'What? With all the people around?'

'Yes. They are shouting "shit."'

Some people, not understanding the command, stand bewildered and hear again, 'Shit, shit.'

'Come.' Greta takes Bella's hand and leads her under the train.

Humiliated, people are turning away from one another, hiding their shame. Closing her eyes, Bella lowers her head, as though this makes her invisible. Men have to squat to urinate, but one old man's legs won't hold up; he goes down on his knees wetting the edge of his coat.

Now the soldiers start loading people into the boxcars. They push and yell, 'Go, go!' People are helping one another, lifting the children, the suitcases. The old man and his wife aren't able to pull themselves into the boxcar. Two younger men hoist the woman, then her husband, lowering them gently into the train.

'My bag, my bag,' the woman is saying in a whisper.

'It's on the train already. This lady took it up for you.' The man points to Bella.

The Germans load as many people as they can squeeze into each boxcar. When it fills up, the soldiers push the sliding door and lock it with a metal bar.

It is dark inside the boxcar. Sporadically, beams from soldiers' flashlights come through the cracks between the boards, illuminating the interior.

Bella and Greta put their suitcases in the corner next to each other. They are tired, but they cannot fall asleep. Now, at least, they can talk. Bella tells Greta about her children and husband on the Soviet side. Greta's fiancé is waiting for her in Kiev.

Greta, the only child of an affluent couple, has known many privileges, but she is no stranger to perseverance and struggle. A javelin thrower, through sheer determination she defeated the odds, overcoming severe shoulder injuries to compete in the Olympics in Germany. Greta speaks a fluent Hochdeutsch, the language of the German educated classes. Her German-born parents moved to Krakow before her birth. Like Bella, Greta is a secular Jew.

'Greta, are we moving?' Bella asks surprised.

'Yes. The train has been rolling slowly for a while.'

'I didn't feel it!'

'You are tired.'

The two women talk late into the night, then finally doze off. Eventually, the heavy metal bar is lifted, the door slid back, and daylight floods the boxcar. Everyone rushes to the opening to breathe the fresh air and to find out where they are. The train is in a field different from the night before. On one side are pine trees; farther down are birches blending into the snow.

The Germans order the people to get off and crawl under the train, as they did the night before. Bella finds a patch of fresh snow, scoops up some to eat, then rubs her face and hands with the rest. Snow has been the main source of water during the past few weeks, and she has become adept at using it in many ways.

After a few minutes the people are loaded back into the train, but the doors of the boxcars are left open. Searching in her bag for a handkerchief to wipe her hands, Bella discovers a crust of forgotten bread. Keeping her hands in the purse, she breaks the bread in two and places one piece in Greta's hand.

'Where did you get this?' Greta whispers.

'I found it in my bag.'

The women suck the dry bread quietly, so as not to be noticed by the others.

'What will the Germans do with us?' a woman with a toddler in her arms asks no one in particular.

'They will bring us to some Polish city and just dump us. What do they need us for?'

'Then why are they just keeping the train in the fields?'

'You know how they are, they have to get exact orders from their Führer.'

'They will take us into labor camps. We'll help them win the war.'

'What about the women and children?'

A loud whistle sounds, and everyone falls silent. Two soldiers appear at the door of the boxcar and toss in loaves of bread. One, two, three. People rush for them, falling over one another. A man is struggling with a woman for a loaf that fell on the floor. As he grabs it, she rips off a chunk. People are shouting and pushing to get to the bread.

'People, stop it!' a woman yells. Her loud, angry voice startles everyone.

'You grab the breads like animals. Shame on you. We are all hungry.'

Those who've succeeded in catching a loaf are hanging onto it.

'The Germans treat us like beasts, and you behave like such!' the woman bellows. She is no more than four feet ten, and thin as a starving child, but her indignation and resoluteness hush everyone.

The woman gives orders to a man near her, 'Take away the loaves from those who grabbed them and bring them here. We will divide the bread among all of us.'

'Pani,' she says to Greta, 'Count how many we are.'

'Sixty-eight,' Greta counts.

'We will divide the bread equally.'

'What about the kids? They don't need as much as an adult man,' a man in a fur hat hollers.

'Everyone gets the same,' many voices answer.

The bread is divided. This is the food for the day; no other food is given. In the evening, everybody is unloaded to relieve themselves. The German soldiers appear less vigilant; they don't rush the people right back into the boxcars.

Coming back into the boxcar, Bella turns to Greta. 'They are going to kill us all; I feel it in my bones. I have to run away. Do you want to come with me?' The two women whisper for a long time.

The next day the same routine, but this time no one grabs at the bread tossed in.

Bella chews the bread slowly, her thoughts on the plan she and Greta have made. It is risky, but she is determined to get away. During the evening unloading of people, Bella and Greta, while unbuttoning their garments under the train, keep moving towards the pines and brush, keeping an eye on the black boots. The pair of boots next to them moves away. No other boots in sight. Bella grabs Greta's hand. Swiftly, both women cross the track and huddle behind snow-covered bushes. They wait for a few minutes, glance around, and creep away from the train. Some people under the train notice Bella and Greta escaping, but give no sign. Again, Bella takes Greta's hand and they silently advance farther into the woods. Now Bella can see the people being shoved back into the train. Hidden among the trees, the women wait until there are no soldiers in sight.

Still uncertain of their invisibility, they crawl until they are a good distance from the train. Not knowing in which direction they would find a train station, they choose the more densely wooded area along the track.

They walk as fast as their feet can carry them, too fearful to look back, though by now, if they were to turn, the train would no longer be seen. They must have been walking for over an hour without a human being or beast in sight.

'Let's sit down here.' Greta points to a fallen tree. The women have no luggage, only their handbags into which each had stuffed a few easily accessible things.

'Okay, Greta, now we do our masquerade,' Bella says with a smile. Out of her tapestry bag, she pulls her silver-fox collar, the head and tail intact, as though the animal had just dozed off. Then comes the rhinestone brooch. She pins the brooch to Greta's beret, tosses the fox around her friend's neck, and steps back to assess the results.

'Greta, you need lipstick.'

'I don't use it.'

'A lady who has traveled from Warsaw to find a decent maid must wear makeup.'

Fumbling in her bag, Bella locates a lipstick and rouge. She removes the lipstick cover and outlines Greta's full lips.

'No, you don't need rouge,' Bella observes. 'You look gorgeous. No German son-of-a-bitch will be able to resist you.'

'I don't want to look too good to them. This lipstick feels greasy on my mouth. How do women eat with this stuff on?'

'Don't worry, we have nothing to eat,' Bella reassures her. The friends look at each other, realizing the irony.

'Now is your turn.' Greta hands Bella a black kerchief. 'Tuck all your hair under it. No, no, lower over your forehead.'

'Where did you get this *shmate?*' Bella asks.

'I bought it from one of the peasant women.'

Looking Bella over, Greta concludes, 'Your coat looks too good for a maid. We need to rough it up some.'

'It is all wrinkled already; it wasn't made to serve as a blanket.'

'It still looks too rich for a maid, we should tear it a little.'

Greta twists her finger into the sleeve of Bella's dark-gray tweed coat and yanks. The fabric pulls but doesn't rip. Picking up a stick, she pushes it through the fabric and pulls. This time, it gives. Then she rips some of the seam where the sleeve meets the shoulder. Remembering Pan Bornstein, the tailor, assuring her that the fabrics would last forever, Bella bursts out laughing, covering her mouth to muffle the sound.

Not knowing what's so funny, Greta looks on with a smile. Abruptly, Bella's laugh turns into tears. She sobs as intensely as she was laughing moments earlier. Greta watches her friend silently. Bella's thoughts are racing and images float before her eyes: Srulik walking fast, the girls following him in the forest. How are Irka's feet? What are the girls doing now? She envisions her husband's startled face finding the no man's land empty of people. She never doubted that he would come to get her.

'Greta, we need to keep moving.'

In the darkness, it's hard to see the ground, but the women keep walking.

Stepping carefully so as not to trip over a fallen branch, they follow the railroad tracks, hoping to reach a train station. After walking what seems many hours, they see a dim light in the distance and hasten their steps. Alongside the tracks stands a small wooden shack, an oil lamp in the window, not much else visible. Greta knocks on the door. A man wearing a black cap with an insignia of a bell emerges.

'Does the train to Warsaw stop here?' Greta asks.

'Yes, it does.'

'When is the next train due?'

'At twenty-one and a half.'

Greta, pulling Bella along, enters the cabin that serves as the train station.

'May we wait inside?'

'It ain't a place for a lady. No chair, dirty.'

'That's okay. Thank you. We'll wait right here,' Greta says, plopping herself down on the wooden bench against the wall.

'Olga, sit!' Greta orders Bella. The women haven't discussed a name for Bella; Olga is the first that sprung to Greta's mind, just as good as any Polish name.

The station attendant looks the women over with great curiosity.

It is a long silent hour waiting for the train to arrive. A coal-burning oven behind the attendant's chair is radiating welcoming warmth, helping to illuminate the room. The rusted metal bench where the women sit, a small wooden table with chipped corners, and a wooden chair are the only furniture in this train station.

'She's coming, I can hear her,' the station attendant announces.

'Do you sell the tickets?' Greta asks.

'No, I have no tickets. You have to buy them on the train.'

Pulling Bella by the sleeve, Greta boards the train as soon as it comes to a stop. Bella's heart is thumping like a racing engine. The possibility of meeting a German soldier face to face horrifies her. She, the dumb maid, will have to be silent during their journey to Warsaw, but will she be able to quell her terror?

The first compartment is crowded with peasants headed for one of the villages on the way to Warsaw. Their burlap wrapped bundles and metal buckets leaning against their muddy boots fill up the compartment floor. In the second compartment sits a woman reading a book, her old Persian lamb coat partially open, revealing a red turtleneck sweater. Next to her are two older men, one sound asleep. Greta moves to a third compartment occupied by two old peasant women sitting next to the window and facing each other. She walks in, followed by Bella. Silently the friends sit next to each other, stowing their handbags under the seat. Above each wooden bench is a luggage rack, but it is simpler to put their bags next to their feet. They have no idea where they are or how far from Warsaw. Asking is too dangerous.

Eager for the train to take off, Bella feels her tension mounting. Greta looks composed and aloof.

After a few minutes, an old man in a blue uniform with a canvas shoulder bag walks in. 'Tickets, tickets, tickets.'

'Two to Warsaw,' Greta says, reaching into her bag.

'Twenty-two *złote.*'

'When do we arrive in Warsaw?' she asks casually, handing the money to the man.

'Same as always. We run on time.'

Bella hears a whistle, sees a low beam of light passing a few times by the window. The train moves slowly, then faster and faster, and off it goes.

'I must be strong, I must control my fear. Showing how afraid I am will give me away,' Bella keeps repeating to herself.

Half an hour later, a stop. One of the peasant women gets off, carrying in each hand a bundle wrapped in black cloth.

Her eyes downcast, thinking of her life before the Nazi occupation as if it had been someone else's story, Bella is startled by a loud German voice. 'Your papers?'

Greta stands up and turns to the soldier. 'She is my maid, she is mute.'

'I want to see her papers.'

'I will find them in her bag,' Greta says, reaching under Bella's seat.

Overhearing this brief exchange and surprised by the elegant German, an officer steps into the compartment.

'Don't disturb the lady,' he tells the soldier, and with the wave of his hand sends the soldier out.

'Thank you,' Greta nods.

'Sorry for the soldier's ignorance.' The German officer stands at the door of the compartment, gazing at Greta. His eyes travel from her face down her firm breasts and along the rest of her body, pausing at the strong shapely legs in thin, navy wool stockings, the latest of European styles, and back to her mouth where a smile barely curves her lips.

Greta sits down. The German officer eases himself into the compartment.

'Where is Fraulein headed?'

'To Warsaw.'

'Is this where she lives?'

'Yes.'

'Interesting,' the officer observes.

Greta's smile grows slightly more generous, but she says nothing, wondering what is so interesting about her living in Warsaw. Bella's heart is pounding; she is glad to be mute. The officer stands there a minute longer, then leaves the compartment, bowing politely to Greta. Seeing the passenger across from them closing her eyes, Greta reaches for Bella's hand. The women grasp each other's palms, holding on for only a moment. The passenger appears to be asleep, but Bella doesn't dare to speak. Maybe the woman is faking sleep; maybe she suspects that Bella is a Jew and is just waiting for an opportunity to summon a German soldier. They sit in silence, Bella gauging the distance they have traveled on this train headed to Warsaw.

Though it is cold outside, the train feels warm to Bella. The 50-watt lightbulb hanging from a wire in the center of the compartment feels luxurious.

The door opens. The German officer is back. This time Bella looks at him for a brief moment, then averts her eyes as from a disturbing glare. The six-foot-tall man is probably no older than twenty-five. How many Jews has he already killed? she wonders.

'Fraulein must be hungry. Will she have dinner with me in the officers' dining car?'

Greta is startled by this invitation. She is frightened by this man, but also afraid to refuse, and she is painfully hungry. She and Bella haven't eaten in two days.

'It would be my pleasure,' Greta nods to the German officer. 'I can't, however, leave my maid. Should another soldier come inspecting, she can't speak.'

'We can take care of that.'

He pulls a small folder from his breast pocket, tears out a brown sticker, signs it, and sticks it to the glass door of the compartment.

'No one will inspect this compartment any further.'

'Thank you,' Greta nods politely.

'Please Fraulein,' the officer says, offering Greta his arm. The passageway is too narrow for the two to walk abreast, so he walks ahead, from time to time glancing back at Greta.

Is he suspicious? Who does he think Greta is? What about all the other soldiers in the dining car? What will she do if he asks for her papers? Bella can't stop worrying. Yet the idea of eating makes her head spin and she is envious of Greta. What will they eat? Will Greta have hot tea?

The officers' dining room is well illuminated. Fine china and silverware on a white tablecloth reflect the light of two glass chandeliers. Three German officers seated in the center stand and salute Greta's escort, right arms out in a "*Heil Hitler!*" The salute makes Greta shudder, but she shows no emotion. Greta's escort leads her to the table in the farthest corner of the dining car and helps take off her coat, hanging it on a hook.

The waiter, in broken German, lists the items on the menu.

'Will Fraulein have Wiener Schnitzel or Sauerbraten?' the officer asks.

'Sauerbraten sounds good.'

'The same for me,' orders the officer, adding 'soup and beer.'

As the waiter leaves, the officer introduces himself.

'I am Hans Muller. And Fraulein?'

'Greta Burger.'

Greta smiles, and for the first time looks directly at the German, meeting his eyes. Blond hair flattened by the hat he removed, gray eyes, together with a few freckles sprinkled around the nose make this German look almost human. Greta looks at the stars on Hans's shoulder. Do they signify that he has distinguished himself by killing more people, more Jews than the others? Her insides are churning, and sweat is now sticky on her neck, but Greta maintains her composure and smiles politely.

'Is Fraulein German?'

'I am German, but I live now in Warsaw.'

Eager to change the topic, Greta observes, 'This is a very nice dining car. Do you frequent it?'

'I'm only occasionally on this line. Do you travel a lot?'

'No, I just came to get a maid. They are not easy to find in Warsaw. This one comes with recommendations, reputed to be honest and a hard worker.'

Hans looks at Greta, his eyes glistening.

'Fraulein has the hands of a musician—such elegant long fingers,' he says, stroking his own hand.

'I play piano.'

'What music do you like?'

Is this a test, a pitfall? Greta wonders and quickly comes up with a German composer.

'I play a variety of music, however, Wagner, Ravel, and Bizet are my favorites.'

'Ravel is also my favorite,' Hans comments.

'Do you play an instrument?'

'The violin. I teach at the conservatory.'

For a moment, Greta sees before her a handsome man she isn't afraid of. Hans's eyes seem soft and reflective, and the rumpled blond hair, unusually long for a soldier, falling across his forehead, gives him the appearance of a grown boy. Greta has an urge to run her fingers through his hair, but of course she doesn't. Her comfort lasts only until Greta's eyes fall again on the green uniform with the officer's insignia. Can the hands that play a violin shoot a baby? Can they stab an old man? What will he do if he discovers that I'm a Jew?

'Why does Fraulein now live in Warsaw?'

'For family reasons. Oh, it's a little complicated. I'd rather you tell me about yourself. What conservatory do you teach in?'

'Before the war I taught in Berlin. I haven't played the violin or heard beautiful music for quite a while.'

The mention of war heightens Greta's tension, yet she must engage in conversation.

'Music brings its reward even in difficult times, Herr Muller.'

'Yes, it does.'

He is eager to know more about her.

'Does Fraulein go to concerts in Warsaw?'

'Occasionally,' she lies. Does he assume we party and just have a jolly time? What does he know about life in Warsaw now? What does he understand about being a Jew?

When the food arrives, Greta has to exercise enormous self-control not to attack it. She is now the athlete focused inward, tuning out all external sounds and images, controlling her feelings through the power of concentration.

Good manners require a little conversation before dipping into the soup.

'Please, Fraulein,' Hans points to the soup.

Placing her white linen napkin on her lap, Greta starts eating, waiting for two counts before dipping her spoon again into the soup. Despite the anxiety churning in the pit of her belly, Greta delights in the hot food. Sauerbraten with red cabbage—where do the Germans find it? It is February, where do they find cabbage in February?

The taste of beef brings memories of dinners with family and friends, followed by conversation and music. All this was in a lifetime before the war.

Thinking how hungry Bella must be, Greta asks, 'Can I buy something to eat for my maid?'

With a movement of his hand, Hans calls the waiter. 'Bread and *Schinken* (ham) for the Fraulein's maid. And a beer,' he adds.

'I would like to buy it,' Greta protests, well aware that now no food is being sold on trains.

'My pleasure, Fraulein Burger.'

'Thank you.'

Greta and Hans eat in silence. She is eager for the encounter to end.

The waiter delivers Bella's sandwich in a linen napkin. Before leaving the dining room, Hans turns to Greta, 'It would be my pleasure, Fraulein Burger, to drive you and your maid to your house in Warsaw. I'll have a car and driver waiting for me at the train station.'

A surge of blood to her head makes Greta dizzy. How is she going to get out of this?

'It is very considerate, but I don't dare to impose, you must be a very busy man.'

'It would be my pleasure. Not often does one meet such a refined lady in Poland.'

Controlling her agitation, Greta bestows a warm smile on the officer. Hans walks her to the compartment with the brown no-control tag stuck at its entrance.

'The Fraulein will please wait for me in the compartment. As soon as we arrive at the Warsaw station, I'll come.'

'Thank you, I will be very grateful to you.'

Hearing the officer's instruction and Greta's response, Bella is puzzled. What does it mean? The inability to ask, to talk, is upsetting her. Gazing at the ham sandwich and beer that Greta places in her lap, Bella forgets about her fears.

'Eat. It's for you. I ate already.'

Bella smells the warm ham, inhales the aroma before taking the first bite. Slowly, slowly, she tells herself. Never before has Bella had a glass of beer, but now, no drink could have been better than this dark, bittersweet dense liquid smelling of molasses.

Greta is calculating how to avoid Hans. They can't continue on this train to Warsaw, but when do they get off, what next? She isn't familiar with this territory, her hometown being Krakow. Seeing Greta's perplexed expression, Bella bends down to her handbag under her seat, tugging Greta's sleeve. Their heads lowered, Bella whispers into Greta's ear, 'What's going on?'

'We have to get off as close to Warsaw as possible. I'll explain later.'

The other passenger in their compartment looks asleep, but the women don't risk talking further. Bella nods.

Half an hour later the train attendant announces Falenice. Bella grabs their handbags and Greta's hand; the women get off the train as soon as it comes to a stop. They walk away from the train as fast as they can without appearing to run, turning a corner into a narrow street. There they wait till the train moves out of the station.

Greta tells Bella about Hans's intention to drive them to their home in Warsaw.

'God, can you imagine him delivering us to my sister Fela in the Jewish quarters? Was he trying to figure out if you're a Jew?'

'I don't think so. He believed that I am German, he wanted to believe I'm German, but when he offered to drive us, I almost fainted. Where are we now?'

'I know this area, it's the last stop before Warsaw. We might be able to get a *droszka* (horse-drawn cab) to take us to my sister Fela.'

The train having pulled out, they enter the station looking for the station master.

'Is there a *droszka* around?' Greta asks.

'If there is one, it will be down the street,' the man says, pointing.

'Thank you.'

The friends walk rapidly, Bella almost running, trying to keep up with Greta.

'Here it is!' Bella says excitedly.

On an elevated bench, in the front of the carriage, leaning against the canopy sits the driver. His cap covering his eyes, the man snores noisily. Bella hops onto the running board, puts her hand on the driver's arm and shakes him. The man, still disoriented from sleep, pulls the cap off his face and peers at Bella.

'*Do Warszawy*, Zamenhofa 30,' she tells him.

'It's gonna cost you 50 *złote*.'

'Okay, go.'

The driver stretches his arm, palm up, 'Money first.'

Bella digs into her handbag, pulling out a twenty and a ten-*złote* bill, but before she can find the rest, Greta hands her a wad of bills.

'No, no, Greta, I'll pay.'

'Don't be silly. I have enough.'

Bella takes a twenty-*złote* note from Greta's hands, gives the money to the driver, and climbs into the carriage. Greta follows. It takes a few minutes for the driver and the horse to wake up, but once they do, they take off at a gallop. It is pitch dark, but lanterns on both sides of the carriage give off sufficient light to see the road. The hood of the carriage obstructs Bella's view, but she doesn't mind, she is eager to hear about Greta's dinner with the officer.

'Greta, I was so scared for you. I thought what will happen if he finds out you are a Jew.'

'I, too, was scared. I am surprised he didn't hear how my heart was pounding. I will tell you all about it when we get to your sister's house, I am very tired."

It takes only a few minutes and both women are asleep. Bella is startled by the driver's abrupt stop and loud announcement: 'Zamenhofa 30.'

She sticks her head out the carriage, looks around as if in a dream—her sister's building. It feels as though she left it just yesterday, and yet it is in a different world, a world she has almost forgotten.

'Come,' she says to Greta.

Bella opens the gate to the building, switches on the light in the hallway, and heads for the elevator to take them to the fourth floor. Though Fela and her family live in an elegant building, most houses in the Jewish section don't have elevators.

It is past midnight. The Geller family is already asleep when Bella rings the doorbell. No one answers. She waits a minute and rings again. After what feels like a very long time, she hears shuffling feet and sees movement at the peephole.

'Who is it?' Fela sounds frightened.

'Fela, it's me, Bella.'

'Bella? Bella?'

Opening the door just a crack, Fela sticks her head out, peering intently at Bella, then at this strange tall woman next to her. Suddenly she flings the door open.

'My God, it's you, Bella! I didn't recognize you,' Fela says, pulling both women inside the apartment.

Realizing she is still wearing the black kerchief, Bella pulls it off and stuffs it in her coat pocket.

'What are you doing here? What happened? Where are the girls and Srulik?'

'They are probably all right.'

'Probably? Where?'

'Later, I'll tell you later. This is my friend Greta.'

Still holding both women by their arms, Fela leads them into the living room, her face puzzled and expectant.

'Bella, what happened?'

'It's a long story. In a while.'

'Are you hungry?'

'No, just tired and filthy. I would like to wash,' Bella says.

'Zosia, please fill up the tub,' Fela instructs her maid, a Catholic peasant woman who has been living with the Geller family for twenty years. At sixty-one and in poor health, Zosia isn't of much help, but Fela assured her that she could live with them as long as she wants. As the woman has no family, Zosia's home is with the Gellers."

"Mom, can we continue tonight?"

"I am tired, Naomi. I have to get up early for work tomorrow. It will have to wait till next Sunday."

4

Interlude

Sundays became the day for telling Naomi my Holocaust life experiences. Today she showed up later than usual.

"Mom, can we start talking before lunch?"

"It isn't easy for me to talk about my Holocaust years. I enter a different world, I become the little girl with all her painful experiences. I cannot start talking, interrupt, and then go back to it, it's too difficult. We can have an earlier lunch and talk thereafter. I have fresh salmon we can broil, good bread and a salad."

"Okay, Mom. Let me start making the salad."

After a leisurely lunch we sat down in my most comfortable spot, on the brown leather coach.

"Mom, dining with the German officer on the train must have been a very scary experience for Greta."

"Yes, Naomi, it must have been. She described the scene in detail and how scared she was. I assume that being extremely hungry helped her to accept the challenge. My mother tried to add some humor when telling me her version of the story, mimicking the formality of the German language that does not address a stranger with a direct 'you.'"

"For eight weeks Bella hasn't bathed, for eight weeks she hasn't changed her clothes. Her dry skin feels sore to the touch. She is eager to shed clothes that are stuck to her, almost glued, yet uneasy with her nudity, her body now old and haggard-looking, she thinks. She avoids the tall mirror on the wall.

As though reading Bella's thoughts, Zosia observes, '*Mój Boże* (my God), Pani Bella is so skinny.'

'Zosia, please burn all my filthy clothes.'

'The gray skirt is of fine material, just needs a good wash. I will do it. And your blue sweater looks like new. A shame to throw it out.'

'I just can't look at them now, but thank you, Zosia. If you want to wash them, please do it.'

The warm water is a marvel of luxury and pleasure. Bella's thirsty skin, like a desert plant, absorbs the moisture. For a moment, time stops—there are no yesterdays and no tomorrows—her head, light as a feather, floats on a cloud.

Fela enters the bathroom carrying a white flannel nightgown, sheepskin slippers, and her brown quilted robe. 'Put these on, Bella.'

Bella notices wrinkles on Fela's forehead and around her mouth, her hair heavily sprinkled with gray. At forty-two, Fela looks much older and smaller than Bella remembers. Before the war, five feet two Fela used to be full-bodied, but not now. Then there was a strong resemblance between the two sisters who are twelve years apart in age; now each has changed in a different way.

It has been a long time since anyone has taken care of Bella. Her sister's loving attention makes her feel nurtured and safe. The flannel, soft and warm against her skin, feels weightless, like a powder puff.

Refreshed and alert, Bella walks into the well-lit living room. This room is as familiar to her as her own home. Against a long wall is the dark tapestry sofa, and next to it the piano. A big grandfather clock that chimes on the hour is right next to the balcony overlooking Zamenhofa Street. The walnut credenzas with fine china for special occasions, the mahogany cellarette, supported by two cherubic figures resting on a stand, are behind the dining table.

The living room used to double as a dining room for bigger gatherings of family and friends. On Saturdays, the brick fireplace kept the *chulent* slowly roasting, giving out an aroma of the meal to come. Bella can almost smell the blend of beef, potatoes, beans, and a stuffed *kishka*. Her eyes well up with tears as she remembers the family gatherings.

'Greta, I emptied the tub. You can bathe now,' Bella says, entering the living room.

Maryla walks in rubbing her eyes. Sixteen years old, the youngest of the three Geller children, Maryla is no taller than her mother. With her shoulder-length chestnut hair, a slightly pale complexion, big hazel eyes, and high cheekbones, she moves with the grace and fluidity of a dancer.

'I woke up scared, hearing voices. Ciocia Bella?' Maryla looks startled.

'Go back to sleep, we will explain tomorrow.' Fela leads her daughter back to her bedroom.

Fela can find nothing in her wardrobe to fit Greta and goes to look in her son's room. Most of Ślamek's things still hang in his closet; he left carrying only one suitcase.

Fela pulls out of a drawer cotton pajamas and wool socks, and moves to her husband's closet for a warm robe. Her husband and older son Heniek aren't home.

She knocks on the bathroom door, waits for a response, lightly opens the door, and lays the clothes on a stool.

'Thank you, Fela. Sorry we woke you up.'

'That's okay. We often wake up during the night.'

'Why?'

'The German soldiers.'

'What's going on now?'

'Tell you tomorrow. You and Bella must be extremely tired.'

Indulging herself for a few more minutes in the warm water, Greta thinks about her parents in Krakow. Have they been all right? Have the Germans harmed them? Do they have enough food? Her parents encouraged Greta to follow her fiancé to the Soviet Union, but now Greta feels guilty for leaving them alone with the Germans all over the city.

Greta joins the women in the living room.

'Fela, where are Heniek and Moniek?' Bella inquires.

'Go to sleep. We'll talk tomorrow.'

'Are they OKAY?'

'They're fine. Bella, you will sleep in Slamek's room and Greta in Heniek's.'

'I'm not tired anymore.'

'Then I'll stay up with you.'

The others go to sleep, but the two sisters sit on the sofa talking for hours of what has happened in their lives since they last saw each other.

'A cup of tea, Bella?'

'Yes, that would be good.'

In the kitchen, Fela sets the teakettle on the gas burner. Bella's eyes move to the scales on the counter with the weights—miniature brass cylinders, stored on a wooden plank. Her little Irka used to love playing with the scales, finding things to weigh so that she might pull out the cylinders and line them up like gilded soldiers.

After a few minutes the kettle whistles. Fela drops a tea-spoon of loose leaves into a small, blue porcelain teapot and lets them steep for a few minutes before pouring some into individual glasses and adding boiling water. She pulls a loaf of dark bread from the drawer.

'So where are Heniek and Moniek?'

'Moniek is staying with his mother; she is scared, but doesn't want to come live with us, so he sleeps there a few nights a week. The Germans are bursting into Jewish homes in the middle of the night, shooting, killing indiscriminately, or dragging out young men who are never heard from again. Brother Hershel's two sons, Moshe and Jakow, are gone more than three weeks, and we don't know where they are. We sent Heniek away to stay with Śliwowski, our former shoe supplier who lives on a farm; Heniek will be safer there.'

'What about the store?'

'The store is gone. One morning two Gestapo soldiers pulled up with a truck, kicked the doors in, pointed their ri-fles at Heniek, and screamed 'Filthy Jew, load it, load it all!' meaning all the shoes in boxes, on shelves. Moniek came out from the backroom to see what was going on. One soldier grabbed him by the arm, twisting it behind his back, and yelling, 'You were hiding, you swine? Get going, load it!'

'The pain was excruciating, the brute pulled Moniek's shoulder out of the socket, but my poor husband had to con-tinue loading everything on the truck. Before the soldiers left the store, they smashed the windows and anything else they could lay their hands on. Moniek passed out as soon as those beasts were out of sight. When Heniek brought his father home, Moniek was still pale as a ghost.'

'What are you going to do, Fela?'

'What can we do?'

'Come with me. We'll all cross the border.'

'No, Bella. We aren't going anywhere. What would we do with the Soviets? You are a *farbrente* (passionate) believer in them, but not I.' The sisters sit silently for a few minutes.

'Let's go to sleep, Bella. It's been a long day for you.'

It feels strange and luxurious to get into a bed with sheets and blankets; Bella falls asleep as soon as her head hits the pillow.

Luckily, the Gellers have a supply of logs stored in the attic and are able to keep the living room fireplace going. Coal is unavailable to them.

The household is quiet, everyone is asleep, but Bella wakes up startled, hearing loud voices in the street. Pulling the drape aside slightly, without turning on the lights, she sees three German soldiers screaming, 'Go, go, move!' as they are using their rifles to beat a running group of men, some with coats hastily grabbed and still unbuttoned. The third from the front is a boy of eleven or twelve. Frightened, the boy keeps turning and looking up. Did he notice her in the window, or is there someone in the building he's trying to spot? One of the soldiers swings his rifle, hitting the boy on the head. The boy hunches over, grabbing his bleeding head with both hands, but does not utter a sound, just hastens his pace. Bella feels her muscles tensing, hands tightening, ready to grab that brute, choke him. But all she can do is stand at the window, watching until the group of men is out of sight. What will they do to this frightened child? Bella can't get this image out of her mind. She goes back to bed, but has trouble falling asleep. It must have been early morning when she eventually falls back asleep.

'Fela, why didn't you wake me, it's almost five in the afternoon?'

'You needed the sleep.'

98

Bella, now slimmer than she used to be, puts on her sister's tweed skirt and gray sweater, rolling up the sleeves and holding the skirt in place with a belt. The sheepskin slippers keep her feet warm. Greta, outfitted in Ślamek's trousers and pullover, is sitting at ease on the sofa.

'I'll get you something to eat,' Fela says as she goes to the kitchen.

'No, thank you—just tea.'

Fela's husband Moniek, having returned from his mother's, joins the women in the living room. His little potbelly gone, his five-foot-eight frame frail, he looks aged.

Earlier in the day, Fela went shopping for food. Pani Goldbergowa, the shopkeeper, saves special finds for her old-timers; Fela has been her customer for twenty-five years. Today it is white beans.

Pulling out the little package of beans from under the counter, Pani Goldbergowa glances around to make sure no other customers are watching.

'Sorry I can't offer you more. Tomorrow I may have potatoes.'

After a supper of cooked beans and bread, the family gathers around the fireplace, the last log for the evening still burning.

'Greta, I'll try to cross the border as soon as possible. Will you come?'

'No, Bella, I'll return to my parents.'

'Will you rest here a few days before you go?' Fela turns to Greta.

'You've taken me in like family, but I'm eager to see my parents.'

The Gellers' telephone isn't working. Phone service is no longer available to Jews. Greta has no way of finding out how her parents are doing.

'I'll take a train to Krakow tomorrow,' Greta says.

No one tries to dissuade her. They sit silently.

'Greta, we stored some shoes in the attic, I'll see if I have a woman's shoe in your size.'

'Thank you, men's shoes would be just as good.'

When Greta wakes up the next morning, the house smells of coffee with chicory. Coffee being expensive and scarce, Fela mixes a small amount of chicory with coffee to give it the aroma of the real stuff. With bread, it tastes almost as good as real coffee.

Seeing Greta dressed, ready to leave, Bella feels a rock in the pit of her stomach and a strange pressure, going upward, choking her. What will the future hold for each of them? When will they meet again? Will they be alive to ever meet?

Bella rushes into her room, returning with the fox collar and rhinestone pin. She tosses the fox around Greta's neck and once again pins the brooch on her beret.

'I can't take it. These are all that's left of your things!'

'I want you to have it, Greta; I'll feel good knowing you'll be wearing them.'

After breakfast, Bella and Maryla follow Greta to the train station, walking a few paces behind her. Greta stops at the entrance to the station, waiting for Bella and Maryla.

'Please don't wait with me for the train.'

'Why?' Bella asks.

'The station is swamped with German soldiers. It will be safer for all of us if I am alone.'

No one would suspect that Greta is a Jew.

As if grounded in cement, unable to move, Bella stands motionless.

'Please, Bella, go.'

Bella and Greta gaze at each other in silence. Then, as if pulled by a magnetic force, each takes a step towards the other. Embracing tightly, eyes closed, their bodies sway in a gentle rhythmic rocking for a brief moment as tears flow down their faces.

'Bella, we'll meet after the war, at Fela's.'

'Yes, after the war,' Bella cries, kissing Greta's face, ignoring the danger of a German soldier spotting them. 'I'll write you as soon as I find my children.'

They hug again, then part.

'Come, Marylka, let me hug you. You are such a sweet and pretty girl. If it's safer in Krakow, come stay with my parents and me. I'll write to you,' Greta says.

Bella and her niece walk silently but alertly, scanning the streets for signs of danger: shooting, an explosion, or random arrests. People walk fast, eyes downcast, wanting to be invisible in the daylight, yet agile like cats ready to dart into an open gate or courtyard at the sound of a whistle or a German voice.

Hanging onto Maryla's hand, Bella walks as fast as her legs will carry her. She is now a stranger in this city where she was born, where her mother and grandmother had been born. The Warsaw she had explored with excitement as a teenager, where she married and raised her children, is now a hostile place, its air hanging dark and heavy.

Entering the gate at Zamenhofa 30, Bella feels a great relief. Here, in her sister's apartment, she feels safe. Yet she has to leave them as soon as possible; she must find her children and husband, but first she must locate a guide.

'Śliwowski may know someone trustworthy,' Fela says. 'But it would be risky for any of us to show up at the farm—the neighbors don't know Heniek is a Jew.'

Fela decides to send her maid with a birthday invitation.

The family is sure the recipient will understand the message, and he does. Pan Śliwowski finds a man with a known reputation as an honest and capable guide who has smuggled many people through the borders. In three days, he will conduct a group of four people across; Bella can join them as the fifth. His price is steep, yet Bella has no choice but to accept the money from her sister.

'Someday, Fela, I'll pay you back.'

'Yes, yes, don't worry.'

'No luggage, just one small backpack, heavy walking shoes, warm clothes, a coat with pockets, and nothing in your hands,' are the guide's instructions.

Bella's three days of waiting for the guide are filled with a storm of emotions. Her sister's love fills her with warmth and longing, but she must go to find her children and husband. She isn't afraid of the border crossing; whatever happens, she will endure.

Fela packs and unpacks the backpack that once belonged to Heniek. She walks through the house, looking into closets for anything her sister might need on her journey.

The backpack ends up with a collection of clothing belonging not only to Fela and Maryla—there's also a ski hat from Ślamek's closet and Heniek's heavy woolen gloves.

The night before Bella's departure, Fela cooks a festive dinner. With the last of the dried mushrooms saved from before the war, she makes a barley soup with a carrot in it. The soup and baked potatoes make a delicious dinner.

It has been a short night for all of them. By four in the morning the whole family is up. The guide is to pick Bella up at four-thirty.

'Bella, did you put on the black socks? They are the warmest.'

'Yes, I did.'

'Do you need some change?'

Bella puts her arms around her sister. 'Fela, my dear, I have everything I need.'

'God will watch over you,' Fela whispers, holding her younger sister, tears welling up in her eyes.

Seeing her mother and aunt in tears, Maryla starts crying.

'Fela, where is Moniek? I want to say good-bye to him.'

'My Moniek isn't good with good-byes. He's probably in the study. Maryla, Sunshine, bring your father.'

Moniek walks into the living room looking haggard—he hasn't slept a wink.

'Be careful, Bella.' They embrace.

'Good-bye, Zosia. Be well.'

The maid crosses herself and kisses Bella's hand.

A tap on the door.

'He's here,' Bella whispers.

'Kiss and hug the girls and Srulik for me,' Fela tells her.

'Fela, this can't last forever. The Nazis will lose. I'll be back, you'll see.' Again, the sisters fall into each other's arms with Maryla and her father looking on.

'I am sorry I couldn't see Heniek and our brothers. Say goodbye to them for me.'

Bella opens the door, turning back for yet another look at every face before her. With the sudden realization that she may never again see her sister, a shudder passes through her body, as though hit by an electrical current. With each good-bye the hollow space in her soul grows bigger, and nothing can fill it.

In the hallway, the guide pulls out what looks like a piece of an old linen sheet and wraps it around the backpack, making it look like a bundle carried by local peasants.

'Pani Millerowa, hold the backpack like this on the train.' The guide hands her the bundle. 'And pull the kerchief lower over your face.' And they are gone."

5

A Mountain to Climb

"Mom, wasn't she concerned that this new guide might dump her someplace and not take her across the border?"

"She was determined to look for her children and husband and had no other option but to join a group with a guide."

"Did she consider staying in Warsaw with her sister?"

"No, absolutely not."

"In addition to Bella, there will be three men and one woman. Coming from different parts of Poland, they are to meet in Siedlice, about 120 kilometers from Warsaw. The group will try to cross the border 100 kilometers south of Białystok where the terrain is rough, but the border less carefully guarded. For an extra fee, the guide has picked up Bella in Warsaw. Fela insisted that her sister should not go unaccompanied on the train.

Bella's heart is racing as she boards the train headed for Siedlice. It is ten past five in the morning; she hopes the German soldiers will not be traveling that early.

Only a few passengers are in the section where Bella and her guide enter; they have a compartment all to themselves. Bella is glad for the guide's silence. She doesn't want to talk— what could she talk to him about? Closing her eyes, she leans back in her seat hoping to doze, but sleep does not come. For the first time she takes a good look at her guide, whose face is turned to the window. He is in his early forties, slim, of medium height. Blond bristles, a few days' growth, cover his face. Bella assumes the man's hair is blond as well, but it is hidden under a snugly fitting ski cap. His brown wool turtleneck, tweed trousers, and leather boots look of good quality. The man has an intelligent face, Bella concludes, hoping it's also an honest face. She has entrusted her life to this man.

At the second stop, a number of people get on, but no one enters Bella's compartment, and she is grateful. This once gregarious woman with a wonderful sense of humor, eager to tell a joke or to hear one, the focus of social gatherings, is now fearful of strangers. In each of them she sees a potential threat to her life. Will they recognize that she is a Jew? Will they betray her to a German soldier?

The three-hour train ride is uneventful. No German soldiers entered their compartment. Getting off the train, Bella follows the guide closely, fearing that he might abandon her in this unknown town. After fifteen minutes of fast walking they are out of the station and the guide slows his pace. The group of five is to meet at Górna, a street of two- and three-story buildings dating back at least two hundred years. Number 20 is a gray building with heavy metal gates leading to a narrow courtyard with a line of shrubbery, now covered with snow. The hallway is dark; it takes Bella a few seconds to make out the stairs and a door. The guide lifts the metal ring attached to the door, knocks three times, pauses, and knocks again once. Vigorous steps approach the door, an eye appears at the peephole, the door opens. A burly man in his late forties ushers them in. The guide doesn't introduce Bella.

'Things went okay?' The man asks the guide.

'No problem, Janek.'

'You can hang up your coat; we'll stay here till night falls,' the guide tells Bella. 'The others will be coming in the afternoon.'

Bella knows nothing about the 'others' except their gender. The guide has spoken only when absolutely necessary, and she doesn't care to question him, though she is eager to meet her traveling companions.

Both men leave the room, ignoring Bella. She doesn't mind being left alone; she welcomes the silence. Looking around for clues about her husky host, Bella concludes that no woman lives in this house; nothing in the room reveals a woman's touch. The long birch table and benches in the center of the room, a shelf with boots and hats in one corner, and a wood-burning stove with a pipe going through the ceiling are the only objects in the room. The white walls are bare, save a few hooks for coats.

She can't figure out her guide or her host, but it doesn't trouble her. They are rude, but why should she care? All she needs is to get across the border. She will find a way to her family. All the Polish Jews are housed in just a few locations that used to be summer camps or estates around Białystok. She also knows Ślamek's address as of a few months ago.

'I bring you food.' The guide places a tray on the table and leaves the room.

Bella is hungry—she had left Fela's house without eating. The dark coarse-grained bread with butter tastes wonderful. The salty piece of farmer's cheese and hot tea make a delicious meal. Bella feels energized and ready to go, but there are many hours to wait. She waits in the room alone; periodically the guide or Janek walks in to stir the fire or to add a log. As the day wears on, Bella grows restless and suspicious. Does the guide have honest intentions? Are there truly others who will join her on this journey? Maybe it is all some sort of scheme? But why would he feed me? Why would he be stalling if he has evil plans? 'Bella, don't be ridiculous, everything will be fine,' she keeps repeating to herself.

Her thoughts are interrupted by a knock on the door. The guide, after determining who is there, opens it and lets in a tall, slim man in his early thirties. 'Good afternoon,' the man greets Bella.

'Good afternoon. Are you one of the people in our group?'

'Yes, Adam Zieliński is my name.'

'I'm Bella Miller.' She offers her hand. 'The guide said we have to wait for the others and for nightfall.'

'It's safer in the dark.'

Zieliński? Is he a Jew? Bella wonders. His hair is light, but so is Srulik's. But a name like Zieliński? Either the man has changed his name or he has other reasons to fear the Nazis. It is inappropriate to ask, but the question troubles her.

Within the next hour the others arrive. The woman, Agata, is the last to appear. In her mid-twenties, six-feet-tall, broad shoulders, a ruddy complexion, hair cropped just a few inches long, she looks to Bella like a wrestler, or a bullfighter. The guide gathers the group around the table.

'We'll start off as soon as it gets dark. You will leave through the back door a few minutes apart and wait for me at the end of the road, next to the red barn. You'll each get a chunk of bread and farmer's cheese—keep it in your backpack. We'll do a lot of walking, there will be areas of deep snow and a lot of climbing. We can't wait for stragglers. You must keep pace with me. If you think you can't make it, take a train back home. We won't carry anyone.' He looks at Bella, the shortest in the group.

He is not going to intimidate me, Bella thinks, meeting the guide's eyes.

An uncomfortable silence fills the room. Bella searches for a friendly face, but they are all averted.

Janek walks in, carrying a bowl of boiled potatoes in their skins in one hand, a plate of bread and butter in the other, and a small pouch of coarse salt under his arm. He sets them all in the center of the wooden table and returns to the kitchen. A minute later he is back with a metal teakettle, six blue enameled metal cups hooked on the fingers of one hand, and five tin plates under his arm. 'Eat now,' the guide instructs, leaving the group around the table.

'I'm Bella Miller from Warszawa,' she introduces herself.

'Adam Zieliński, from Lublin.'

A long pause before a man in his late thirties says, 'Icek Nabel, from Osiedlice.'

'Agata, from all over.'

Again a pause, waiting for the last man to introduce himself.

'Aaaaallek (Alek) Uurbach, from Warszaaawa.'

'Glad to meet you, Pan Urbach. We are from the same city,' Bella says, walking over to the other end of the table. She picks up the plates and cups and passes them around, starting with Alek. She does the same with the bowl of potatoes and bread. Adam reaches for the big teakettle and fills everyone's cup.

Peeling the potatoes with their fingers, peasant style, they dip them in salt. Bella's hungry companions dig into the bowl with vigor.

'I wonder how many kilometers it is to the border,' Bella says to break the silence that's disturbed only by the occasional shuffling of boots under the table or the smack of a tongue trying to dislodge a piece of dry potato.

'About eighty, but it depends on which way the guide takes us,' Adam responds.

The silence makes Bella uncomfortable. After a few minutes, she makes another attempt at conversation. 'It's getting dark—we'll probably leave soon.'

'Yes, we probably will,' comes from Adam, but no one else responds.

The host and guide re-enter the room, carrying portions of bread and cheese wrapped in old newspaper.

'Put this in your backpacks. Use the outhouse before we go,' the guide points the direction. Adam reaches out to help as Bella is getting into her coat. She wraps a burgundy scarf around her neck, pulls on the ski hat and gloves, and straps the backpack on her shoulders. She feels energized and eager to go get to her family.

Adam is the first to leave, followed a few minutes later by Bella. Next to the red barn they wait for the others. She is glad to be alone with Adam for a few minutes, the only friendly person in the group.

'Our guide is not a very sociable fellow,' Adam observes.

'Nor are our companions.'

'I'm sure they'll be okay on the road. They must be a little anxious about the crossing. Here comes Alek.'

'Are you going to be warm enough, Pan Urbach?' Bella asks.

The man gives her a warm smile and nods. One by one, the others join them, the guide coming last.

'Follow me,' the guide beckons.

He leads them through side streets with old warehouses and junkyards, and hardly a person in sight. Rusted, broken remnants of a plow, a potbelly coal oven with two legs and the door missing, a head of a sewing machine retired with age, are all heaped in front of a shed.

It doesn't take them long to get out of town and off the road into a snow-covered field. The earth underneath their feet is rocklike. Protruding shafts left from the harvested wheat are the only sign of life in this frozen soil.

The night air is cold; with each breath comes a puff of vapor. How does the guide find his way—in this utter darkness, the flat fields all look alike? This would be a hell of a place to get lost, Bella reflects.

To keep pace with the others, she must run to catch up at times. Once they enter the woods it becomes increasingly difficult to keep up. Fallen branches, ditches full of snow, roots of trees, and trees themselves obscure Bella's view of her fellow travelers. They walk and walk, and walk, all in silence. Initially light, Bella's backpack now feels heavy. Periodically, she adjusts the straps to relieve the pressure on her shoulders. How long have they been walking, three hours, four hours? No matter how much she pushes herself, Bella is always at the end of the group, Agata in the front.

Seeing Bella fall behind, Adam slows his pace.

'Pani Millerowa, don't worry. We won't leave you.'

'I appreciate it, but I refuse to endanger anyone's life or to be a burden.'

'We are together.'

'No, we are not. You heard the guide.'

'He just has a loud bark to feel in control.'

As the march goes on, exhaustion overcomes Bella. It becomes almost impossible for her to pull her legs out of the deep snow and thrust them into it again, over and over. Unaware of a ditch, she trips and lets out a loud cry, realizing immediately that making noise endangers all of them. Adam and

Alek rush to help her, pulling her out of the shoulder-high snow. The guide approaches Bella and her rescuers and hisses, 'Once more you slow down to bail someone out, and I cut you out of the group.'

They say nothing, just keep walking.

'Are you okay?' Adam whispers.

'Yes, thank you.'

Bella's legs now weigh a ton each, and lifting them requires a Herculean effort. She tries to shuffle her feet instead of lifting them, but it doesn't work.

Is daylight breaking or are her eyes playing a trick on her? Half an hour later, the guide stops by a tall pine and waits for everyone in the group.

'Two more kilometers, and we break for the day. We'll stop in a barn; you can sleep there. At nightfall we start again. Tonight was easy, it's going to be tougher tomorrow. We'll cross the border at five in the morning.'

The anticipated rest renews Bella's energy, making it possible for her to endure the additional two kilometers.

An old mare and two cows are the only animals in the barn. They look as tired as the weary travelers.

'You can sleep on the hay in the loft and also at the other end of the barn.'

Too exhausted to climb the ladder, Bella looks for a spot away from the livestock. All she wants is to get off her feet and sleep. She finds a corner with a pile of hay, takes off her backpack, kicks off her shoes. She burrows her feet into the hay, curls up in a fetal position, and falls sound asleep. It is three in the afternoon when Bella awakens. Brushing the hay off her coat, she looks for the others. All but Icek are up, sitting near the livestock.

'Come, Pani Millerowa, it is warmer here. We waited for you to milk the cows,' Adam says with a smile.

Bella wants to reach over to him and pull the loose pieces of hay out of his hair, but it would be improper for a woman to do so. She glances at his face with its soft gray eyes looking straight at her without making her uncomfortable, his full mouth now curved in a mischievous smile.

'It's a brown cow; pull a teat and hot chocolate might squirt straight into your mouth,' Agata retorts.

'This would be my first miracle,' Bella tells Agata.

'Dream, lady, dream.'

The guide walks in carrying paper-wrapped portions of bread.

'We'll set out in an hour. From here we can exit together.' He leaves the barn door ajar. Bella walks outside to see what is around. About a quarter of a mile ahead, standing in the open field, not far from the woods, is a small farmhouse, but nothing else in sight. What an isolated, lonely place to live in, she reflects.

Her companions seem to be in a better mood today. Even Agata has a smile.

'Anything exciting outside?' Agata asks.

'Fields and woods, fields and woods,' Bella replies.

Bella moves away from the group, pulls out of her backpack a pad of paper and a pencil, and writes the names of her husband and daughters. Not knowing their address, she describes where she assumes them to be, in a camp for Jewish emigrants near Białystok. She writes the same information on another slip of paper and puts one slip in each of her coat pockets. Should she be found dead, maybe a kind soul will let her husband know about it. Deep down, Bella knows that her companions will not abandon her, but the Germans and the Russians are lurking on both sides of the border.

They leave the barn at dusk. 'Yesterday was easy,' Bella remembers the guide saying. What will this night be like for her, if yesterday was easy? 'I'll make it, I'll make it,' she repeats to herself over and over.

They walk for a few kilometers across open fields, then turn back into the woods. At about nine in the evening, three hours into their walk, they find themselves in a burned-out part of the forest near a country road. Abruptly the guide stops, gesturing for the group to halt and be silent. His finger on his lips and the other hand still raised, he kneels, putting his ear to the ground. As he gets up, he gestures for the group to follow him quietly and fast. Now Bella has to run. The guide is rapidly walking away from the road, back towards the dense woods.

One, two, three blasts of a machine gun. They are still in the burned area with little cover. The guide drops to the ground, gesturing to the group to do the same. Seeing her fumble with the straps of her backpack, Adam grabs Bella's hand and pulls her to the ground next to him. Now they hear heavy vehicles on the road. Tanks? Trucks? Bella doesn't dare raise her head to look, but she hears the grinding wheels of the vehicles and feels vibration in the ground. Then come loud German voices, commands. She tries to lie motionless, breathing into the snow. Suddenly, a light shining nearby startles her, bringing a moment of panic—a flashback to the invasion of the no man's land. Are they coming? She lies silently, holding her breath as if playing dead for an approaching bear.

The roar of the heavy wheels is subsiding, the voices growing fainter, and finally they can hear them no more. Bella waits for a sign that it is safe to lift her head. She opens her eyes. Everyone is still flat on the ground. It is comforting to see Adam next to her, now looking at her. After a few minutes, the guide gets up and, one by one, touches them with his foot. They follow him forward, deeper into the woods.

'We'll have to alter our route. We must stay under the cover of trees. It'll take us two hours longer.' Bella feels adrenaline flowing in her body. No matter how long it takes, she is bent on making it. She trips a few times, but hastens to keep up with the others.

'We will take a few minutes' break. Go into the woods, if you need to, but not far.'

Her backpack on, Bella goes a few paces to where she thinks she cannot be seen. The pause is welcome. Hungry, she pulls out the bread and cheese while waiting for the others.

The guide has warned them that today would be tough; he was right. To beat the daylight and cross the border while it is still dark, they are walking faster than before. In Polish territory, their major concern is to avoid German soldiers, but at the border they must stay clear of Soviet guards.

Bella's breath is labored as they climb uphill. She is determined to hang onto her backpack, though it is becoming heavier and heavier. Adam reaches for Bella's hand and she doesn't resist, despite her determination not to be a burden. For a few minutes, Adam's pull offers her a reprieve, and then she lets go of his hand.

The incline is getting steeper and steeper, and there are areas of deep snow she has to avoid. It is early March, a time when the snow is beginning to melt in Warsaw, but here it is still firm and piled high. Bella has no idea where they are. She tries to picture the map of Poland, but that doesn't help.

'It's almost six. We must be close to the border,' Adam whispers to Bella.

'I hope so.'

Now, the walk all downhill is easier. An hour later, the guide stops, waiting for everyone.

'We'll walk twenty meters apart. Move fast and quiet.'

What's going on now? Why this directive? With this man there's no way of knowing. He's a rude bastard, but he knows what he is doing and so far hasn't misled them.

Another hour passes. The guide stops again.

'You have crossed the border. You are now three kilometers into the Soviet side. You can talk and do what you want. Two kilometers from here is a train station. I'll walk there with you, and then you're on your own.'

'We made it, we made it!' they shout. Tears are flowing down Bella's face.

'You were a good sport, Bella,' Agata tells her.

Arms crossed over her chest, Bella looks at Adam and nods: 'Thank you.' He smiles, shrugs, and says nothing.

In the distance they see rooftops and chimneys billowing smoke. It feels incredible: they are approaching a city and can just walk undisturbed in the daylight.

The conversation grows animated, as though all their thoughts of the last few days burst into words, and there is no way of stopping them. Everyone is talking. Even Icek, who has scarcely said a word for two days, now comes alive.

Adam will go to Kiev; his friend has been waiting for him there. Bella wants to unravel the mystery of this man. Why did he flee Poland? What is his plan? What is his occupation? But to inquire would be improper. Polish etiquette considers such questions rude, particularly coming from a lady. Most of all, Bella wants to know whether he is a Jew, but you don't ask such a thing. Bella has told Adam about her husband and children and her escape from the no man's land.

'You are a very brave lady' was his only comment.

Now they can see Białystok unfolding before them and can hear the whistles of trains and the chugging of locomotives.

'Around the corner is the train station. I take off here,' the guide tells them.

'Thank you.'

'Thank you.'

'Thank you.'

'Thank you.' All shake hands with the guide.

When the guide leaves, the five stand for a moment, leaning against a gray building that's in need of a coat of paint, uncertain what to do next.

'Good luck to all of you,' Bella says, shaking hands first with Alek, then with the others. Adam moves over to Bella and stands a moment facing her, his arms slightly outstretched, not knowing what to do with them. As she is looking at him, Bella's arms move towards Adam, but they stop midair. She wants him to hug her, she wants to embrace him, but it is improper.

'Are you going to be okay?' he asks. 'Can I help you?'

'You helped me more than I had a right to accept. I'll be okay. How about you?'

He stops a moment, then lifts his hand, holding it suspended in the air before placing it on Bella's shoulder. 'Yes, I'll be fine.'

They both smile, for lack of knowing what else to do, then turn, each in a different direction to catch their train.

It has been a long time since Bella was last alone. She delights in the freedom, yet misses a pair of protective wings, like a cloak to swaddle her. It would have been nice to have Adam with her on the train, just for a little bit. She is a married woman, what right does she have to harbor such wishes?

An unexpected surge of anger in the depth of her soul startles her. 'Srulik had it easy. He was safe all along. He had the girls with him. Did he even wonder what has been going on with me?' No sooner does she put her anger into words than she feels guilty for it.

Suddenly Bella feels ravenous, but first she has to buy her train ticket. At the counter she buys a ticket to Ignatki. Polish currency is still used in Białystok, a part of Poland until September of 1939 when the Soviets occupied the area.

The train is scheduled to leave at ten-thirty in the morning, in two hours. Ticket in her pocket, Bella is looking for a grocery store. Still unaccustomed to the freedom, she feels exposed in open spaces and walks close to buildings, mindful of gates and entrances. Next to one gate, a few steps down below the street level, she notices a door propped open by a wooden barrel and next to it a basketful of loaves of bread. She enters the dimly lit room, shelves stacked with an array of boxes, four barrels against the wall, and nearby two burlap sacks, one filled with rice, the other with flour. The place smells of herring, pickles, and freshly baked bread. Uncertain whether the woman behind the counter understands Polish, Bella gestures at the Kaiser rolls and the salami on the counter.

'Do you want me to slice it?' the woman asks in Polish. Relieved, Bella asks the price of a roll with butter and salami.

The woman pulls a pencil from behind her ear, struggling to push back the paisley kerchief covering her hair. As she leans over a piece of brown paper, her big breasts, bulging through her heavy blue sweater, rub against the counter. She scribbles something on a scrap of paper, crosses it off, and scribbles again. Her gray gloves, with the fingers chopped off, carry traces of every kind of food in her store.

'Twenty *grosze*.'

'Please give me two. I'm very hungry.'

While slicing the rolls and salami, the woman sizes Bella up; a backpack on her shoulders, hair tucked under a ski cap, a heavy scarf around her neck—this must be one of the Polish Jews from the other side, she figures.

'Can I buy something to drink?' Bella asks.

'Just milk, but you have to have your pot.'

'No, thank you.' Bella pays for the rolls.

'Wait a minute, lady,' and the woman goes to the back of the store. Bella looks around, fascinated by the display of food on the shelves. It is a tiny store, but the shelves are full. She spots a few bars of chocolate. She will buy one for her girls. The woman returns with a steaming metal cup. 'I had my teakettle on; I got you a cup of hot tea.' Overcoming her pride, Bella accepts the cup.

'You can sit on the barrel; the lid is strong.'

The food tastes wonderful. What a luxury—salami. Every bite is pure pleasure. Bella eats one roll, then the other.

'How much do I pay you for the tea?'

'Oh, no. Nothing.'

'Thank you, it is kind of you,' Bella says, blushing.

The chocolate bar she bought in her backpack, Bella leaves the store smiling. The world is smiling back. The sun is out, snow is melting on the sidewalks, and people are walking with energy and purpose. Pulling off her ski cap, Bella runs her fingers through her thick black hair, the crisp air tingling her scalp. In the dim, dust-covered display window of a haberdashery, Bella catches her reflection. No one would guess she is only thirty. Bella removes her backpack. Rummaging inside, she pulls out a comb and a lipstick. Carefully, she outlines her lips, rubs them together, then puts a dab of lipstick on her finger and applies it to her cheeks, leaving just a touch of color on them. She takes out the pins securing the thick knot of hair at the nape of neck, letting her long hair fall down her shoulders. Spreading her fingers, she rubs her scalp, tossing her hair as though wanting to shake out the experiences of the last few days, or maybe the last few months. Her head feels light and bouncy. She hasn't let her hair down since she was a teenager. She will pin it up again on the train."

"Next week, Naomi, we will return to talking about my life in the camp."

6

Reunion

"It must have been very sad and scary for you not knowing whether you would ever see your mother again."

"I don't remember thinking much about my mother during the daytime; I was always busy inventing some game. Without knowing it, this must have been my escape. At night, however, I often cried myself to sleep."

"Life in camp Ignatki, our new home, starts to feel normal. Tata found work in Białystok something to do with carpentry, I don't know exactly what. He catches the train every morning at seven and returns when it's dark. I am fed up with Halina telling me what to do, and she is probably tired of being my Mama—I can be stubborn sometimes. We reach a compromise: I help her cook, do the laundry, and gather wood, and she doesn't pester me to find out where I am going. I am free to roam the area, looking for kids from other cabins. At times, though, Halina suddenly remembers that she is my older sister and should take care of me. Rebelliously, I reject her authority: 'I can do what I want; you're not my Mama.' But I don't want Halina to be angry with me, so sometimes I tell her where I am going.

Pani Zingerowa, who shares a cabin with us, sometimes invites all of us, to eat dinner with her and her husband. The cabins have no kitchens and no bathrooms, just two little rooms with wooden floors and wooden walls. Pani Zingerowa cooks in a pot hanging on a heavy wire with a fire beneath it. She always wears pretty dresses and brushes her hair smoothly. Even though she is plump, she walks with a bounce. Pani Zingerowa's room is pretty, with pictures of flowers and doilies on the windowsill. Ours looks ugly with just a tiny table with two stools in the center and nothing else. The outhouse is far away, and I am scared to go there after dark. Sometimes Halina goes with me, but I think she too is afraid to go there alone in the dark. We decide to always go together, supposedly for my sake.

One night I dream that Pani Zingerowa wants to be my Mama, if my real Mama doesn't come back. I wake up feeling bad. My Mama will come—I just have to be patient—but I wish Pani Zingerowa would come to tuck me in. She is old and has no children. Why couldn't she tuck me in, or read me a story? I hate when Pani Zingerowa closes the door to their room, leaving me alone with Halina and Tata. My sister's cot is next to mine, but she doesn't talk much, and Tata, on his mattress on the floor under the window, never talks.

During the day I'm busy and think little about my mother, except when I get hurt, but in the evening I often grow sad. My sadness comes when the lights are out and I'm lying alone on my cot. Tata comes home tired and not very talkative. He eats supper, reads the Yiddish newspaper, speaks with Pan Zinger, and that's about it.

Sometimes I worry that Mama died and no one wants to tell me. If she's alive, why isn't she coming? Pani Zingerowa tells me many times that my Mama is very brave, that she loves Halina and me. But Mama doesn't come.

'Come, child.' One morning, Pani Zingerowa takes my hand. 'No one in this little cabin can take care of your long braids, you don't want to get lice.'

I don't know what lice are, but if Pani Zingerowa thinks that I don't want to get them, then I don't want to have them. She leads me outside, drapes a sheet around me, unbraids my hair, pulls out her scissors, and starts chopping. I turn to see a clump of long hair fall to the ground, then another and another. My head is now feeling light and cold.

'Will my Tata recognize me?' I ask in a panic, suddenly realizing what Pani Zingerowa has done to my hair.

'He will recognize you; he'll love your short hair.'

We return to our cabin, and I hold back tears. I run my fingers through my hair. It feels strange, unlike my head. My head comes with long braids.

'What have you done to your hair?' Halina yells at me.

'I don't want to get lice.'

'What lice? Who has lice?'

'I don't know, girls with braids.'

I get very sad thinking that Mama won't like me now, and I tell Halina who cut my hair. But all she says is, 'Tomorrow we have to do a big laundry, the sheets and the towels.' I hate doing laundry. My hands burn and get tired, but we have to do it.

After breakfast Halina and I lug in the big wooden basin, like a huge barrel, but shallow. We set it on a stool borrowed from Pani Zingerowa, heat pots of water, and pour them into the basin. Pani Zingerowa helps me carry the pot.

'My God, such a little child carrying boiling water!'

Halina and I take turns rubbing the wet clothes against the washboard. While one of us uses the board, the other rubs the smaller things by hand. Sometimes, when I scrape my fingers on the board, they bleed.

'Be more careful, you'll stain the white sheets,' Halina scolds. We must've poured in ten pots of hot water. The basin is full, and soap bubbles are overflowing onto the wooden floor.

'Girls, be careful not to get the floor too wet. It takes a long time to dry,' Pani Zingerowa warns us.

Sleeves rolled up to my elbows, my sweater all wet, I scrub and scrub. I hate doing Tata's underwear; I would rather wash pretty lacy slips like those Pani Zingerowa has hanging on the line.

'You're such a slowpoke. We'll be doing this laundry forever,' Halina gripes.

'I don't see you doing it any faster, and you're older.'

'So what if I'm older? You have two hands just like me.'

'You just complain and complain. You always complain. Halina, is someone knocking on the door?'

'Who would be knocking on our door? Anyway, my hands are wet.'

'Come in,' I yell.

The door opens slowly, as though the person isn't sure she wants to come in.

'Mama?' I scream. 'Mama! Mama!' I run to her with a pair of wet, drippy underpants in my hand. 'Oh, Mama you came.' I cry and I laugh and I grab her by her arm. I jump up and down and want to tell Pani Zingerowa that she was right, that my Mama has come, but Pani Zingerowa isn't in the cabin. Halina runs up and puts her arms around Mama. Mama cries and hugs us; first she hugs me and then Halina, and afterwards she bunches Halina and me together—all three of us in an embrace. We haven't seen Mama for many months. She is a little thinner then when I last saw her. In flat shoes, gray skirt, and brown sweater, she looks like a girl.

Mama glances around the cabin. 'Where's Tata?'

'He works in Białystok,' Halina tells her. 'He'll come late, probably about seven.'

Mama runs her fingers through my hair, not commenting about my missing braids.

'I didn't want to get lice,' I explain.

'Of course, you don't want to get lice. You look pretty in short hair.'

I feel relieved that Mama isn't angry about my missing braids.

Mama eyes me closely and, before taking off her coat, peels off my clothes—the blue sweater, the shirt with little flowers, the navy skirt, my stockings, and my underpants. She drops them on the floor, picks me up, and sets me in the basin with the laundry. I don't ask why she is dunking me in the laundry tub. It's funny, but it feels good. I will let her do anything—she came back. My Mama is back!

Mama takes off her coat, rolls up her sleeves, and scrubs me and scrubs me with a bar of soap. She asks me to kneel in the basin and dunks my head into the water, scrubbing it with her fingers until my scalp is tingling.

'Do you have more warm water?' Mama asks Halina.

'Yes, I'll get it, Mama,' Halina offers, running out to fetch the last pot on the stove. Mama sticks in her finger to make sure the water isn't too hot. No, it's fine.

'Stand up, Irka.'

Mama gets on her tiptoes and makes a fountain out of me, pouring the water over my head and letting it flow down my body.

'Halinka, do you have a clean towel?'

Halina obliges. I feel wonderful in my pajamas, though it isn't night; we could find no warm, clean clothes for me.

'Halina, you too, my girl, could use a good scrub, but we'll save it for tomorrow.'

By now the floor is soaked with water.

'Mama, Pani Zingerowa said we shouldn't make the floor wet,' Halina comments.

'We'll wipe the floor dry. It'll be fine. Who is Pani Zingerowa?'

'She lives in that room,' I point to the open door.

'I look forward to meeting Pani Zingerowa.'

Remembering that she still has her ski hat on, Mama removes it and looks around for a place to put it away, but all she can find are a few nails sticking out of the wall. She hangs her hat and coat, setting the backpack on Tata's mattress. I watch with great curiosity as Mama looks in the backpack. What could she be looking for?

'See what I got for you—a chocolate bar.' Mama holds up the bar. Oh! A chocolate bar! My mouth is watering, I love chocolate, and I haven't tasted it for a very long time. As Mama unwraps the bar, my eyes follow every motion of her fingers. She breaks it in half, handing one half to Halina and the other to me.

'Can we eat it now, Mama?' I ask.

'It's yours. Eat it whenever you want.'

Halina picks up the red wrapping paper off Tata's mattress, takes a tiny bite of the chocolate and rewraps the rest, putting it in her pocket.

'You want a bite of my chocolate, Mama?' I ask.

'No, it's all for you, I had some.'

I want to eat it slowly so it will last long, but my mouth doesn't want to slow down. In no time my chocolate is gone, but my insides feel wonderful.

Mama sits with me and Halina on Tata's mattress and tells us why she couldn't come to us sooner. We knew about the Germans taking her from the no man's land, but nothing more. She tells us only part of her story, the rest she saves for Tata. I'm so happy to have Mama back that I don't listen much to what she is telling us, I just keep looking at her. Mama's face is pale, her eyelids are puffy, but otherwise she is the same—my Mama.

Halina reminds me that we have to finish the laundry, but now that Mama is back, I ignore her instructions.

'Halina, that's okay, I'll do the laundry. You just change into something dry.'

Mama does it very fast, and we show her where to hang it on an outside line. It takes a few days for the laundry to dry because it is so cold. After a very cold night I like looking at the hanging laundry; the shirts and the pants are so stiff they could walk away with no person in them. Mama is going to make supper, I don't have to peel potatoes. Pani Zingerowa offers to go with Mama to the grocery store and I want to come along, but I'm in pajamas. Seeing Mama leave, I feel a pain in my stomach and tears flood my eyes—suppose she doesn't come back? Remembering that Pani Zingerowa has gone with her eases my fear.

Tata comes home from work, and it's the first time I see my parents hug and kiss. Their hugging back home must've been like their secrets—in Yiddish and not meant for Halina and me to understand or witness. Come to think of it, I've never heard them argue, or be really angry either, other than once when Mama yelled at Tata for hitting me. She was so angry that she forgot to do it in Yiddish. 'Don't you ever lay a hand on the child!' she yelled in Polish.

Now Mama and Tata are talking and talking and can't stop.

'What happened? Tell me what happened in the no man's land?'

'Later, Srulik, later. We'll have lots of time to talk. Let's have supper.' Looking at the table with only two stools, Mama knocks on Pani Zingerowa's door to ask whether she may borrow two chairs.

'Of course, we ate already.'

Mama made a stew from cow's lungs, kidneys, and some other innards. The potatoes are soft and tasty.

Tata doesn't read the newspaper tonight, and doesn't talk much with Pan Zinger. He is eager for Halina and me to go to sleep early so that he can be alone with Mama. It was a big day; I am ready to crawl under my green military blanket. I fall right to sleep, but wake up a few times in the night. In the dark, I find my way to Tata's mattress, stooping to see whether Mama is there.

'What happened, Irka? Did you have a bad dream?' Mama asks.

'No, I just want to see if you are here.'

Mama leads me back to my cot and sits with me until I fall asleep. I dream often that she is gone and wake up frightened. After a while she doesn't ask me what happened, she just tucks me back in. When I go outdoors, I tell Mama where I'll be, and I don't stay out long. A few times a day I come back to see if Mama is home. When the cabin is empty, I wait until Mama returns, then go out to play again.

'Irka, I'll be with you all the time. I'm not going anywhere,' my mother assures me, but it takes a while before my heart believes her.

The nails on the wall are replaced with wooden hooks Tata made. We soon have shelves for clean laundry and two more stools. I'm not excited about the scarf Mama brought me from Maryla, so she hangs it on the wall like a picture. Pani Zingerowa and Mama become friends and help each other; Mama even invited the Zingers for latkes — potato pancakes. Mama is smiling a lot and sometimes hums while she is cooking or cleaning the cabin.

It is about two months since Mama came to Ignatki; my scary dreams of her going away come less often.

Mama gave me a book about Cinderella. I don't know where she got it but I became excited, until I started reading it. A few days later she asks, 'How did you like your book?' adding, 'I read it when I was a little girl.'

'It's okay.'

But I think it's stupid. It's a book for little kids who believe in fairy tales. Who ever heard of mice turning into horses? I read everything I can find with Polish print. Pani Zingerowa has a book, and when she leaves it on the table next to the door, I sometimes read a little, but some things I don't understand.

Walking in the woods with my friend Pola, I find a wet page from a magazine and pick it up.

'What do you want it for?' she asks, but I don't want to tell her that I like to read things.

'It has a nice picture. I'll dry it and maybe hang it on our wall.'

Eager to dry and read the page, I run to our cabin, planning to spread the sheet next to the stove. As I open the door, I find Mama, looking sad and tired, sitting on a chair, Pani Zingerowa next to her. Something is wrong. She didn't hear me come in, and I stand silently at the door.

'God, I can't believe it — I can't. I knew so many of them. Whoever heard of such brutality?'

'It's horrible, horrible, Pani Millerowa. You were so brave and smart.'

I know that Mama wouldn't want me to hear her, but I remain standing just inside the door. I want to know what they are talking about, but I can't ask. Mama is in a no-kids mood.

'I wrote to my sister, I wrote to Greta, but haven't heard from them.'

'No one is getting mail from Poland.'

'I'm so worried. Who knows what's going on there?'

I sit on the floor, trying to be very quiet, but my knee knocks the shovel off the hook as I'm spreading out my wet page. Mama turns, facing me, but says nothing. She just sits. Hearing Halina's footsteps, I walk outside.

'Mama is sad. Something very bad happened with some people, but I'm not sure exactly what. I don't think she wants to talk to us now.'

'How do you know?'

'I heard her talking to Pani Zingerowa.'

I feel better having Halina with me. I don't have to sit quietly, just looking at the walls. Since Mama came back, Halina has found friends in our camp, and she is much nicer to me.

'Mama, you want me to help you make supper?' Halina asks when we go inside. Mama shakes her head no, no, but continues sitting. We have bread, pig's head sausage, and hot tea for supper. I don't like it when everyone is quiet. It feels as though something terrible will happen soon. I go to bed early, but can't fall asleep.

'Srulik, they killed all the people who were on the train with me from the no man's land. In cold blood, they butchered them, even the children.'

'How do you know?'

'Yesterday someone crossed the border, a cousin of the Bornsteins, four cabins down.'

Unsure who killed the people and why, I am scared that the killers will come after us. Halina and I don't know how Mama escaped from the no man's land. She came back, and that's all that matters.

Mama is sad for many days, silent most of the time. I want to make her feel better, but don't know how.

Mama forgets that I know a lot about death, that I saw people killed by bombs, people starved or frozen to death in the no man's land. She treats me like a little kid, and I help her keep believing that I am a kid. I don't talk to her about the things I understand or things that frighten me.

Since finding out what happened to the people from the no man's land, Mama is talking a lot about her sisters and brothers in Warsaw. She worries what the Germans might do to them. But for me, life is good. My Mama is with us, my feet are not hurting, and I'm no longer hungry. The snow has long ago melted, it's getting warmer, the trees are budding, and the area starts looking like a forest. My friends and I play outside, and we meet new children who live some distance away. The older children talk about the Russian soldiers who took a man away in the middle of the night. 'Why would they do it?' I ask, but they have no answer. I give it no more thought until I hear Mama and Pani Zingerowa talk about raids at night. I think my mother and her friend must be talking about the German soldiers, but the children outside spoke of Russian soldiers. I ask my mother about the raids, but she sends me out to play. Every time Mama sends me outside to play, I know something is wrong, something she doesn't want me to know, and that makes me more anxious. Again, I hear my parents speak their Yiddish secrets. They have so many secrets that by now I already understand a little Yiddish. But they whisper, making double sure I can neither hear nor understand.

Tata continues going to Białystok and sometimes doesn't return in the evening. Mama tells us that he has to work late at night and is too tired to take the train so late. This happens now quite often. By now the children in the camp also know about the Russian soldiers raiding the Jewish immigrants' camps and taking away the young men.

'You were the great believer in communism, that it is the best for the workers. Look what is going on here. Is this what we devoted our lives to? Is this what we sacrificed for?' I hear my mother ask Tata.

'I can't understand what's going on. There must be something more to it.'

'Don't fool yourself, we've been blind,' Mama continues.

There are now many more women than men in the camp. I no longer ask why Tata isn't home at night. They don't tell me, but my body senses imminent disaster. I must have developed an extra sense for danger.

During the past few days, there has been a lot of talk among the people of Ignatki, with constant churning and movement, like a beehive with the queen missing. One day Mama tells Halina and me that she is taking the train to Białystok and will spend the night with Tata. They will be back home in the morning. I get more anxious; she's never done that.

'Pani Zingerowa will stay with you,' she tells us.

In the middle of the night, we hear loud banging on our cabin door.

'Halina, what is it?'

'Shh, don't say anything,' she whispers to me. The banging continues. Pan and Pani Zingerowa don't answer. I'm frightened, yet want to know who is outside. Tiptoeing, I head for the Zingers' door, but Halina grabs me by my foot, knocking me down to the floor. I climb on her cot and we lie quietly, holding our breath, hoping the intruders will go away. A hard kick with a heavy boot shatters the silence, and the door is bashed in. Two Russian soldiers with guns stand in our cabin. Halina pulls her blanket up to her chin. I am so scared I can hardly breathe.

Pan Zinger comes out in his striped pajamas, barefoot, followed by his wife.

'What do you want?' he asks the soldiers.

'Get dressed! Get your things and get outside!' one of the soldiers yells.

'Why?' Pani Zingerowa asks.

'Don't ask questions, woman.' The soldier glares at Pani Zingerowa.

'These your kids?' the other soldier asks, pointing to Halina and me.

'No. Their parents are in town.'

'Up, up. Pack.' The soldiers gesture to Halina and me.

'Get dressed, Irka,' Halina instructs me. I do as she says. My skirt is on the floor but not my other things, I must've put them with the dirty laundry. I grab a shirt off the shelf, not looking to see whether it's Halina's or mine. We dress as fast as we can, with the soldiers in the cabin.

'Girls, do what they tell you,' Pani Zingerowa instructs us, as she gets busy packing her belongings, including the pictures on the wall and the doilies on the table.

'Pack, pack!' the soldier yells. 'I'll be back to get you.'

'Get you? Where is he gonna take us?' I ask Halina.

'We aren't going anywhere until Mama and Tata come,' she assures me. For a moment I feel comforted. Halina and I are going to wait here for our parents. She's almost adult; she'll protect me. We both tell Pani Zingerowa that we'll wait here for our parents.

'A good idea, but pack your things,' she tells us. We find the black bag and stuff into it everything we can find.

One soldier takes the Zingers out, and the other turns to Halina and me: 'Come!'

'We are going to wait here for our parents,' we tell him.

'Everyone has to wait next to the train station.'

'Our Mama and Tata will not find us,' I speak boldly, even though I fear the soldiers.

'We'll make sure they find you. What is your name?' he asks Halina. She tells him. 'Galina,' the soldier pronounces my sister's name in the Russian way. 'I'll tell your parents where you are.' The other soldier returns, shouting, 'Get going, little girl, move faster!' and he pushes me towards the door. Squeezing between his parted legs, I grab one of our stuffed bags, Halina takes the other, and he pushes us out of the cabin. We drag the bags along the grassy area—they are too heavy for me to lift.

It's still dark; though by now I know the camp well, I've never walked it in the dark. With their powerful flashlights, the soldiers light up the area. I now can see all the Ignatki people outside with their bundles. The soldiers have herded them to a few central spots and now lead them to the railroad tracks, a kilometer away.

It's May, the night is warm, but the ground feels cold, and there are no stars. I look up, but find none. They are either hiding in the trees or it is going to rain. I hope it doesn't rain— I'm barefoot. I forgot to put my shoes on and don't remember where they are.

'Halina, I want to go back for my shoes.'

'Stay here. What did you do with them?'

'I don't know.'

'They must be in the bag, there was nothing left on the floor.'

By the time we reach the railroad track, daylight is peeking through the green leaves, and I can make out hundreds and hundreds of people standing with their suitcases, bags, and bundles in front of the long freight train. The soldiers are starting to load the people, shoving them in, one after the other, as many as each boxcar can hold. They don't count the people, but peer in, yelling, 'Move back, move back!'

Halina and I stand on the pavement looking in all directions, unsure where our parents will come from. As fewer and fewer people are left standing with us on the pavement, my heart races faster and faster. A Russian soldier comes up, lifts our bag, and pushes us towards the train.

'No, no!' Halina and I scream. I grab the bag, but the soldier is stronger than I am, and he pulls it with me still hanging onto it. I kick him in the shin. He drops the bag and with his fist hits me hard on my back. My eyes well up with tears, but I try not to cry. Halina jumps up and grabs the bag. 'We are not going without our parents,' she cries, and now I'm crying too.

'We contacted your parents,' another soldier tells us. 'They said you should get on the train, and they'll meet you at the next station.'

'No. We will not go without our parents,' Halina repeats.

By now, almost everyone is on the train. A few people are being loaded at the other end and that's it. I look around, Mama and Tata aren't here. The soldiers are so much stronger than we are. I no longer believe my sister can protect me. She looks as scared as I am. We hold hands and cry. Everyone else is on the train. Only Halina and I stand on the pavement. Seeing a soldier coming towards us, I freeze and shiver inside, fearing that he will dump us into the train, and we'll never again see our parents. What will happen to us?

'You are bad girls, not listening to what your parents told you to do. If you don't get on willingly, we'll have to carry you and throw you in.'

'I'm not going, I'm not going!' I scream, holding onto Halina's hand.

I turn my head away from the soldier. I want to deny his existence—if I don't see him, he doesn't exist. A small truck appears in the distance. I keep looking and looking and can now see a hand waving at us. As the truck gets closer, I see two people standing in the back and waving.

'Halina, look!' I shout. 'It's Mama and Tata.'

We start running towards the truck, but the soldiers grab us. 'Wait here.'

'It's our Mama and Tata!' we scream and jump.

'They'll find you. I told you I'd help them find you.' I no longer listen to what the soldiers are saying.

Our parents jump off the truck and run to us with outstretched arms. Tata takes Halina's arm and grabs the bag from my hand. Mama lifts me off the ground and we all follow the soldier.

'Hurry up, hurry up! You delayed us long enough!' the soldier yells. He sticks his head into one car, turns away, and leads us to another. 'Get in!' he commands, stopping before the door of one of the boxcars.

'Did you tell us to wait for you at the other station?' Halina asks Mama after we find a corner for our bags.

'No. Who told you that?'

'The soldiers,' I tell her. 'We didn't believe them. We screamed—we didn't want to go. I kicked a soldier in his leg.'

'He hit her hard in the back,' Halina adds.

'No. We didn't talk to anyone. As soon as we heard rumors that they're evacuating everyone, we rushed to get to you. We had to find someone to drive us. Everything will be fine now, everything will be fine,' Mama keeps repeating, her eyes flooded with tears. I don't listen to her words.

Seeing all the frightened people clustered on the floor of our boxcar, things don't feel fine, but I am so tired the events of this morning feel like a dream. Leaning against the wall, I sit numb, unable to talk, unable to think. Mama and Tata are here and that's all I want—to be with them."

7

To an Unknown Destination

"Naomi, my girl, my experience with German soldiers and with Russian soldiers, deaths I had witnessed, and the fragments of stories about killings I had overheard merged into a generalized fear that clung to me like a crust on my skin. At times I would feel like crying, not knowing why, but the tears would not flow. I'm sure that the diminished trust in my parents' ability to protect me contributed substantially to my anxiety. Though I couldn't yet understand and appreciate his role as a daring activist and labor union organizer, my father had always seemed omnipotent to me—he could do anything; he was tall and strong; he would keep me safe. Witnessing his powerlessness in the face of the Germans and Soviet soldiers, my father became less and less a protector."

"After sitting the whole day in the hot, smelly train, without food, without water, not knowing where we are headed, the soldiers slide the wooden boxcar's door shut, drop the metal bar across it, and we are cut off from the rest of the world, left only with the light and air that enter through two small holes at the top of the freight car and between the cracks of the boards. The stink of cattle and mold blend with the smell of sweat and fear. The bewildered people don't talk; they just sit motionless on whatever they carried out of their cabins.

Tata, the tallest person inside, stands up to peek through the hole.

'Pan Miller, what can you see there?'

'Nothing but a few soldiers pacing the pavement.'

'What the hell do they want from us? What did we do to them? They pack us in like criminals, like animals. We escaped the Nazis to find this?' Angry voices mingle in the dark.

'We are a dangerous element, enemies of the people, we're the bourgeoisie of Poland,' someone says ironically.

'But you, Pan Miller, you are a carpenter—a working man.'

'I'm sure we'll soon find out what it's all about. There must be a good reason for all this.'

'They're no better than all the other Jew-haters,' a woman adds bitterly.

'I never trusted these *redniks*.' Voices are coming from all directions.

'It will be easier on all of us if we stay calm and wait for an explanation. We'll accomplish nothing with anger and speculation,' my father advises, at ease with talking to groups of people and tempering emotions. The voices calm down. People start rearranging their bags, settling in for a journey of unknown duration. It makes me happy when Mama finds my red shoes inside the bag, the shoes from Ciocia Fela, which now fit my healed feet.

Finally the train is moving—lazily, but moving. I am so tired I can't keep my head up. I curl up on the floor, my head on the rolled-up black bag, and fall asleep. I sleep through the night and part of the morning.

'Wake up, Irka.' Mama strokes my head. 'You need to eat.'

The boxcar is open. It's bright daylight. People are sipping something from metal cups.

'Have some soup and bread.' Mama hands me a cup and a piece of black bread. I'm not hungry, but very thirsty. The soup is so watery that I gulp it down with a few swallows. The few pieces of cabbage sink to the bottom, but I don't bother to fish them out. Mama saves my bread for later.

We are in a village train station. People in the outside world, walking on the unpaved grassy path, look at us with curiosity. A thin elderly woman, head wrapped in a brown scarf, gazes at me with kindness. She wants to talk to me, but the soldiers pacing back and forth in front of the train stop her. Are these the same soldiers who loaded us into the trains in Białystok? I don't know, they all look the same to me, faceless uniformed men.

'Where are you taking us, *tovarishch?*' Tata asks the soldier.

'You'll find out, and I'm not your comrade.'

Tata takes my hand and seats me in front of the opening, my feet dangling out of the boxcar. He continues holding my hand while I kick my feet with great delight. There are no children my age in our car; I'm the youngest.

The soldiers tell us to get off. People get excited, hoping we've reached the end of the journey. Maybe the Soviets needed the camp where we'd been and found another place for us, maybe even a better place. But no sooner do we all climb down than the hopes fade—the soldiers order everyone under the trains to relieve themselves. This will become the pattern for every morning and evening stop the train makes.

We stand on the tracks for hours without an obvious purpose. The adults are getting worried, but I enjoy it for as long as the car is open. At dusk the soldiers lock us in and we are in a black world. I need to use a toilet, but where? The doors are locked already. A piece of the floorboard is ripped out, but I can't do it in front of all these people.

'I'll keep my coat around you,' Mama tells me.

'But the people can still see me.'

'Irka, we have no choice.'

I hold it in until I can wait no longer. Mama spreads her coat around me. I feel humiliated and close my eyes; at least I don't see the others looking at me. We all sleep a lot and talk little.

The next morning, as soon as daylight breaks, Mama, with Tata's help, arranges an enclosure around the hole in the floor. The little toolbox Tata carried from Białystok contains nails. He pounds a few nails in the ceiling, Mama parts with her precious sheet, and the result is a private squatting toilet. People in the boxcar are delighted—a luxury, a reason to feel good.

The soldiers open our boxcar. We must've traveled during the night—the train now is in a station of a different village, or a small town. The sidewalk is paved, though just a few feet from it grows tall green grass sprinkled with red poppies. Chimneys in houses nearby billow black smoke; the people must be cooking. I wonder whether this is our destination.

'Get your bowls and cups!' the soldiers yell. A few minutes later they show up carrying buckets. They ladle out soup into bowls in our outstretched hands; no bread today. I peek into my bowl; the contents look like dirty dishwater with a shriveled piece of cabbage floating on top—no different from yesterday's soup. This, apparently, is a standard prisoner's soup prepared at every feeding stop. A cup of soup and sometimes a piece of bread, will become our daily rations for five weeks. If you're lucky, you might find a piece of potato drowned at the bottom of the bowl. In some stations we wait for hours, not knowing why and with no one to ask. People have stopped speculating where we are headed and when we will get there.

When daylight and the summer breeze enter the boxcar, I want to capture them and save them for the gray and black hours when the doors are slammed shut and barred. I envy the people walking outside; other than for bathroom use under the train, we can't get down—the soldiers don't let us. My legs feel stiff, I want to walk and run, but all I can do is sit or sleep on the bare floor.

A week into our forced journey, when the doors are slid open, we are in a train station with water pumps along the grassy walkway. I stick my head out and see people roaming freely. Coming from under the trains, we are allowed to wash ourselves at the pumps. What an excitement, splashing water all over myself. I pull off my dress, kick off the shoes, and sit under the pump asking Halina to pump hard. My sister thinks I am ridiculous, but she complies, and I am giggling as the water tickles my ears, my back, and all my skin.

'Little girl, that is enough. Move. Others want their turn,' someone scolds me. I get out from under the pump, but am so excited I can't contain my joy—I jump, twirl, and hop on the grass near the water pump. Mama shows up with a towel, but I don't let her dry me—I like the water dripping down my body and my wet underpants clinging to my skin.

'Well, it's warm, you can dry in the sun,' she says, defeated.

The soldiers allow us to linger around the pumps and on the grass; I hate them no more. After a while they send us back into the boxcars, but the doors remain open. As our car fills up, I realize that Tata is missing.

'Tata is trying to buy food for us,' Mama tells us.

The thrill of maybe having a piece of bread is now marred by my anxiety for my father. I keep asking my mother when Tata will return. Mama tries to calm me, but I sense that she too is getting anxious. The soldiers are in front of our car, ready to slide the doors closed.

'No! No!' Mama, Halina and I are screaming. 'My husband is out. Our Tata is out. Don't close the doors!'

The soldiers ignore us and go about their business of locking us into the grayness of the boxcar. 'Wait! Wait!' we protest and continue screaming, pushing our faces against the smelly wooden boards of the cattle car. The train starts moving as we scream and cry. Our companions make no effort to comfort us. How do you comfort a wife and children when they may never again see their husband and father?

After a while, Mama goes back to our corner on the floor. Halina and I follow her. We sit crouched without uttering a word. Mama ignores us. She is in a world where we don't exist. After remaining there awhile, she stretches her arms and pulls Halina and me closer to her. I want to tell Mama how frightened I am. I want her to reassure me that Tata will find us, but looking at her sitting like a stone statue, I say nothing. I'm sad and feel like crying, but tears don't come. I had been a child who seldom cried, and now the war has almost turned off my ability to cry. As though the tears are confused, they flow into my throat, but not to my eyes.

We sit together in silence until the grayness turns into blackness. Arranging our bags on the floor, we huddle for the night.

As soon as the doors are pulled open the next morning, I stick my head out, but can see little. The sky is dark and laden with ominous clouds. Standing next to the opening feels almost like being outside, but that's as far as I am allowed to go until the soldiers let us out. Suddenly the clouds burst and the skies are weeping for me. I used to like summer rain, to run barefoot outside the summer cottage, to splash in the puddles, even if it made Mama a little angry. Like a tree in a dark forest, I'm hungry for light, for sunshine.

'Eat your soup,' Mama tells me, but I can't. I'm not hungry. She saves it for me for later. I'm not hungry the rest of the day. 'Tata will find us, you'll see,' Mama tries to cheer me up, but she herself doesn't believe it. How does one find a cattle train that has no name, no known destination, and no cattle in it?

I ask Halina what she thinks happened to Tata and whether he'll find us. She shrugs and tells me she doesn't know.

'You look tired. Take a nap,' Mama advises. I go to sleep and don't get up till next morning.

'Would you like me to pick you up so you can see what's outside?' Pan Posner is asking me, but I don't want to be picked up.

On the third day without Tata, we are allowed to stay out of the train for a few extra minutes. The sun is out, it's warm. Taking off my shoes, I rub my bare feet against the grass, enjoying the softness of the warm, moist green blades. It tickles. Before getting back on the train, I pull out a handful of grass and carry it with me into the boxcar.

'What do you want the grass for?' Halina asks me, but all I can tell her is that I just want it.

We now are used to being always hungry and dirty, accustomed to hearing the sounds of people's efforts on the toilet behind the hanging sheet that's no longer white. There's little conversation among the passengers in our car; they try to be cordial to one another, but at times tempers snap. People get a bit more spirited when the soup comes with a piece of bread, but this happens no more often now than in the beginning of our journey.

On the fifth day after Tata's disappearance, we stop in the train station of a town bigger than the others. The soldiers carry bags of ripped-off chunks of bread and give us each a big hunk. We aren't yet allowed to get off the train, but I sit with my feet dangling out and watch the people on the outside.

'Where are we?' I ask a young soldier.

'You are in big city, little girl. Put your feet in or you'll fall out.' He tickles the soles of my feet. I giggle and pull my feet up.

'Mama, we are in big city.' I pass on the information, meaningless to me.

There is a commotion on the ground. Women carrying baskets are coming closer to the train, and the soldiers don't push them away. Some people in our boxcar are buying things from these women. Loud, angry voices are coming from behind the train, but I can't see the people. I sit taking it all in, amazed at the hustle and bustle of this place.

'Irka, Irka.' A voice is coming from the distance. Unsure whether I heard my name called, I crane my neck, now really careful not to fall off the train.

'Irka,' I hear again, this time sure it's my name someone is calling. With the third call, I hear running feet. 'Tata?' I ask startled. It sounds like Tata. He saw me from a distance and he's running.

'What did you say?' Mama asks.

'Tata called my name!'

A minute later my father stands before me, his face covered with a reddish beard I haven't noticed before. He appears clean, but tired, and looks taller than five days earlier. 'Tata, Tata!' I shout, hugging Mama and Halina. Tata jumps onto the train. We all hug as our boxcar companions cheer. 'A miracle, just a miracle that Pan Miller found his family.'

I'm so happy to see Tata that I can't let go of his arm. Maybe if I hang on, he will never get lost again. Mama talks and talks so fast I can hardly understand her, but seeing her animated, I believe now everything will be okay. Tata brought two large loaves of bread and a small chunk of farmer's cheese wrapped in a white cloth. We save the bread for the days when we get only soup.

Everyone in our boxcar wants to know where Pan Miller has been, what he saw, and whether he heard where the Soviets are taking us. No, no one knew where the train was headed. He met some friendly comrades, but they were afraid to talk, or just didn't know.

Now, I am happy and feel again that Tata is all-powerful and will take care of us: he knew how to find us, he brought two large loaves of bread and even farmer's cheese—not many fathers can do such things.

Our days pass with the same routine: barring and unbarring of the boxcars; relieving ourselves under the train; watery soup; similar train stations; and the waiting, the waiting for what is to come. My dress is dirty and hanging loosely; we all lose a great deal of weight and sleep a lot, or try to sleep—there's not much else to do. Mama finds a treasure—a pad of paper in Tata's bag. I try to write very small letters so the paper will last a long time. I don't dare use it to draw pictures—pictures take up a lot of space. I write a poem about a girl who knows to fly like a bird, asking Mama how to spell words. My parents whisper—quiet secrets. The adults in our boxcar easily get angry with one another; someone is using the toilet too long, or takes up more floor space than others. 'Don't stick your legs out when I'm walking, don't gripe all the time, stay away from the crack—you're blocking the light,' people snap at one another.

After a few weeks of travel, the weather gets a little cooler, and the grass, what little we see of it, looks coarser. The days are getting much longer until there is hardly any night. In some stations the peasants are bold enough or the guards less watchful, and we buy bread, sometimes rock-hard salty cheese, which I lick like a lollipop. Mama even bought a salty dry fish—what a treat. In the distance, I see the outlines of mountains—or maybe these are just clouds. No, mountains they are.

'We must be close to Siberia—go to sleep in daylight and wake up in daylight,' someone suggests.

'You don't have to be a professor to know it. Of course we're near Siberia. Look out the door, see the Ural Mountains?' Everyone is running to the partially opened door.

'Pan Miller, what do you think?'

'Yeah, I assume we are headed to Siberia.'

'So why didn't you say something before?'

'What for? We'll all find out soon enough.'

People become animated and talk all at once, hardly hearing one another: 'Isn't Siberia where they ship all their criminals?'

'Some are no more criminals than you and I.'

'Who else would ever want to live in that God-forsaken place where birds freeze on trees?'

'Pan Bernstein, you are not a bird, so don't worry,' a little woman speaks up.

'It's no time to be funny.'

'What better choices can you suggest?'

'They may need workers to help the war efforts in Europe, against the Nazis,' my father suggests, trying to justify our predicament.

'Are you naive, Pan Miller? Stalin has himself a sweet deal with Hitler—he got more than half of Poland for promising not to interfere with the Germans' march into whatever country they want. Stalin will do nothing against the Nazis, he wants to protect his ass and to hell with everyone else.'

Two days later, after weeks of stench and darkness in the boxcar, we arrive in Siberia, to a city whose name I don't remember.

No sooner do the soldiers open the doors of our boxcars, than people sense the end of our journey. We are in a train station larger then all the others, yet a strange quiet surrounds us. The workers in the station move purposefully, but there's no conversation—not a word exchanged. People look somber and each in his own world; no eye contact, not a glance wasted on anyone or anything.

It's hard to judge the ages of the people around us. They all seem a little stooped and are wearing similar drab, dark cotton slacks and dark shirts. Uniformed soldiers are the only ones eagerly showing their faces. Nobody but the soldiers look at us. For all the others, we don't exist. But even the soldiers' faces appear expressionless.

'Go under the train, but do it fast and get right back on,' the soldiers instruct us.

We each receive a piece of bread, some water, and a small lump of sugar. The sugar tastes wonderful—for weeks we've had nothing sweet. We stay inside the cattle car for hours, anxious and eager to get off and face the world around us. The adults speculate and disagree, but are willing to accept any verdict rather than live with the uncertainty. In the late afternoon, the soldiers tell us to get off with all our belongings and stay next to the train. My family, having little to unload, is among the first in our car to get off. It feels exciting and wonderful to breathe the cool air and to have the clear blue sky high above us, a freedom I have not experienced in a long time. Taking small steps, almost marching in place, I move around, stretching my arms, wiggling my shoulders, arching my back like a cat.

'Stay still. Don't make so much commotion,' Mama impatiently tells me, but I can't stand still. I have to move, though I do it less obviously.

'Follow me with your bags,' a soldier directs us.

Each family, clustering together and carrying its bundles, follows the soldiers. After walking for an hour, we arrive at the bank of a river, where barges—open wooden platforms with tiny cubicles in the front—are waiting for us.

'Get on, get on.' The soldiers load us onto the barges, packing as many people as the platforms will hold, not much more than standing room. When the first barge is full, the crowd is urged forward to the second vessel.

'How long are we going to be on the boat?' I ask.

'No one knows,' Halina jumps in angrily, as if it is my fault that she doesn't like the accommodations.

'Just sit down, Irka, and don't ask so many questions.' Now Mama is mad at me as well. Our barge floats on the river for a few days. We are cold and hungry—the bread and water don't fill me for long. My family huddles together at night for warmth. We pass small villages, but hardly a person can be seen and not much greenery, just tall trees, lots of trees in the distance.

'Don't get too close to the edge,' Mama keeps warning me, but there's not much more to do than watch what is ahead.

Everyone gets excited when, in the distance, we see a city. Is this Syktywkar, the end of our river journey? We are not told what will happen next. After a few hours of standing on the deck, we spot a group of men in old army fatigues coming towards the barges. They talk with our guards and board the platforms. We are ordered to pack our bags and disembark. The men in fatigues are our guards for the last leg of the journey, this one on foot. The guards carry no guns—where would anyone try to escape to in this isolated part of the world that no train or bus can reach?

In a mess hall with long wooden tables and benches, old women carrying metal buckets and ladles fill our bowls with hot soup. I look into my dented tin bowl and find myself face-to-face with a fish head, the eyes staring straight at me. I am very hungry, but turn away, unable to imagine eating this fish-face in my bowl.

'Eat while the soup is hot,' Mama tells me.

'I can't.'

'What do you mean you can't?'

'The fish is looking at me.'

'So close your eyes and eat it. We have to get used to eating whatever is there to eat.'

I start off with the two pieces of potatoes and the broth. Seeing me hesitate, Mama takes my bowl and with her spoon smashes the head and eats the fish eyes.

'There is no head now and no eyes. Eat it, it's very good.'

We walk for about five or six miles along a dirt road, carrying our belongings. The guards seem as tired as we are and follow the pace of the old, who fall behind. Exhausted and dirty, we finally struggle in through a gate bearing a big sign: "*Dyrnowski Kirpichny Zavod*"—a brick factory. This brick-producing labor camp will be our home for the next two-and-a-half years."

8

The Siberian Taiga

"A forest so dense that light hardly enters, a constant night churn-ing with life becomes our backyard. A misleading silence keeps the se-crets of the forest from newcomers — city-dwellers ignorant of what hides in the taiga. Yes, Naomi, this is where the birds freeze on trees, if they lose their way, and where breathing sometimes feels like swal-lowing sharp objects."

"Our labor camp is located on a patch of land cleared in the forest. Tall cedars, pines, spruces, and aspens dwarf the two-story wooden buildings clustered a minute's hop from the edge of the dense forest. You can still smell the fresh pinewood of the roughly finished boards of our building, as though the trees were sawed into lumber and shaped into dwellings while we rode the train and now are ready for our occupancy. Maybe our journey was slowed down to allow the workers to finish the houses.

At the entrance to each building hangs a big portrait of a man in a military uniform. He looks stern and powerful.

'Mama, this is the same man whose picture we saw hang-ing in all the train stations. Who is he?'

'Stalin, the leader of the people.'

'Of all of us?'

'Children just have to mind their parents. Now run upstairs.'

My family is assigned to the second floor. The stairs creak and wobble, but it is fun to run up and down, up and down. My legs are eager to run and jump after the many weeks of sitting crouched on the train and then cramped on the barge. I want to be outside, unconstrained by the smelly walls of the cattle car and the pushing crowd on the barge. I inhale deeply to see how much air I can hold in my lungs, as if breathing is a function I have just discovered.

It's July, the sun is out, but it isn't hot. It feels like autumn is just around the corner.

Mama sticks her head out the open window, 'Irka, come help unpack your things.'

I yell back, 'Coming, coming,' hoping to hear a long echo, but I don't, the sound of my voice is swallowed by the forest. Disappointed, I run upstairs.

I don't understand why Mama calls me to unpack; there is no place to stow our things other than back into the black bag or the suitcase. The room is bare of any furniture, not even a shelf or a hook on the walls The cooking utensils, what few we have, Mama sets on the floor by the fireplace.

We share the room with the Grinberg family. They have two daughters, both older than my sister; to me the girls look like adults. The Grinbergs, being the first into the room, positioned themselves with their belongings against the longest wall, uninterrupted by the window or the fireplace. We place our bags against the wall adjacent to the fireplace, an open pit in the wall with a brick floor. No territorial squabbles. In the wide hallway stands a six-burner stove for the use of the seven families on the second floor.

No sooner do we unpack our few belongings than two officials in brown uniforms arrive, sheets of paper in hand.

'Head of the family? Who is head of this family?'

'I am,' Tata responds.

'Names and ages of your girls, and don't lie.'

'Halina twelve, Irena seven.'

One of them points to Halina. 'This one looks more than twelve.'

'If you don't believe me, why did you ask?'

'Galina, how old are you?' the man asks my sister, using the Russian pronunciation of her name.

'Twelve.'

The man asks Tata some other questions, but I move away so as not to hear him. He sounds angry and looks mean.

'Do you expect us to sleep on the cold floors?' Mama asks the man.

'You will get cots and blankets when we have them.'

Every family receives a book of coupons for our food rations which will be redeemed in the government store, the only place available for buying anything.

'The store is still open if you want to buy something to eat,' the uniformed man tells us, pointing out the direction to the store.

For two coupons and some rubles, Mama gets a herring and half a loaf of black bread with the texture of wet clay. She divides the food among the four of us, but I'm still hungry after eating. I wonder if there is something wrong with my stomach. Maybe it is bigger than it should be, making me hungry so often.

'Irka, it's late. It's time for you to go to sleep.'

'But it is daytime, Mama.'

'Here it is light even at night.'

It feels strange going to sleep in full daylight. Not having a watch, I am confused about when it's night and when it's day.

'Is it night yet, Mama?' I ask the second day we are there.

'I'll tell you when night comes, but go to sleep whenever you get tired.'

It is cold sleeping on the floor. The one blanket Halina and I share is not big enough to lie on and to cover us as well, so we sleep with our clothes on.

Adults who have children work in the brick factory. Single young men are sent into the taiga to clear new tracts of land or do other lumber work. They stay out there for days at a time without returning to the camp.

My parents and Halina work in the brick factory. The uniformed man decided that since my sister is almost thirteen, she must work. Mama and Halina look tired when they return from work. Mama makes dinner without uttering a word, while Halina just sits on the floor and doesn't move until food is ready. The whole week we have been eating *przypalanka* for dinner, a soup of potatoes thickened with browned flour. On her last trip to the store, Mama bought potatoes and oil, and we have some flour still left from the week before. We have to ration the food to last us a few days until we can buy something else with the coupons. The man in the store never knows what he will be getting in. Mama buys whatever happens to come in, and according to how many coupons and money she has left. The workers get paid very little.

I am left alone for the whole day, but I don't mind. 'Visit Pani Finbergowa whenever you get lonely or need something you cannot manage yourself,' Mama tells me before leaving for work. Pani Finbergowa is an old woman who lives on our floor, but I never visit her. I am busy walking into the woods, just at the edge, to look at all the different trees. I haven't seen trees that tall, and don't know what they are. I wander into other buildings to ask if they have children. All the houses look alike, and I have to observe the shapes of trees, the distance between the house and the forest to distinguish the individual buildings. If Stalin at least looked different in those portraits—smiled in one, frowned in another, looked to the right or to the left—it would make it easier to identify the houses, but the same stern Stalin hangs in the same spot above all the entrances.

Across from our house stands a very tall pine with a broken branch on the left side, and next to it a stump where I can sit; the pine and the stump make it easy to remember where I live. A few boys and girls live in the third building to the right—finding that house is no problem. I'm allowed to visit the houses in our cluster, but not the others that are far away. The labor camp sprawls over a wide area, but I don't know who lives in those other buildings. In our cluster of buildings live only the people who arrived with us on the train, all Polish Jews.

Some older children tell me that a few miles down the road is a school, and in the center of the yard lives a bear in a big cage. When the workers were clearing a patch of forest to build the school, an angry, big black bear leaped out of the woods ready to pounce on them. The workers shot the bear but saved the cub they found nearby and built a cage for him in the schoolyard. Never having seen a live bear, I'm eager to see him, but also afraid.

'Can the bear break the cage and get out?' I ask my new friend Shmulek.

'They probably made the cage very strong.'

'Maybe the bear likes to live at the school,' I try to comfort myself.

Eagerly, I run home. 'Mama, will I be going to school soon?'

'I hope so.'

Even though it's still summer, the white nights are much shorter and getting colder. We sleep on top of our winter coats, and it feels a little softer than on the bare floor.

'They got in cots and blankets in the store. Run before they give them all away,' a neighbor urges my mother as soon as she returns from work.

Mama grabs her wallet and book of coupons.

'They're giving us the cots—you don't have to pay for them,' the neighbor advises Mama.

'As soon as Tata and Halina get home from work, send them to the store,' Mama instructs me.

From that night on we sleep on cots, and Halina and I each have our own blanket. It has been so long since I slept on something other than a floor that it feels strange, but I get used to it in no time. What a luxury to have my own blanket and a cot!

One day Halina comes home crying, her hand wrapped in a gray towel.

'What happened?' I run after her up to our room.

She keeps crying and doesn't answer, just holds her right hand. I try to remove the towel but she yells out, 'Don't touch it!'

'What happened, Halina? Tell me—I have to know why you're crying.'

'I cut off my finger.'

'Your finger? How?'

'The machine, at work.'

'Does Mama know?'

'No, they wouldn't let me see her. They just sent me home.'

I run to Pani Feinbergowa. 'My sister is hurt, she cut off her finger!'

Pani Feinbergowa says nothing but follows me to our room where Halina is still crying and clutching her hand. A big patch of blood blooms on the gray towel.

'Come, my child,' Pani Feinbergowa gently takes Halina by her other hand. I follow. We end up in a nurse's office, a tiny cubicle with white walls and a small cabinet. There's only one chair, and the nurse directs Halina to sit down.

'Didn't they tell you at the factory to come and see me?' the nurse asks.

'I don't know. Maybe they did, but I didn't hear them, and I didn't know where your office is.'

I squint in order not to see the wound when the nurse, a young Russian woman, unwraps Halina's hand, tossing the bloody towel into the corner of the room.

'It hurts.' Halina is crying loudly. Tears are flowing down my cheeks too.

'You cut off the tip of your finger. It will heal. You'll be okay, but don't put your hand in water until you come to see me in two weeks,' the nurse instructs my sister.

We leave the nurse's office with Halina's hand in a heavy white bandage and a form to excuse her from work.

'How could they send a child out alone bleeding and not take her for medical help?' Mama is outraged when she comes home and discovers what has happened to Halina. Mama's calico dress is smudged ... but she ignores it.

'Those bastards, I will speak to the foreman tomorrow.' Tata seems equally angry about this incident.

'What good will it do, Srulik?' Mama pauses, looking sad. 'We're in the perfect land where workers get fair treatment. These are our comrades, right? Our child is put to slave-labor, and we can do nothing about it.'

'Bella, I find it all so hard to understand.'

'We were duped—just idiots believing and struggling for something that turns out to be the greatest lie, an ugly lie.' Mama leans against the wall for a while saying nothing. 'These are our comrades? This is what we dreamed about? This is what we endangered our lives for?' Mama abruptly stops, puts her hand over her tightly closed lips. 'I forget—the walls have eyes and ears. You never know who'll snitch on you to gain favor with the Party leaders.'

This is the first time I hear my parents openly criticize communism and comrades. They don't even switch to Yiddish. Now the talk is not kept secret from Halina and me, but from the soldiers, the factory foremen, the Party members. Without being warned, I know never to repeat what my parents speak of between themselves, particularly when they talk in whispers.

I've already learned a little Russian and understand when the roaring husky voice on the loudspeaker repeats over and over: '*Mat-rodina*, the motherland needs your labor. It is an honor to serve our great comrade Stalin, our leader.'

All workers are encouraged to become *stachanoviets*, worker-heroes who perform beyond the required norm. From time to time, posters of men and women who have achieved the status of *stachanoviets* are plastered on the outside of our building. I don't understand fully what it means, but seeing my parents sneer when they utter these words, I know it isn't something good and that I shouldn't ask Mama to explain. When my mother doesn't want to answer my questions, she sends me someplace: go upstairs, go outside and play, gather wood for the fireplace. I don't ask her, but question older children in the camp who don't treat me like a little kid. My friends and I gather in front of one building or another; most of the time we walk, or sit on the grass and talk.

'The communists hate Jews. They just want us to work for them and starve us to death, my Tata says,' Shmulek tells us.

'Why do they hate Jews?' I want to know.

'I don't know, they just hate us.'

'The war will be soon over, and we'll go home,' Zygmund declares.

I understand there's a war, but it feels unreal, I don't see any fighting. The German soldiers are already in Warsaw, so what more could they want?

'Do you think the war will be over before it gets real cold here, before the birds start freezing in the trees?' I ask.

'Maybe.'

The older children discuss what their parents talk about, who hates the Russians, who argues with his neighbors, and who is just a mean person to be avoided. Mama doesn't realize how well informed I am about what's going on in our camp, and how closely I follow the conversations of adults around me.

Summer here lasts only two months: July and August. There is hardly any fall and it's getting very cold. By September I'm wearing my winter coat. School starts next week. I'll be walking with the other children; Shmulek knows how to get there. I'm happy about going to school and I mark off each day on a piece of paper, counting how many are left till Monday.

'I am not hungry, Mama, I have to go!'

'You have to eat, take a piece of bread and some tea. Shmulek will wait for you,' Mama urges me on Monday morning.

I gulp down a few sips of hot tea without sugar, grab the bread Mama holds out to me, and run.

Eight of us children will walk to school together, but only four are out in front of Shmulek's house. We wait a few minutes for the others to show up. It's three miles to school, but I don't mind. I hop, as I always do when I feel happy. From time to time I put my hands in my coat pockets to warm them, and to check whether the sheet of paper and my pencil are still there. Yes, they are there.

My legs feel very cold and they hurt when the wind blows under my coat; I have no tights, I outgrew them. Mama will cut off the sleeves of her brown sweater to extend my tights.

The school is in a wooden building whose white paint is chipped in many places, particularly around the door. The unpaved outdoor area has a tall wooden fence at the forest side, but nothing else can be seen. No bear in a cage. He died, the Russian kids tell us. Most of the Russian children wear gray jackets, either too big or too small on them. My friends are dressed in a variety of clothing. Shmulek's pants now reach a few inches above his ankles, the blue jacket with sleeves that hide his hands is his mother's. I'm holding back a giggle, watching Shmulek try to get his hand out to push back a few of his black curls that hang over his forehead.

An old thin woman in a mid-calf-length gray skirt and khaki-colored tunic made from an army blanket, her hair pulled back and pinned into a round bun, comes out of the school ringing a bell. We all run to the entrance, but she spreads her arms, blocking the door: 'No running, no talking. Form one line and move forward,' she orders us in Russian. We all obey, eager to see the inside of our new school. There are lots of children I haven't seen before. They're from other labor camps in the area; most speak Polish or Yiddish, but some speak only Russian.

The entrance hall is big enough to hold all one hundred kids, mixed ages standing clustered, some look almost as old as Halina.

'I am Ilena Mikhailevna Borodina, your principal. You are expected to work diligently and be obedient. No talking in the classrooms, no moving from your seats without your teacher's permission.' She pauses and glances around.

'All children through age ten move to the right. Children older than ten, go to the left.'

Shmulek ends up in my group on the right and in the same classroom.

Tania Petrova, our teacher, is a young Russian woman. The room has two long wooden tables and benches for the forty-eight pupils in my class. The wood is so rough we have to be careful not to get splinters. Tania Petrova stands behind a small table facing us. In the next room is the class with the older children. Stalin, in this picture hanging in our class-room, looks a little friendlier than all the other pictures of him I have seen.

Tania Petrova knows no Polish or Yiddish, just Russian.

'We are to speak only Russian, the language of the moth-erland,' Pietrova instructs us, waggling her finger in the air.

All the Polish and Yiddish-speaking children came to the labor camp the way my family did, awakened in the middle of the night, loaded into trains, and never told where they were being shipped. The Russian children, however, never talk about their journey, or where their parents are from or why they came to Siberia. Any question we ask about their parents or about their past gets the same answer from each of them: 'I don't know.'

Red-haired Sonia, who becomes my friend, also answers 'I don't know' to most questions. When I once asked why her parents came to Siberia, she answered, 'They just wanted to come to Siberia.'

I can't imagine anyone wanting to come here to work in a labor camp. These kids are not ignorant, but everything seems a great secret, even where they were born.

We each are given a thin notebook and a pencil and instructed to copy the Russian alphabet from the blackboard. Some letters look strange, not at all like the Polish letters I know. I peek at the notebook of the Russian-speaking girl next to me to see how she is writing the difficult letters.

Our classroom also serves as the lunchroom. At noon, an old woman in a black babushka covering her hair, carrying a big bucket, shows up in our class, ready to ladle out soup into each of our metal bowls. From the bag tied around her waist, she distributes a piece of bread to each of us. All the soups here taste the same—fish heads and a slice of potato—but now I eat the fish head and am pleased when the old woman gives me a big one. Maybe this one will keep me from being hungry. I am hungry most of the time, and sometimes I can't stop thinking about food.

'Irka, will you be able to find your way to the store?' Mama asks me.

'Yes, I know where the store is.' There is only one store and everyone knows where it is.

'Go and ask for our bread rations,' Mama instructs me, giving me the coupons and some money.

Tovarish Piotrovich, with a big white apron tied around his waist, looks at me: '*Chto ty chochesh?*' 'I want bread,' I tell him, giving him the coupons. The Russian people I address as *Tovarish* (comrade), and the Polish people Pan or Pani.

Piotrovich takes off a shelf a dark round bread that looks like a huge mud cake. I watch him closely as he cuts a chunk of it and puts it on the scales. 'A little more,' Pietrovich talks to himself, as he grudgingly adds a tiny piece that barely tips the scales.

'*Eto wso*,' this is it, and he hands me the bread.

I carry the bread close to my chest to make sure I don't drop it. I try not to look at it—looking makes me hungrier—but my eyes don't obey. I would like to eat the little piece. Maybe I will eat it and not tell Mama about it? Will she know that I ate the piece if I don't tell her? It's very small, it would be okay for me to eat it. But this bread is also for Mama, Tata and Halina; it would be wrong for me to take it. I fight with these thoughts all the way back to our room. I want to get rid of the bread as soon as I can to stop struggling with the temptation to eat it.

'Here, Mama,' I hand the bread to my mother as soon as I open the door. Mama takes the little piece and puts it in my empty hand. I eat it slowly, relishing each crumb.

A month after school begins, Tania Pietrova walks into the classroom carrying a stack of books. There aren't enough for all of us, so two kids have to share a book.

Shmulek agrees to be my book partner. On the cover of the book is a picture of a few children with red scarves around their necks. Stalin stands over them, one hand resting on a boy's head.

'The boys and girls with red scarves are *komsomols*, brave and dedicated to the motherland, our future heroes,' Tania Pietrova tells us. On the first page, it states: 'It is each child's duty to serve *mat-rodina* and to study hard.' Our school day starts with all the children lined up and singing a song about our leader Stalin and how we all love him. We also learn a song about a boy who is flying over the beautiful country where he can see the wide Baikal and the deep Amur, the great lake and river of our magnificent Soviet Union. He flies over the Kremlin, waving to Comrade Stalin.

Tania Pietrova tells us that we children should teach our parents love for the motherland and for our leader Stalin. This is the *komsomols'* duty.

I come home excited about having a book, but I never mention to my parents that I am supposed to teach them something. It sounds strange to tell Tata or Mama that I will teach them, and anyway, I wouldn't know how to teach them love for Stalin and the motherland.

Mama looks at my new book and says nothing, but I read her frown; she doesn't like my book. Tania Pietrova told us yesterday that pupils who get high grades will be able to borrow a book from the school library; I want a book, and work diligently to deserve it.

It turns so cold outside that I freeze in my coat and shoes. The Russian kids come to school wearing *fufaiki* and *valenki*, heavy quilted jackets and knee-high molded boots made of some pressed rough fiber. The *fufaiki* are all dark navy, and the *valenki* a dirty beige. The foremen in the factory and the Party leaders walk around in huge fur hats, and their coats are lined with a long-haired fur.

'You can't go to school until we get warm clothes for you,' Mama tells me.

My imploring is to no avail. Mama keeps me out of school until our store gets a shipment of *fufaiki* and *valenki*. I am proud of my new boots and *fufaika*, big on me, but I know I will grow into it. A heavy scarf over my face, huge mittens, and a thick sweater under the *fufaika* keep me warm and cozy but make it hard to walk. I have to get used to walking in the *valenki*; they're stiff, so I can't bend my feet as I walk, and the soles are a little rounded, giving each step a rocking motion from heel to toe and back. I carefully observe how the Russian kids walk and try to imitate them, raising my feet off the ground. It's hard to do it fast, but I must keep up with the other children walking with me to school.

Snow is so high I can walk only in places that have been shoveled by the men in our camp, otherwise I would drown in the snow. Even in my new *fufaika* and *valenki*, at times I can't walk the three miles to school. My hands and feet hurt badly when I am outdoors for a little while. My fingers get so stiff that I can't bend them to hold my notebook. If Mama, Halina, or Tata are home when I get indoors, they tug off my mittens and boots, and rub my hands and feet. The temperature here drops to minus 50 degrees. We are all taught to observe one another's faces: if a nose or ear turns white, it means it's frostbitten, and you have to rub it immediately and vigorously with snow, and not come indoors until it turns red and feels hot. Otherwise, your ear will fall off or get rotten, I'm told.

Yesterday a man yelled after Halina, 'Girl, girl, wait, your ear is frozen!' Before she could do anything, the man grabbed a handful of snow and was rubbing her ear. She didn't even know which ear the man was talking about. People watch out for one another and also help out when someone gets stuck in the snow while walking.

Most evenings we hear the howling of wolves — 'wooo, wooo,' a long, almost crying sound that seems to carry for miles. Sometimes it stops, and then there are a few cries again as loud as if the wolves were almost in our backyard. The howling frightens me, particularly when the wolves sound so close. The Siberian gray wolves are big and covered with bushy long fur. Once, on the walk to school, we spot one in the distance, and we stop, frightened. Zygmunt, who is ten years old, reminds us what the teacher says — a single wolf will never attack. They hunt only in packs.

'Yeah, they roam in packs and attack people if there's nothing else to eat,' Shmulek tells us.

'You're just trying to scare us.'

'No. It's true, Irka. Didn't you hear that two days ago a man from another camp was killed by a pack of hungry wolves?'

'Mama, is it true that the wolves ate a man?' I ask anxiously when I get home that afternoon.

'Don't listen to all the stories people tell.'

This isn't the end of my wolf anxiety. I hear the same story repeated by adults, even mentioning the name of the victim. Someone questions why the man found himself alone in the dark, but it's now dark most of the time; daylight lasts only a few hours.

I spend a lot of time indoors, either in our room or in a nearby house. It is so cold outside you can hardly breathe, but indoors it is warm; we have wood to burn in the fireplace. Tata and Pan Grinberg have stacked up piles of wood for burning, but we may not have enough to last us through the winter, Mama keeps warning, when Halina wants to toss in another log. There is a forest all around us, but in minus 40 or 50 degrees, you can't chop down trees.

It is four in the afternoon, dark outside. I have no book to read, no paper to write on, no one to play with, and I am hungry. When I am alone and have nothing interesting to do, I feel the hunger much more, and can't talk myself out of it. I look out the window that faces the forest. Snow covers the ground, and trees glow in the darkness as though a distant light were illuminating the area. I try to make up a poem in my head about a girl who got lost in the taiga, but she wasn't afraid, and the wolves were friendly and helped her get home safely. As I stare out, thinking about the friendly wolves, I notice something that looks like two round light bulbs flashing outside our house. The light bulbs are moving to the right, stopping, then moving closer to me. Suddenly I realize that these are the eyes of a big animal. A bear?

'Mama!' I yell, forgetting that she's at work. I'm alone in the room and scared that the bear may come inside. I run across the hall to the neighbors and grab Pani Feinbergowa by her hand.

'Please come with me, I'm scared!'

'What's wrong, Irka?'

'A bear, a bear!'

'Where?' Pani Feinbergowa hesitates.

'Come, come,' I pull her to the window. The animal is still there glaring at me with the eyes like little lanterns.

'It is some big beast, but I'm not sure it's a bear.'

'What will we do if he comes inside the house?'

'Don't be afraid, Irka. The outside door is closed, and animals are afraid of people. He won't come inside.'

Seeing that I'm still scared, Pani Feinbergowa takes me to her room, and I chat with her while she darns socks stretched over a glass.

'Would you like to learn how to darn socks?' Pani Feinbergowa asks me.

'Yes, let me try it.'

'We'll need to ask your Mama if she'll let you use a needle.'

'She will. I am not a little kid, I can be careful. I peel potatoes with a knife.'

By the time Mama returns from work, the animal is gone, but I tell her all about it. For the next few days I'm afraid to be alone outside in the dark. Shmulek's father walked me home yesterday and the day before, but after a few days I forget about the bear and walk by myself until another incident catches my attention. Lusiek, a young man who worked with the taiga team, has been killed by a bear. Everyone in the camp knew Lusiek, a slight fellow of nineteen. Mama doesn't try to comfort me with denials, everyone is discussing Lusiek's death with great sadness. They were deep in the taiga and the workers weren't trained adequately, the adults are saying.

'These sons of bitches must've left the boy alone, not caring what happened to him,' Shmulek's father complains angrily to his neighbors.

Mama warns me to stay indoors when it gets dark, but it gets dark at two in the afternoon. What am I to do alone in our room? Besides, it's dark in the morning when I walk to school. Daylight doesn't come until ten.

Toward the end of the winter, our wood supply is running out. Tata gathers small frozen twigs that fall off the trees; they smolder and smoke, and make me cough.

'Next winter we will know better,' Mama consoles us.

On the days I don't go to school, Mama takes me along to the canteen for the soup of fish heads and potatoes. The workers can buy a bowl of soup cheap. It is warm in the canteen, and I like being with the workers. I sometimes bring my book with me and read after the workers have finished eating.

In late April, the snow finally starts melting, and daylight lingers much longer.

Each family is granted a small plot of land for growing potatoes. We have to save enough potatoes for seedlings; keeping them in a warm place speeds up the sprouting. It is Halina's and my job to cut the potatoes into as many chunks as possible, leaving one eye in each piece.

Our plot is quite far from home, but now it's getting warm and walking is fun. With a bagful of potato pieces, all four of us head out to plant them. Tata borrows two shovels from a neighbor so each of us can have our own.

'The hole has to be as deep as this stick is long,' Mama tells me, handing one stick to me and another to Halina.

'How many potatoes will grow from one piece, Mama?'

'I am not sure, but definitely a few.'

I enjoy planting potatoes, knowing that one small piece can turn into several whole potatoes.

Every week or so, Tata, Halina, and I visit our plot to see how our potatoes are doing. On one of our visits we find the plot covered with little green, leafy clusters.

'Is this how potatoes grow, Tata, on those leaves?'

'Potatoes grow in the ground, like carrots. You can't see them until they are harvested.'

Tata forgets that I've never seen anything edible grow. Nothing grew on our street in Warsaw.

In the summer, the forest becomes an additional source of food and an exciting place for me to explore. There are various berries and mushrooms, all kinds of mushrooms.

I love picking mushrooms, but am never allowed to go alone. We go in groups of a few people to help keep one another from getting lost in the forest. It is easy to wander into the forest and be unable to find your way out, unless you mark the trees or observe them carefully.

It is dark all around in the dense taiga. The trees grow close to one another as though they're huddling together to protect themselves from the winter frost. Not having fur coats like the Party leaders, they grow a thick bark to keep themselves warm. I crane my neck, but can see no sky; the trees form a roof over my head and no light enters. I feel dwarfed like a tiny bug in this giant green world. It is extremely quiet, so quiet that if I stand still, I can hear myself breathing. The only sound one ordinarily hears is the movement of a small branch brushed with an elbow, or the crunchy leaves and needles under our feet. If I am lucky, I will sometimes glimpse a red fox, a snowshoe rabbit, running fast to get away from people.

It seems unbelievable that in this giant place small things like mushrooms are growing. It looks more like a place where you would find a bear, not a mushroom. But, as I bend down and examine step by step what is on the ground, in time I come to know which moss to turn over and look under, and which trees most likely have mushrooms near them. A new world opens up—the hidden world of wild mushrooms: big, flat, yellow, white, pointy, dark-brown, round mushrooms, and many other kinds. The darker the place, the more likely I'll find mushrooms.

Oh! What a big one, and next to it two more, and another, almost on top of one another. I drop them in the bag Mama sewed for me, then turn around as in a swivel chair to check under the other dark patch of moss. Here they are, another small cluster—one, two, three nice ones. Next to this fat tree with the rough bark, surrounded by damp dark-green moss, must be good ones. No, none here. I scramble up and look further. The area to the right looks like a good possibility. I walk fast, eager to see whether I am right. Yes, but only two of medium size. I want to fill up my bag. I want to find more than Halina, more than Mama. I have my method: I sit on the ground and rotate my body. Where I uncover a cluster, there are likely more just a few feet away.

An invisible force draws me deeper into the forest to look, to find— if not in this spot, probably in the one next to it, on and on. I forget there are others with me in the forest, I don't feel branches scratching my arms, I forget I was hungry when we came to the forest, and I'm not worried about getting lost. Time passes and I don't know how long I've been in the woods. There's magic all around me, and time has no meaning until I hear Mama calling to me. 'Stay closer. I must always see you.'

The search itself becomes a fascinating challenge. The forest has the power to pull you in deeper and deeper to seek its bounty. It has a tantalizing, hypnotic force over one searching for its treasures. The finds, however, are reserved for the discriminating adventurers. You must know and understand what you find, otherwise, you will not survive the eating.

Mama stops me. 'Let me see what's in your bag.'

'I know, Mama, which are poisonous, the pretty ones with the red dots, the silver- colored ones that shine in the dark.'

'There are many others that are poisonous.'

'I know them all, Mama.'

People in the camp have been teaching one another which mushrooms are safe to eat, which to avoid. Some of that know-how has been passed on from those claiming to be experts, and based on the experiences of those who got sick eating the wrong kind. One neighbor almost died from eating the silver mushrooms. The man in the store is another source of information—he is a Russian who has lived in Siberia for many years. Some speculate that prior to getting his job, the man served a sentence as a political prisoner.

'You don't fulfill your work quota, and you are accused of sabotage. Maybe this poor *shlomazl* wasn't a great worker and off to Siberia with him,' Smulek's father says.

In the summer, it's my job to cook the family dinner. I do it outdoors, on four bricks, two on each side stacked up, far enough apart to light a fire between them. Before going to work, Tata takes down the iron pot filled with water—it is too heavy for me to carry. At three in the afternoon, I start the fire under the pot elevated on the bricks. For fuel I use twigs gathered from the edge of the forest. The potatoes—sometimes carrots or rutabaga—I peel and drop into the pot while the water is still cold, so hot water won't splash my face. The soup is done when the fork easily splits the potatoes. Usually I'm very hungry by then, but I fight the temptation to eat some of the potato pieces; Mama has to divide it among all four of us. Yesterday I couldn't resist eating a piece of potato. I didn't tell Mama about it, but suspected she could see it on my face, and I felt bad.

When the soup is cooked, I cover it. Tata carries the pot to our room when he returns from work. By now we have a table and two benches that Tata made from leftover pieces of lumber he found next to the new construction site. The table stands in the middle of the room, where both we and the Grinbergs use it.

Two days ago the man in the store got a shipment of bedpans. Everyone was walking from the store with a white enameled bedpan in hand. We're using ours as an additional pot for cooking; it's much lighter than the iron one.

'The soup we eat is like *pishachs* anyway; it may as well come out of a bedpan,' Mama comments with a smile to Pani Grinbergowa. I already know a lot of Yiddish words and don't think it funny that Mama compares our food to pee water. In the summer, we eat much better. Some days we have cabbage in the soup, and carrots, and, of course, mushrooms give the soups a great flavor. Soon it will be time to harvest our potatoes, and we'll put more of them into the soup, Mama tells me. When I look at the green, leafy plants, I have no idea what goes on in the ground with the potatoes. Are they ready? Are they big?

I'm getting used to going to sleep in daylight. After the dark winter, I'm delighted that it's bright during all my waking time. If occasionally I wake up at night to go to the outhouse, it's light and I go outdoors by myself. In winter, we stay inside and use a bucket.

Like camels in the desert storing water in their humps, we need to store summer's light to sustain us through the long black winter.

'When Tata comes back from work, you can go pick some potatoes with him,' Mama tells me one afternoon. I'm so excited, I can't wait to pick our own-grown potatoes. I made a sign with a few twigs so I'd remember which ones I planted. I'll dig up my potatoes.

'Not with the shovel, you'll damage them,' Tata warns me. 'With your hands, gently move away the dirt around the plant. Yes, just like that, a little deeper. Stick your hand in as deep as you can. Grab the plant and shake it some. Now tug a little. Is it moving?'

'Yes, I feel it move. It's coming, it's coming!'

'Now yank it out.'

'Tata, look at this bunch of potatoes. Let me count: one, two, three, six of them! All from that one sprout I planted!'

I marvel at how the potatoes have multiplied on their own. We pull out a few more and carry them home. My fizz and bubble over this miracle lasts for a while. I tell Halina and Mama and any kid willing to listen to me.

'Don't make such a big deal, that's just how things grow,' Shmulek cuts off my enthusiasm, making me feel ignorant, but only for a moment. Yeah, he is a big shot; he grew up in a *shtetl*, with a vegetable garden behind his house.

Before we harvest all our potatoes, Tata builds a partition in the corner of the room to store them; he does the same for the Grinberg family. The potatoes have to be kept indoors, or they will freeze.

Today we celebrate our good potato crop. Mama bought a salty herring, and we will bake potatoes in the fireplace, and I can eat as many as I want, Mama tells me.

'Will they last us the whole winter, Mama?'

'No, not the whole winter, the winter here is very long, but they'll keep us for a while.'

It is my eighth birthday, Mama reminds me. We have no calendar and I don't know how she remembers, but she does. Strange that Mama mentioned my birthday, I don't remember what we did before the war for our birthdays.

'Let's pretend, that there is no war, Irka. What kind of present would you like for your birthday?' Mama asks.

'A big loaf of bread that I could eat as much of as I want.'

I am puzzled why a tear is rolling down my mother's face.

'What is it, what happened Mama?'

'Nothing, just something fell in my eye.'

Praying and other religious practices are forbidden by law, but some people pray anyway. In one of the buildings, men gather on Saturday mornings and pray quietly, their *taleses*—their prayer shawls—wrapped around their shoulders. Many people know about it, but no one mentions it; it's a communal secret respected even by atheists like my Tata. Though my father is an unbeliever, he considers religious practice an act of defiance against oppression. No government should have the right to interfere with how a person lives his life, as long as he causes no harm to others, Tata believes.

My parents no longer consider the Soviets their brothers in struggle; they no longer use the word comrades. My father no longer shouts in his sleep about workers uniting. At times I hear my parents talk with pain about their disillusionment with the communist system. 'Who would ever believe Stalin's terror, people being afraid of their own shadow? They don't trust even their own brother. People being snatched by the NKVD and never heard of, who would believe this?' There are heated discussions, all in whispers, about the treaty Stalin made with Hitler and why it failed. The Nazis attacked the Soviet Union anyway. The adults speculate about how long the war will last, and they're eager for news of what is going on at the fronts. Rumors abound about the German army taking this or that Soviet city, but no one can confirm them. The government radio we are allowed to listen to tells us about the brave Russian soldiers defending the motherland.

'Men and women in the country must sacrifice for the good of the motherland. We are a strong nation of dedicated comrades. We will conquer the evil attackers. Work hard, comrades, work is your weapon, as strong as the guns of our brave soldiers,' the husky voice on the radio declares.

'The Soviet Union will be Hitler's grave. He is taking a bite of a dish too tough for him to swallow. He will choke on it, particularly when winter comes,' Tata declares to a group of men standing next to our building. The war becomes more real to me. It is in the Soviet Union where we now live, and I worry that the German soldiers in their marching boots may show up at our labor camp.

'Shmulek, do you think the Germans will come to Siberia?' I ask.

'It is too far. I don't think they will get here.'

I tell Shmulek what Tata said about the Soviet Union becoming Hitler's grave, and we compare notes about what our parents say regarding the war.

'But our problem now is the locals, not the Nazis. The Nazis didn't ship us to Siberia to labor camps.'

'Don't complain. You're alive, and who knows whether our brothers in Poland are.'

These conversations among adults continue. Sometimes I have difficulty understanding what they are talking about and ask my friends, but my friends can't figure it out either. Strange how adults ignore us; they think we're just kids who don't need to know, we don't worry about anything anyway, all we want is to play. The adults will do the speculation and the worrying. But the less I understand of what I hear, the more I worry.

'Someone must have squealed about the Sabbath prayers. Party officials came to inquire about religious services,' Pani Grinbergowa is telling Tata.

'How low can some people stoop for a crumb of a privilege?' Tata reflects.

One day, totally unexpected, our old friend from Warsaw, Mietek, shows up at our house. Both Mama and Tata rush to him, excited.

'How did you find us? Where are you coming from? What goes on with you? We had no idea what happened to you. Oh, it's good to see you!'

'I have my sources. I'm doing fine. How are you?'

'Doing okay, as good as can be expected,' Tata answers.

'Sorry, Mietek, I have nothing home today to treat you with, but I can bake a potato if you're hungry.'

'Thank you, Bella. It's perfectly okay. I'm not hungry.'

Mietek got fat since I saw him last in Warsaw, his potbelly pours over his belt. He looks shorter than I remember, barely reaching my father's chin.

'Bella, you don't have to be the perfect hostess. Do what you need, I'll hang around with Srulik.'

Mama looks a little puzzled, but says nothing. Seeing that Mama isn't leaving the room, I plop myself on the floor ready to listen to whatever will be going on. Mietek turns to

Tata, 'Come, Srulik, I need to stretch my old legs. Let's get a bit of fresh air.' And without waiting for a response, he grabs Tata's shirt and tugs. Tata follows. About half an hour later, Tata returns without Mietek.

'Where is he? What happened?'

'Hell knows where he is.'

'Why was he so eager to get rid of me? This whole visit puzzles me and makes me uncomfortable. There was something strange about him. I can't put my finger on it, but it was there,' Mama declares.

'Bella, it was more than strange. I was ready to kill the bastard! It took a lot of self-control not to kick the hell out of this *fertzele* (pipsqueak.)'

'What did he do?'

'Can you imagine the chutzpah of a man asking me to tell him who is conducting the Sabbath prayers, and who performed a ritual circumcision in our labor camp? What degradation, a man who tries to collect this information from a friend! I am to be his stool pigeon so he can find favor with the Party. He's telling me that he's an active Party member and thought he could count on my loyalties to the cause. I didn't ask him what shitty cause he was talking about, I was afraid of getting violent. Can you imagine the idiot telling me that religion is the opium of the poor? 'You son of a bitch,' I told him, 'if the poor want opium it is none of your business nor mine. I would rather myself grow *payes* (sidelocks) and put on *tfilim* (phylacteries) than serve as your spy among my fellow Jews. Get the hell out of here, and I never want to see you again,' I told him.'

'And what did he say?'

'To hell with him and what he said.'

'But what did he say?'

"You're making a mistake, Srulik,' or 'think it over,' something like that.'

'Do you think he might make trouble for us?'

'What kind of trouble can he make? He is probably just a peon in the Party.'

'You know the Yiddish saying that one fool can drop a stone in the river, and ten wise men can't pull it out. Did you see how fat he's gotten, certainly not from hard labor.'

'Don't worry, Bella, he'll do nothing.'

***

The whole labor camp is wild with excitement. Women are hugging one another, men are slapping their neighbors on the back, disregarding all previous standards of dignified and polite behavior.

'What is going on, Mama? What is it?'

'We are free, we are free people! What wonderful news.'

'Free to do what, Mama?'

'Anything we want to.'

I run to Shmulek to find out more about this freedom that everyone is so excited about.

The Polish Government in Exile, or whatever it's called, has signed an agreement with the Soviet Union that includes a stipulation that Polish citizens are free to leave the forced labor camps. Polish representatives have been assigned to assist in this process and to work out the logistics of travel and so on. Within two or three weeks, people will be able to buy their transportation tickets. The camp is humming like a beehive: 'Where are you going? What is the best place to go until the war is over? Where can you get work? Where is the safest place, considering the German war with the Soviet Union and the heavy battles raging in some areas?'

180

A week later, in the midst of all this excitement, two Party members from the investigating division show up looking for Tata, Pan Grinberg tells us. With no one willing to tell them where Tata is, the men look around, wait a bit, and then leave. Tata hasn't wanted to worry us, but he's had some indications that he's being accused of sabotage or some other such crime for refusing to spy on the religious Jews.

'Srulik, we must leave at once and take no chances. That son a bitch set you up.' I know Mama is talking about Mietek.

That evening we pack and at night leave what has been our home for two and a half years. Tata tells the Grinbergs we're leaving, but not exactly where we are headed. Mama won't let me say good-bye to my friends.

'You tell no one, not even your best friend Shmulek. He might repeat it to someone and word will get out.'

'But I feel so bad, Mama, running away without saying anything to my friends.'

'I understand, but we must be careful not to endanger Tata.'

Tata's friend Zygmund Rostov and his family are stationed in a labor camp five or six miles from us. We head there to wait until we can get tickets out of Siberia."

9

Uzbekistan

"Mom, why would this so-called friend, Mietek, want to harm your dad?"

"I was too young to know the character of the man, but apparently neither did my parents know who he was, or who he could become to gain favor with the party leaders. Mietek didn't look the same man I remembered from Warsaw, coming with ends of salami or slivers of cake. I was scared of him, and my excitement over going to Uzbekistan was tamed by my fear of what might happen to my father."

"We are all excited about going to Uzbekistan. It will be warm all the time, very warm, Mama tells me, and there will be lots of fruit.

The only fruit I think I remember the taste of is *złote renaty*, the wonderfully aromatic yellow apples Mama kept in the linen closet to give the linen a nice smell. Even though slightly sour, they were so good and juicy I wanted to keep the bite in my mouth for a long time before swallowing it. Often the juice would drip on my chin when I bit into the apple. Oh, I would like a bite of an apple. I lick my lips and feel my mouth watering. Maybe they have *złote renaty* in Uzbekistan. They probably have everything you want.

'Mama, do they also have bananas?'

'Yes, even bananas.'

I have never eaten bananas. When I was a little girl, I thought bananas were only for the sick and the very rich, just like pineapple and marzipan. I liked the Polish sound of *ananasy* and *marcepany*, that sounded very sophisticated and exotic. Tata was the only person in our family who ate bananas. Often he would get diarrhea, and bananas helped him. I know now that some people eat bananas even when they are not sick. Rich people eat pineapple and marzipan whenever they want.

My paternal grandmother used to scold me for disliking the noodles she made with farmer's cheese and sugar, 'You must be a very fancy girl who only eats *ananasy* and *marcepany*, nothing else is good enough for you?' Maybe in Uzbekistan I will even taste pineapples and marzipan, I fantasize.

My elation about all the good things we will have in Uzbekistan, and that the Rostovs will be our neighbors, is suddenly gone. I have not said good-by to my friends, not even to Shmulek. I feel so bad just disappearing without letting my friends know where we are going. I can't believe that Shmulek would tell anyone, but when Mama mentioned endangering Tata, I didn't want to argue with her.

We are packed and have the tickets for the barge.

'Be at the waterfront at five in the morning,' the Jewish representative informs us.

My parents don't talk about it, but I'm afraid that Party members may find Tata and take him away. I wake up many times that night fearing that I overslept, or having dreamt of someone chasing us with guns or knives in hand.

At four in the morning we leave the house and walk to the river with our belongings. It's a long silent walk with bundles on our backs. Mama gave me the lightest one to carry, but after a while it becomes heavier and heavier. Periodically

I adjust the straps that are cutting into my shoulders. Tata is walking fast and Mama, breathing heavily, is trying to keep up with him. With her tiny little steps she always looks like she is running.

Seeing my parents' tense faces, Mama's back arched, I know they are worried. From time to time Mama anxiously looks behind to make sure we are not being followed by the police, or by the NKVD.

I fear what will happen if the NKVD catches us. For me, NKVD are angry-looking men in fur coats and the power to do anything they want, men who take pleasure in harming Polish Jews. I still don't know why they hate us.

Though it is summer, the sky looks gray and the air feels dry and cold. Nothing to see on this dirt road but potato fields and a dense forest in the distance. We walk for an hour without any talk, and probably look like people running away from something.

'Halina, look, the river.'

'I can see it.'

'It will feel good to dump these bags.'

She doesn't answer. More important than dumping the heavy bag is the relief that the river will protect us from the NKVD. They do not know that we are leaving on the barge and will not be able to find us.

Stepping on the small barge with a rotten floor, I wonder whether it will carry us safely to the train station. I am careful to avoid stepping in the floor holes the size of big balls.

The barge is tightly packed with people trying to hang onto whatever rails or bars there are. I turn to look, but all the passengers are strangers—not a single familiar face. They all look angry, or scared of something. Their lips are tight, eyes downcast, arms close to their bodies, not talking to one another. Most women are draped in black shawls, and babushkas cover their hair. Some of them carry big bundles tightly wrapped in some dark cotton cloth. Everything, the people, the barge, the sky, is so dark and so sad. I think I am going to cry. No, no, I mustn't. It would be very embarrassing to start crying, I must hold it back. By now I have learned very well how to hold back tears. I close my eyes tightly, breathe deeply, and try to think of one person I like. Not always, but most of the time this works.

My eyes must have been closed too long, I didn't see the workers untying the barge, but I can feel we are moving, a slow swaying back and forth, back and forth. I sit down on the floor to keep from falling on the people next to me. I can see my family from some distance, but don't feel like getting closer to them. I want to hide, to be invisible, and to be silent.

Mama is talking to Halina. My sister is headed in my direction. I lower my head, pretending to be asleep.

'Irka,' Halina whispers, but I don't answer. She pauses for a minute, and goes back to Mama.

I don't remember much of the ride, I must have been dozing off and on, but when I wake up seeing big logs floating on the river, I get frightened and confused.

'Are we in *Kirpitchny Zavod?*' I shout in Russian, pulling the pantaloons of the woman standing above me.

'*Niet,*' she answers, looking at me puzzled and annoyed.

I get up and move to Mama.

'Are we still in *Kirpitchny Zavod?*' I ask. 'Look at the floating logs.'

'Oh no, we are not. We have been floating for hours. This is how they ship the logs to other locations,' Mama tells me. 'You have been sound asleep; we didn't want to wake you.'

'Mama, what are we waiting for now, aren't we getting off here?'

'We will get off, but we must wait for the right official to do something.' I have no idea what that something is, but have a hunch that neither does Mama. Tata, unlike himself, is so quiet; I didn't see him talk to anyone. Not until we leave the barge and get on the train do the tension and the silence lift.

'Bella, we can take a deep breath now. We are free.'

'These slimy, sneaky bastards might still be around, even when we get on the train,' Mama tells him.

'We lost them. I'm not important enough for them to chase after me forever.'

'I hope you're right.'

We did lose them, or they lost us.

***

We are on the train, off to Uzbekistan. This train has benches, and we are free to get off at some of the stations. It's a little tough sleeping on the hard benches, but no one complains.

Mama buys food from vendors who come up to the train at most stations. Bread and farmer's cheese, or *brinza*, a salty, hard white cheese, are our staples. Occasionally Mama buys boiled potatoes that are still warm, or dried salty fish.

I have nothing new to read, no one to talk with. All I can do is look out the windows.

'Mama, can I have the rope from around the brown suitcase?' I ask.

'What do you want a rope for?'

'I will use it as a jump rope when we get off at stations.'

'You can't sit quiet a minute; you always come up with something!'

'Please, Mama.'

'The things will fall out of the suitcase if we untie it.'

'The suitcase is on the back shelf, nothing can fall out.'

Mama sits for a while saying nothing, and I am trying not to bug her. I know if I pester her too much, she will get angry and not do what I am asking.

'Srulik, give her the rope off the suitcase,' Mama turns to Tata, pointing at me.

As we get further south, the grass is taller and more dense, the flowers bigger, and the food more varied. The bread looks like thin, flat pancakes. The salty cheese is hard like a rock and looks like one. Either you lick it with your tongue, scrape it with your teeth, or soak it in a cup of water to soften it.

'Mama what's this?' I point, puzzled by the thing an old woman walking alongside our train is wiggling in the air.

'I don't know. Let's look at it closer.'

A yellowish twisted object about a foot long, looking dry yet sticky. She has many like it in her basket. The peasant woman is having trouble explaining what the thing is. I bend down to smell it, but it has no smell. The vendor woman scrapes off a tiny piece and puts it in my mouth.

'Hmm, this is sweet and tasty.' Mama buys two of them, still not knowing what they are.

It is sweet and wonderful. We try figuring out what this delicious thing is. 'Look, it is a twisted melon,' Halina yells out. I have never eaten nor seen a melon. This Uzbekistan must be a place of all kinds of wonders, and Tashkent, the city of bread, is the best of all of the cities. I try to imagine what new, unexpected marvels will welcome us, but all I can think of are things to eat. I am sure everything will be there. My predictions become more believable as we find dried figs for sale — something else I have never tasted before.

'Halina, how can she do it?' I stop, puzzled, watching a woman carrying a huge basket on her head and above it, on a flat board, a big bundle.

'I don't know,' Halina replies, apparently uninterested.

My eyes follow the woman. Her shoulders are pulled back, back straight, hips swaying a bit in the loose striped cotton dress that reaches her ankles. She walks as though utterly unaware that she has this tall load on her head. Back in the train, I look for big objects to place on my head to see whether I can walk like this woman. All I have is a small stack of books, but they keep on tumbling.

'You have to get used to it little by little. These women have been carrying things that way since they were kids,' Pani Rostovowa tries to console me.

'I'm a kid, but I can't do it.'

'It took them time to learn.'

Mama gets annoyed with me when I go on asking too many questions, but I want to know whether there is no winter at all in Tashkent. Why do the women wear long-sleeved dresses down to their ankles when it is hot here? Why do they carry loads on their heads? Many other things intrigue me, and nothing I have to read explains these things.

'We are entering Uzbekistan,' Tata announces.

'But we are going to Tashkent, Tata, right?'

'Yes we are. Uzbekistan is not a city, but a whole state,' Tata smiles at me.

I feel relieved. I have built up many expectations for our life in Tashkent. A city with all those riches will have schools, I will learn all kinds of things. Everything will be perfect: enough food, warm weather, and nice people — no traitors.

From a distance I see pale-green unfamiliar-looking trees. Tata tells me they are olives, and the others are dates. I have never seen olive or date trees, nor have I eaten their fruits.

The following morning we arrive in Tashkent, but we are not allowed to get off the train. Soldiers along the track stand guard to make sure no one leaves.

'What is going on?' Mama asks, puzzled and anxious, her eyes straining to see into the train station as far as she can, her lips closed tightly as they are when she gets angry or upset. No one answers. Mama is pacing the floor, talking Yiddish to Tata, ignoring Halina and me. I stick out my head to see what is happening on the platform, but Halina grabs my arm and pulls me back in. After sitting for hours, not knowing what we are waiting for, a soldier comes on the train and tells us to follow him. He leads us to a big hall where people are sitting on the floor next to their suitcases or bundles made of blankets and other wrappings. The soldier points to an empty corner, 'Sit.' Without giving any further instruction or explanation, he takes off. At the end of the hall, three men sit behind a long table strewn with papers. The men all wear the same brown uniforms with some insignia on the chest. Men in uniforms frighten me—they always do us some harm—but I say nothing.

After sitting for an hour or so, Tata gets up and heads towards the uniformed men at the table, but a soldier grabs him by his arm and pushes him back to our corner.

'What are we waiting for?' Tata asks the soldier.

'Just sit and wait!' he yells, putting his hand on the rifle slung over his shoulder.

Hearing the soldier's angry, stern voice, I turn around so as not to see Tata's face. I wish he would hit the soldier, or yell back at him.

Two women carrying big baskets approach Mama. '*Kushat, kushat?*' Eat, eat?

One woman is selling bread and *brinza*, the other has a basket full of cucumbers.

Suddenly I feel very hungry. We haven't eaten since early morning and it's nightfall.

Mama puts half of the bread and *brinza* into her big canvas bag and divides the rest into four portions. We eat sitting on the floor. The men at the desk pack their papers into a box and leave. Night falls and we stretch on the floor, knowing that nothing will happen today.

We spend an additional four days and four nights on the floor of the train station, allowed to get up only for the toilet, always under the watchful gaze of the guards.

Our turn comes to talk with one of the men. Tata and Mama in front, Halina and I follow with our bags. Strangely, my pack that felt so light initially is now too heavy for me to pick up, and I drag it on the floor.

'We plan to stay in Tashkent,' Tata tells the man.

'No one is asking you what you plan. You will go where we assign you.'

'We were assured freedom to leave Siberia and go south to where we choose,' Mama adds.

'I don't know who promised you what, but no one goes where they want. You go where we tell you to go.'

Surprisingly my parents did not know that in the Soviet Union no one has the right to choose a place of residence without official written permission, and such permissions are never given without high connections and hefty bribes.

'Where are you sending us?' Mama asks.

'You are going to Laish.'

'Where is that?'

'You will find out when you get there.'

We return to our spot on the floor to wait for the next train to take us to our destination. The Rostovs are assigned to another location; we don't know how far it is from Laish.

'Srulik, did you ever hear of a place called Laish?' Mama asks.

'No.'

No one has a map to look up our destination. My family sits quietly on the floor, none of us talking. I can build no fantasies about Laish, a strange-sounding place about which no books have been written, and no one knows a thing.

More train rides, another distribution center, and we end up in Laish, a dusty-dry farming village with clay huts and people looking us over with curiosity and suspicion. A gangly man in a striped caftan with a turban on his head meets us.

'Come,' he instructs us, without introducing himself or explaining anything. Four other families assigned to Laish accompany us: an old couple, a husband and wife with their three- year-old boy, a childless young couple, and a family with two teenage boys. I don't know any of these people.

I have never been on a farm, but have envisioned a farm with cows, goats, chickens running around, and lots of green, growing things. But there's nothing of the kind here. No animals other than a scrawny old horse grazing in a dry patch of grass and an ugly barking dog we meet down the dusty road. Some scattered clay huts have brown, round, pancake-like things that look like big polka dots plastered all over the outside.

'What are the round things?' I ask Mama, but all she says is, '*Shh*, don't ask so many questions.'

Two women with huge bundles of wood stacked on their heads walk past us, their eyes averted, but the little kids who follow them stare and stare at us, getting close enough to touch Mama's dress. Impatiently Mama shoves them away. Mama's short-sleeved cotton dress reaching just past her knees, with its small flower print, must have looked strange to the local youngsters. All women in Laish wear loose ankle length heavy cotton tunics with long sleeves.

It is hot outside, yet the few men we come across all wear black or other dark-colored heavy jackets, some tied with a rope around their waist, and small hats, something like the deep skullcaps of religious Jews, but colorful. They keep their gaze glued to us as if we were Martians.

Our host or guide—we don't know who the man is—stops before a long, low building the color of dried mud, with three doors. Diagonally to this building is a smaller one with only one door. The buildings form an L with an open dirt area in front of them.

'Here.' The guide points to my family and the old couple. He moves to the next door and points to the other two families. Seeing that the guide is ready to leave, Tata grabs his arm. '*Tovarish* (comrade), are you the leader here?'

'No, I was just told to show you to your house.'

'We want to talk to the head of Laish. We need work, food, and a school for the children,' Tata continues.

'I will tell him,' and off the man goes.

Mama opens the door to our room and stops abruptly. I peek in. The sour-smelling stench is so powerful that it stops my breath. I turn back and run from it without seeing what is in the room. Halina follows me, holding her nose. Mama swings the door open and stands there speechless. I get closer to her and look inside. Huge bugs crawl all over the walls of unpainted clay, cobwebs hang suspended from all corners of the ceiling, the floor is full of scattered straw, animal shit, and lumps of dried mud.

'Srulik,' Mama yells out. 'How can we live in this place?'

The old couple, the Benders, stay behind us, looking to Tata for a solution.

'We have no one to talk to now. Let's see what the chief says when he gets here.'

'The question is when?' Mama sounds tired.

We sit outside on the dusty ground, leaning against the wall of the building for a long time, but no chief shows up.

'No one is coming. For the time being, let's clean up this place the best we can,' Mama says. We all look around for a broom or some tool to clean this dump with, but there's nothing around. I walk down the building and open the third door and peek in, but slam it instantly, screaming, 'Mama, Mama, look what's in that room!'

'What is it?'

'Snakes, all kind of snakes on the floor, and some kind of strange animals on the walls.'

'We have no time for this stuff now, Irka. Just help clean up this mess.'

Tata has found pieces of boards and a few sticks. We each take one of these and get to work. Being the tallest, Tata starts knocking down the cobwebs with a stick. Next he is scraping the walls to remove as many bugs as possible. The black and brown bugs are huge, with a few legs sticking out on each side of their disgusting bodies. I hate touching bugs, and the idea that they might get on me gives me the creeps.

It isn't easy getting all this trash off the floor without a broom. With my feet, I shuffle the straw towards the door. Halina stoops and moves things off the floor with a flat board, while the Benders try to help but aren't able to do much. It's dark when we finish the work and put our bags inside. I notice a water pump next to the other building and point it out to Mama. She walks over there with me. The pump works. 'At least we have water, if nothing else,' Mama says.

As we are getting ready to go to sleep, tired after all the walking and the cleaning, a short stocky man shows up at our door, holding a stack of flatbreads under his arm.

'I am Moiseyev, the chief. Here are *lepioshki* (flatbread) for you.'

'What about work, school?' Tata asks.

'I don't know... No work, school far away...'

'So what are we supposed to do?' Mama asks.

'I don't know.' And off he goes.

'Srulik, what have we gotten ourselves into?' Mama sounds desperate.

'Let's go to sleep, we will come up with something tomorrow.'

Mama is too tired to unpack, and we sleep on the dirty floor, resting our heads on the suitcase and the bags. The Benders do the same.

I wake up off and on during the night and each time hear my parents murmuring to each other.

In the morning, we give half the *lepioshki* to the neighbors in the next room and divide the remainder among the six of us.

'Halina and Irka, stay here. Tata and I will see what is around.'

Our parents are gone for a long time, and I am getting restless. I ask Halina to walk out with me at least for a little bit in the area. She refuses, 'Mama told us to wait.' When I step outside, Halina yells, 'Don't go away! I won't know where to find you.'

'Don't worry. I'll be just outside the door.'

It is hot inside and hot outside. Not much to see. No trees, no shrubs, no greenery of any kind, just the dry dirt turned gray. I am a little scared of this silence outside with no living creature around.

As I turn facing the small building with one door, a man appears looking straight at me. His loose pantaloons are lowered to expose his long erect penis. He doesn't move, just stares at me. I look at him curiously and then run inside. I don't understand what's going on, but sense it is something strange, wrong, and shameful. I tell Halina nothing about it, but after a few minutes step out again to see whether the man is still there. He is, and again is staring at me. I am afraid of him, though I don't know why; he's some distance from me and isn't moving.

My parents return with a few potatoes and two small flatbreads. Their sad faces tell me things aren't good, no matter how they try to cheer us up.

'The Polish representative will come here soon and help us to straighten things out.'

I don't bother to ask what kind of straightening out Mama is talking about. For the next week, we survive on what my parents can find to buy, but it's very little and we're very hungry all the time. When the Polish representative does show up one day, we're all overjoyed to see him. Now our problems will be over.

'I am sorry, but there's nothing I can do for you right now. There is a war, and most of the crops go for the soldiers. You must do the best you can for the time being.'

Every family is on its own for its survival. I am very hungry, my stomach hurts, and all I can think of is bread. Mama goes out in the morning with a little bag to scout the area. She comes home with a pile of green leaves. She boils these in a pot of water and tastes it with a spoon.

'Can I taste it, Mama?'

'Not now, Irka. Later,' she tells me in a soft voice. I wonder why she is refusing me and feel angry at her. An hour later we all get a bowl of this green water with some leaves in it. Mama even gives a bowl of it to the old couple. For the next two weeks we live primarily on green soup. When the leaves are of a different kind, Mama eats them first and gives none to us until about an hour later. Why she does this remains a mystery to me until one night I hear Tata asking her, 'How do you know, Bella that these things are safe to eat?'

'I don't give them to the children until I have first eaten them myself.'

Green leaves and grass are like the mushrooms in Siberia, I figure. You can get sick or die eating the wrong kind. Mama doesn't want us to die, but I don't want Mama to die either.

Every morning Tata pulls out his hammer and goes out looking for work, but he returns empty handed, tired and sad. This happens for many days in a row until one evening he calls Halina and me to follow him. He takes us into the snake room and closes the door. I look around, the snakes are in all four corners of the room, big snakes, small snakes, gray ones, yellow ones, they are sitting there as if in their own kingdom. The walls are spotted with creatures. Our young Polish neighbor told us that they are scorpions with poison in their tails.

'Watch out when they give out a hissing sound,' the neighbor warned me. I don't move from the door.

'Don't be afraid. I'll watch that no snake or scorpion gets to you,' Tata tells us. Out of his pocket he pulls out two hard-boiled eggs and gives them to Halina and me.

'Eat them here. We don't have enough to share with the others.'

'Where did you get these, Tata?'

'I worked for a man fixing his tables, and he gave me the eggs.'

'Do you have one for Mama?'

'Not today. Maybe tomorrow.'

I hadn't eaten an egg for so long I almost forgot what one tastes like. At times, when I feel extremely hungry and my stomach hurts, I try to remember tastes and smells of food I ate before the war.

'Halina, what does a Kaiser roll with butter, or with strawberry jam, taste like?' I occasionally ask.

Her snappy answer usually is, 'I don't know how to describe a taste,' or 'Don't ask silly questions!'

There are no children to play with. I used to walk into our neighbors' room to entertain their three-year-old boy, Moshe. I would tell him stories I made up and liked to see him giggle and look at me as if I were a magician. Lately, poor little Moshe is so listless that it isn't fun being with him. Seeing him makes me sad and uncomfortable. I wish I had an egg to give him.

Mama finds out that in the next village they have onions for sale. She leaves us in the morning with a pillowcase filled with some of her clothing in hand. She is gone most of the day, and Halina and I are worried. We've gotten used to Tata taking off in the morning with his hammer, but now they're both gone. Late in the afternoon Mama returns carrying a pillowcase of onions.

'We were worried, Mama. Why were you gone so long?'

'The village was far from here, and I had to find my way by asking people along the road.'

Tata makes a fire in the evening, and we bake some of the onions. They are small, but tasty when baked.

The next morning Mama hands Tata whatever money we have left and instructs him how to go to the onion place and buy some more onions while they still have them. Baked onions are our main food for the following two or three weeks. Tata brings home a few *lepioshki* and a piece of *brinza*, his payment for a full day's work at the house of one of the farmers.

Our parents are tense all the time and talk little to us, other than to convey the specifics of daily activities: sweep up the floor, don't stay out in the sun all day long, I'm going out for a while, don't know when I will be back, and so on. I talk to Halina about my concerns and worries. Will Tata find work, will we ever go to school, and do people know when they are dying of hunger?

It is past wheat harvest time, and Mama tells Halina and me that we will go looking for fields to glean whatever was left after the harvest.

'Will the farmers let us?' Halina wants to know.

'They're finished with the harvest and aren't there anymore. All that is left are small bits of wheat they don't need,' Mama assures us. But I'm a little afraid, thinking of the man in the house next to us, whom I have seen now a few more times exposing himself. Is he a farmer? I wonder.

I tie my mushroom bag around my waist—it would be so nice to be in Siberia now to pick mushrooms and berries.

'Come on, Irka. What are you dreaming about?' Halina chides me.

Walking to find the wheat fields, I learn about the big brown pancakes on the houses. We come across local women, with buckets in hand, scooping up horse and donkey dung.

'What do you do with it?' I ask an Uzbek woman.

The woman points to her house with the brown circles on it. They mix the dung with a little straw and slap it on like pancakes. When these dry, the circles fall off the walls, and the women use them for fuel.

'God, it must stink,' I say in Polish.

We continue walking for a while until we find a harvested field.

'Girls, look for the wheat heads.'

Here and there is a full head, but most are just small pieces I toss in my bag. Remembering that Mama told us that, if we have enough kernels to take to the mill, we will have dumplings, or maybe bake flatbread as the Laish women do, I rush to find as much as I can.

I am startled out of my concentration by loud screaming in the Uzbek language I don't understand. Turning around, I see a man running towards us with a long rifle in his hand.

'Grab your stuff and run,' Mama calls out. All three of us run as fast as we can, not turning to check whether the man is still chasing us. After a while, Mama stops, breathing heavily.

'He's gone. We can slow down.'

Was the man going to kill us, I wonder, but say nothing to Mama. All Uzbek men look scary to me.

At home, we empty our bags into one little pile. Not enough to take to the mill, but we will husk the wheat and cook it, Mama decides. We rub the pieces in our palms until the kernels fall out. My hands get scratched, but we can't eat the wheat otherwise. The wheat cooks for a long time and it still is hard when we eat it, but it is our first meal in a very long time, other than onions or boiled grass and leaves.

The leader of the village, whatever his title, shows up one morning with good news. 'I have work for all of you, good work with money.'

'When can we start?' Tata asks.

'Come now, all of you.'

'She is just a little girl,' Mama points to me.

'Good work for little girl,' the man assures us.

'I can do it. I want to come, Mama.'

We don't know what kind of work it is, but we will get money to buy food. After a long walk, we end up in a cotton field. The foreman, an Uzbek who speaks very little Russian, gives each of us a sack and points to the group of working women, their backs bent, ignoring us.

'Like this, like this,' he pulls Tata by his hand, pointing to the woman with a bagful of cotton. We watch the silent woman pulling the white fluffy stuff out of what looks to me like a brown wooden flower; its petals open to allow the white puff to pop out, like a chick from its shell. The woman's bag is tied around her waist, and both her hands are rhythmically moving pulling the white cotton, as if she were milking a cow. Watching the woman, I move my hands the way she does, but when I try to actually pull out the cotton, I can't—I need both hands for each stalk.

Being small is an advantage—I don't need to bend down as my Tata does—but my hands quickly get scratched and sore. The hard open cones are rough and prickly, and no matter how careful I am not to touch them, my hands cannot avoid them, particularly when I try to work fast. Oh! I just cut my hand, and it's bleeding, staining the cotton. I'm afraid the foreman will send me away. We will be paid by the bagful and I want to earn money.

'Mama, do you have something to wrap around my finger?'

Mama has nothing to use as a bandage, but she scoops out a wad of cotton and presses it against the bleeding spot.

'That is enough work for you, Irka, your hands are all scratched and bleeding,' Mama tells me when she sees my hands. I sit down on the ground, holding the cotton in place. My hands feel hot and throbbing. Mama straightens up and rubs her lower back. After a while Tata does the same. Once my hand has stopped bleeding, I'm back to my job. Mama is too busy filling her bag to notice I'm working again. My hands, though, are burning terribly, and I keep myself from crying. A few times I stop briefly to blow on my hands to cool the burning. I ignore the blood and let it drip on the cotton, wherever it falls.

It's a hot day. We each get a cup of water from a standing bucket, but I'm still thirsty. Mama is firm—no more cotton picking for me today. I'm glad to obey and lie down at the edge of the field. Mama moves me into a shady area under an old barren olive tree. At the end of the working day, Tata carries me home on his back. I'm so tired, I don't even feel hungry. My hands are red and swollen, the skin feels tight—I have difficulty making a fist.

There is work for one more day, but Mama is determined that Halina and I stay home. Halina's hands are also scratched all over, though not as badly as mine; it hurts if I touch anything. Mama makes me wash my hands with a burning soap and instructs me not to touch anything today. Halina will help me if I need something.

For the next two weeks we eat much better. We have flour for making *lepioshki*, potatoes, and *brinza*. Mama gives some of the flatbread and a small piece of the salty cheese to the Benders who spend most of their time lying on cots.

We got very little for the cotton picking—our money runs out and we are hungry again. Tata again goes out daily to search for work.

This morning Halina cannot get out of bed. It's hot in the room, but she shivers and cries that she is cold. Mama covers her with all the blankets we have, but Halina keeps shivering and grinding her teeth. It is scary to see her shake so violently. Her face feels burning to my touch and she seems confused, asking for lemonade—I don't remember us ever having lemonade. Mama sits on the floor next to her all day long, gives her sips of water, and wipes her brow. We all sleep on the floor, on top of a blanket.

I am scared and worried that Halina might die. I keep re-arranging her blankets.

'Leave her alone,' Mama tells me, 'Halina is sick.' As if I didn't know.

Tata goes to the chief demanding he find a doctor.

'I'm not leaving until you bring me a doctor, my daughter is very sick.' After about an hour, a skinny man in a caftan shows up, asking Tata about the symptoms.

'Is she cold and shaking all the time? She can't stand up? Her teeth are chattering, yes?' the man asks.

'Yes.'

'Malaria.'

'How do you know it's malaria without seeing my child?'

'I know, I know. Give her lots of water and this medicine, as soon as you get home,' he says, handing Tata quinine.

Since moving to Asia, I have heard about malaria and about people dying from it. Seeing my sister shake violently and then lying exhausted scares me—she will die, she will die, I fear. I feel bad for all the times I was nasty to Halina. I don't know anything about a God, but I pray for my sister to live, and promise myself that I will always be nice to her. After many days of shaking and burning with fever, Halina recovers.

Soon after, though, I get malaria. I feel so sick and shaking that I can't move or lift an arm to chase away a mosquito on my face.

'Mama, my bones are breaking,' I keep repeating, hardly able to speak, my teeth chattering uncontrollably. It feels like the violent shaking is determined to crush and smash all the hard parts in my body, leaving me mushy like a pudding. I don't know how long I am shaking, or how long I'm in bed. At some point I lose the concept of time and maybe lose consciousness. When I open my eyes, I see Halina next to me, vigorously brushing the bugs off my blanket. The ceiling is full of crawling and wiggling things, but I can't see clearly what they are. I see movement, but not shape. I close my eyes, scared that malaria has blinded me.

'Halina, how long have I been sick?'

'For a long time.'

'Did I talk silly stuff like you did?'

'A little bit, but you are better now.'

My legs feel like mush. I don't have the strength to lift them.

'Rest, rest, you are not ready to get up yet.' Halina tries to restrain me.

'I have to see if I can walk, help me get up.'

Hesitatingly, Halina pulls off my blanket and supports me so I won't collapse on the dusty floor.

'Halina, am I as green as you were after your malaria?'

'Just a little, but it'll go away.'

'I wish I had a mirror to see what I look like.'

'You look like before, only a little thinner.'

'I don't know how I looked before. Do you know what you look like?'

Halina pauses. 'It's a long time since I saw myself in a mirror.'

'When?'

'In Kirpichny Zavod. An older girl, Rachel, had a little mirror and let me look into it.'

'You look the same as you did then, Halina. Your eyes are blue like before,' I assure her.

'Silly. The color of a person's eyes doesn't change.'

'What color are my eyes?'

Halina sticks her face so close to mine that her nose almost pokes me. 'Now they are kind of greenish, but sometimes they look brown.'

'Ha, so my eyes do change color! Are they strange?'

'No, they're just regular eyes. Now, just sit and rest. Don't talk. Would you like some water?' Halina asks me.

'Yeah, I'm very thirsty.'

Halina brings the water in a cup and sits with me until Mama returns.

Mama lays her hand on my forehead. 'Are you feeling a little better, Irka?'

'Yeah, I'm fine.'

Mama walks away and returns carrying a bowl of soup with vegetables and browned flour.

Seeing me peek into the bowl with disbelief, Halina tells me that Tata has been working for a few days. Though the soup looks good, I'm not hungry and too tired to eat. 'Later, Mama, not now.'

I strain to see our room; it looks smaller and darker than what I remember. Even the Benders seem to have shrunk. Maybe malaria blinded me and I can't see well, I fear.

'Halina, did I sleep for a long time?'

'Yes, you did. Mama was very worried about you, and I was afraid you might die.'

'See, I'm fine,' I assure Halina, but her blue eyes still look worried.

Tata is making furniture for a rich farmer, or a big shot in the Party. He gets paid little, but he is glad to find any kind of work—cleaning a barn, scrubbing down walls after the dung cakes dry—and he accepts whatever the people are willing to give him in return. Sometimes it is two eggs, a piece of cheese, or even just a few *lepioshki*. This man gives Tata some money and also a bag of flour.

A week after I get out of bed, Mama is going to look for an Uzbek woman who will show her how to make *lepioshki*.

'I want to come with you, Mama. I want to see how they make it.'

'You're too weak. Stay here with Halina.'

'Please, Mama, I can walk.'

'I'll help her walk, or carry her,' Halina offers.

'Yes, yes,' I agree eagerly.

All three of us go. We approach the first house we come to, the dung cakes stuck on its walls. A woman in a gray-striped, long, loose-fitting dress, her head wrapped in a colorful kerchief, is sweeping the dusty porch, sprinkling it with water. We try talking to her, but she speaks hardly any Russian, and we don't know Uzbek. When Mama shows the woman the flour, Halina and I close our palms in the motion of flattening dough, but the woman stands perplexed. I run up to the wall of the woman's house and point to one of the dung circles, repeating the word *lepioshki*.

The woman starts laughing, and we know she understood us. We follow her to the back of her house. She shows Mama how much water to pour into the flour, and with hand motions she directs Mama to mix it. At that point the woman takes over. She forms small balls of dough, flattens them in her palms, and with her bare hands slaps them onto the inside walls of the outdoor clay oven, still hot from her morning baking. The oven looks like a huge container open on top. To my horror the woman tosses into the oven two of the dung cakes. At first, I avert my eyes, but curiosity wins out and I peer in. The cakes are aglow in no time. Surprisingly, they don't smell. When our *lepioshki* start separating from the wall of the oven, the woman pulls on a heavy mitt and removes them one by one. As payment for her labor and the use of her oven, Mama offers the woman a few *lepioshki*, but the woman shakes her head. Mama has nothing to give her. All we can do is thank her with gestures.

We've never had as many *lepioshki* as we have now in our bag, and I can't imagine ever being hungry again. The Benders enjoy the flatbread, though it appears an effort for them to sit up and eat. They're so thin I'm afraid they'll soon die. It's scary.

With two *lepioshki* in hand, I run next door to bring them to little Moshe.

'Where are you going?' Halina asks.

'To see Moshe,' and before she can stop me I'm out the door.

'Moshe!' I shout, eager to see his face as I give him food.

Moshe's parents sit silently on the floor, and I know at once that something happened to the little boy. I don't ask, or say anything to the parents, but run back into our room.

'Halina, what happened to Moshe, where is he?'

'He died. I don't know whether of malaria or something else.'

I don't feel like eating or talking to anyone. Moshe was such a sweet little boy, and he is gone. Neither Mama nor Halina said anything to me about it. Puff, he just vanished.

Two days later I ask Halina, 'Why didn't you tell me that Moshe died? Why did you say nothing to me about it?'

'What for? You were very sick yourself.'

'You should have told me. You just can't bury someone and forget about him.'

'You saw people killed during the war.'

'But this is different. He was a little boy, our neighbor, and it is not a war.'

Halina and I never again talk about Moshe, but I think about him for a long time.

The last day of Tata's job, I have a great surprise: 'The man says I can bring my youngest child with me,' Tata announces.

'How about Halina?' I ask.

'Sorry, only the youngest.'

'Halina, I will bring you something.' I try to comfort my sister, without a notion of what that something might be.

It's winter and cold outside. I borrow Halina's coat, as mine reaches only slightly below my hips, and the sleeves are a few inches too short.

Tata leads me past some areas I've never seen before, though we have been in Laish for nine months. The houses are much bigger than those around where we live, and some are even painted white or a pinkish color.

'This is where the man lives,' Tata informs me. I know which man he is talking about. Tata always refers to his employer as 'the man'—no name.

Our host is wearing black pantaloons, bunched-up fabric hanging in the crotch. A loosely fitting vest embroidered in bright colors over a Russian peasant-style white shirt, and a colorful scullcap sitting on the center of his head complete his wardrobe. He takes us into a room where all the walls are covered with colorful rugs. I've never seen so many rugs. From one of the walls protrudes a platform of cement with a variety of bright pillows on it. The only furniture is a tiny square table in the center of the room, very low, almost resting on the floor. It is covered by a colorful striped cloth. Fascinated, I gaze around as though someone has placed me inside a fairy tale. The host motions me to sit down. Seeing me confused, Tata drops onto his knees next to the table. I try to do the same, but our host tugs at my legs and stretches them out under the tablecloth. Oh! I almost burn my foot, and I bend down to peek under the table. Hot coals or some other burning material are in a pit under the table, giving off heat. I rest my bare feet on the bars of the table and now the heat feels good. I have worn shoes with no socks because the only pair I have left is wet. I feel like a queen with some mysterious little people warming my bare feet. My fantasy grows when our host brings in a plate of fruit and some sticky cakes, grapes, dried figs, dates, and another kind of fruit I can't identify.

In a quiet, yet powerful voice, the man encourages us, 'Kushai' (eat). I don't need much encouragement and reach out for some grapes. I can't remember when I last ate grapes—some time before the war. I am too embarrassed to take too much, but feel as though I could eat everything on the plate. Both Tata and I take some of the sticky cakes; I can taste the honey. After a while the man carries in a tray with tiny cups of strong-smelling coffee and sits down to join us. Tata and the man sip the coffee, but I find it extremely bitter.

'Tata, I would like to bring the rest of the fruit and cake home to Mama and Halina,' I tell him in Polish.

'We'll see.'

Before we're ready to leave, I ask the man in Russian if I could have a piece of cake for my sister. The man walks out and returns with a ripped-out sheet of a Russian newspaper onto which he empties the plate.

On the way back home, I ask Tata if the man lives all by himself in that house.

'He has a wife and two daughters.'

'So why didn't we see them?'

'The family is Muslim, and their women are not allowed to look at strange men,' Tata informs me.

This sounds to me very peculiar, but since the man was so nice to us, I don't question the customs of Muslims.

I hop all the way home, unable to stop talking. I feel extremely grown up and important when I ask Mama and Halina to walk with me into the scorpion room. They follow me, wondering what I want to show them. They are very surprised when I pull the crumpled paper from my coat pocket and show them what's in it.

'It's for you both. Tata and I had some at the man's house.'

'He gave it to you for us?' Halina asks.

'I told you I'd bring you something!'

For days I can't stop talking about my adventure at the man's house.

Without a day's break, Tata goes hunting for other jobs, but can find nothing. The flour is all gone. In winter there's no grass or leaves for making green soup. Mama pulls out a silk scarf that Ciocia Fella gave her and takes off with it in the morning. A few hours later she returns with a few *lepioshki* and a piece of *brinza*. A few days later Mama takes her small handbag and goes to see what she can trade for it.

Unexpectedly, two unknown men show up looking for Polish Jews. It turns out they are from some Jewish organization. They spend a long time talking with my parents. I want to hear what they are talking about, but Mama sends me away to play. I have no one and nothing to play with, but I know already that it means, 'Go away, this is not for you.' Mama makes evasive comments when Halina and I ask what the men came for. Again, my parents are whispering a lot, but they can't turn to Yiddish, as Halina and I understand too much now. I hate it when my parents keep secrets from us, particularly when two Jews come to Laish.

One of the men shows up a few days later to speak with our parents again. That afternoon, Tata and Mama, serious faced, sit down on the floor to talk to Halina and me.

'There are some wonderful things happening. Jewish organizations are setting up schools for children.' Before I have time to get excited, Mama tells us that my sister and I will need to move to another place, a little bit away from Laish.

'Are you and Tata coming with us to live there?'

'No, it's just for children. You'll have food there, children to play with, and, of course, a school,' Mama tells us.

'We'll come often to visit you,' Tata adds.

'Do we have to go, Mama?' Halina questions.

'Yes, it's for your own good, and you'll be happy there.'

Knowing that Mama and Tata will be visiting often and that Halina will be with me makes it easier to accept our parents' decision. I even look forward to all the good things that will happen to us in this new place."

10

My Years in Orphanages

"Mom, since I am on spring break and have no classes this week, can we also talk during the week? I am so eager to hear it all."

These Sunday sessions of going back to my childhood have been painful and stressful for me. My memories and reflections of the Holocaust years kept popping up during the week. I suddenly felt very lonely. The reality that all my extended family had been killed, not a single one left alive, hit me with a new sadness. I wanted to put this chapter of my life back into the bottom drawer where it had been for most of my adult life.

"Naomi, stay with me tonight. I won't go to work tomorrow, and we'll have the whole day to ourselves and talk as much as we want to."

"Oh, that's great, Mom!"

"I will call my secretary to give her some instructions, and then let's go out for Chinese."

"Halina and I arrive in Chelek in a two-wheeled buggy driven by one of the Jews who visited us in Laish. His wool hat pulled over his ears, a brown jacket wrapping his skinny body, the man isn't much taller than Halina. He seems a bit confused about which way to go, but the horse knows the road better than the driver. It takes us about seven hours on the bumpy road, passing one village after another, all looking alike: clay houses, scrawny cows, here and there a horse looking ready to conk out. Chelek, however, is a much bigger village than Laish.

'The children's home is in this village,' the man tells us. I'm eager to see the place, yet feel a lump in my throat that I fear may turn into tears. Laish was my home. Mama and Tata are there. Where is my home now? What is a children's home?

'It would take much less time to get from Laish to Chelek if there were a bridge over the river,' the man comments after many hours of silence. He is not very talkative, but I don't feel like talking either. Maybe he is sad and cold like Halina and me.

Mama let out whatever hem there was in my navy coat, yet my bare knees are still sticking out. Tugging at the coat doesn't help, the sleeves are reaching just a little below my elbows. My big toes have worked themselves through my shoes, so the shoes don't pinch any more. Looking at me in the coat, as we took off for Laish, a neighbor commented, 'She will grow up to be a tall lady.'

Before we leave, Mama reminds Halina that she is the older sister and should watch over me. By now Halina doesn't have to be reminded—at times she is excessively protective of me, and I don't like it. She worries that I won't find my way back whenever I'm gone for a while, that someone will hurt me. Who knows what else she worries about?

'I'll be okay, Mama. I'm not a little kid.'

'Yes, yes, I know,' she says, kissing my cheek, then Halina's.

It is late afternoon by the time we reach the children's home. The low, long building looks like a big block of clay with no life in it. There are no windows we can see, no sounds coming from it, no children outside. Is this where Halina and I will live? The man must've made a mistake. Where are all the children? As though reading my thoughts, the man observes, 'It's cold. They must all be inside.' He knocks on a door. We wait a long time, but no one answers. We move to the next door at the other end of the building where, after a few knocks, a man comes out. Strange, coming from indoors, he is wearing a wool hat pulled over his ears, and a heavy brown sweater.

'You have new children for us?' Pan Fogel asks, smiling at Halina and me.

'These are the Miller girls, Halina and her sister Irena.'

'People call me Irka not Irena,' I correct the man.

'Very well, we'll call you Irka,' Pan Fogel agrees.

'I will say good-bye to you girls,' the little Jew says, turning to Halina and me, looking eager to move on.

Pan Fogel leads us into a big room. Against both long walls, on wooden platforms, wrapped in army blankets, are tightly packed children of various ages. Some of them are lying down, but most sit talking with their neighbors on the platform. The room is very noisy.

'No girls, all boys,' I whisper to Halina. She doesn't answer.

'Children, this is Halina and her sister Irka, your new friends,' Pan Fogel introduces us. Conversations stop and all heads turn to us.

I stand quietly for a moment looking at the kids. Their heads are shaved, and they all wear the same dark flannel shirts. One child smiles at me, and suddenly I realize that on the platform to my right are all the girls. They look so strange with their bald heads, almost scary. I touch my braids and want to hide them, protect them. I don't want to be bald-headed and look like a boy.

A group of older boys sit on the floor playing some board game.

Pan Fogel removes two khaki-colored blankets from a wooden shelf and hands them to Halina and me.

'Halina, we will find a spot for you at the end with the older girls; and you, Irka, put your blanket right here, next to the Carter girls,' he tells me, motioning the girls to scoot over a little to make room for me on the platform.

'Put your bag under the platform,' Ruth Carter tells me. Her hands folded over her chest, her head small and shiny, she looks like a little girl. Placing my belongings on the dirt under the platform, I wonder why the floor is wooden, but there's dirt under the sleeping area. The dirt floor, with stacks of bricks supporting the platform, is dark and dreary. Bags, some old shoes, and a sleeping cat are all I can see.

Seeing me wiping my dirty hands, Ruth Carter explains that the platforms were made by ripping out the boards from the floor and raising them up on bricks.

'Come on up,' Ruth invites me, sliding over to make room. But I don't want to lie or to sit after so many hours in the two-wheeled buggy, I want to move around.

'Thank you, I don't feel like sitting, I sat for many hours and can't sit any more. I'm going outside.' Ruth looks offended.

'It's cold outside,' she warns me, but I just shrug and say nothing. If you aren't under a blanket, it is just as cold in this room as it is outside. There are no heaters, no fireplace, but I don't feel like explaining it, I just head for the door.

'Where are you going? Anything wrong?' Pan Fogel asks.

'Nothing's wrong. I just want to walk outside.'

'Outside, what's outside?'

'I don't know. I'll find out.'

Pan Fogel asks one of the older boys to go with me outdoors. With his broad shoulders, more than a head taller than

I, the boy looks like a man to me, not a kid. But if he is in the children's home, he must be a kid.

'What's your name?' I ask.

'Moniek.'

Moniek doesn't look very eager to be with me. Standing with his hands in the pocket of his coat, which probably fitted him well a few years ago, but is now too short and too tight, he just stares.

'Which way do you want to walk?' Moniek asks me in a terse voice.

'I'll walk myself, if you don't feel like going.'

'It's okay. I'll take you.'

'Are there any people here — farms, or anything else going on?'

'Not much happening here, and the center of the village is too far away to walk, but I will show you an area that has some trees and is prettier than here.'

Polski Dom Dziecka 23, The Polish Children's Home number 23 referred to by most as *sierociniec*, the orphanage, stands in a desolate area. Dirt and rocks covered with snow, a small hut with a nearby skinny mongrel dog too tired to move or bark. On a clothesline is a woman's black dress, nothing more.

We walk for half an hour, and the landscape indeed turns more welcoming than the area around the orphanage. As I step on a rock, my right shoe rips on the outside, flapping as I try to walk.

'Do you have a handkerchief so we can tie your shoe?' Moniek asks.

'No, I don't.'

Strange to ask me whether I have a handkerchief, I have forgotten even what handkerchiefs look like. Moniek breaks a thin twig off a mulberry tree and wraps it around my shoe.

'Thanks, Moniek.' I look at his now friendlier face.

'It's okay.'

'How long have you been in the orphanage?'

'Three months.'

'You look so tall and strong, I thought you were a man, not a boy.'

Moniek proudly pulls back his shoulders, 'I'm sixteen.'

I return to the orphanage, dragging my foot. Halina has been getting anxious since she discovered I was gone.

'Look, Halina, what happened to my shoe.'

'The other is tearing too, but there's nothing we can do. Maybe they'll give us shoes in the future,' says my sister, trying to comfort me. I shuffle, rather than walk, afraid to lift my feet for fear the shoe may fall off altogether, or the other may also tear.

Before the supper of potato soup and a piece of bread, I learn that I am not the only child who soon will be shoeless. Children who have no shoes line up in the center of the long room, and the older boys, including Moniek, carry them to the small dining hut adjacent to the building, a child under each arm and one clinging to the boy's back. Four boys are the carriers, all of whom have shoes laced high and in good condition—no tears, no toes protruding. We all sit on wooden benches like those we had in the Siberian school. It is easier to talk to kids when they're sitting at the table than when they're all bunched up on the sleeping platforms. I learn the names of a few girls and how old they are; I am nine and a half years old and among the younger children in the home, but it doesn't trouble me—I prefer to be with older kids. Many of the children speak Yiddish among themselves. I understand a lot of Yiddish, yet speak very little, but even the Yiddish-speaking kids know some Polish.

'You don't speak Yiddish because you're from Warsaw. The Warsaw Jews are half goyim,' a boy declares.

'You're talking nonsense. I'm a Jew as you are, my parents speak a better Yiddish than you do.'

'So how come you and your sister don't know it?'

'We had no need for Yiddish, but I can learn it fast if I want to.'

Most other Yiddish-speaking children, however, not only don't criticize me and Halina for not speaking the language, but consider us an elite of sorts for speaking a good Polish and being from Warsaw, as opposed to the children raised in small villages. The Carter sisters also speak fluent Polish and are considered to be elite. Their father is in America and when the war ends, they will go there. I try to imagine America, but all I know is the name 'New York,' a city with very tall build-ings. I wonder what happened to the old York.

'Why is your father in America?' I ask Ruth.

'He went to the World's Fair and could not return because of the war.'

'Do you have any pictures of America?'

'No, but I know it is a beautiful country, very big, and everyone is rich. No poor people in America.'

I am not poor, just often hungry, but I feel a pang of envy that Ruth, who is only a year older than I, will travel to Amer-ica. I'd like to see all the beautiful places. I cannot visualize this big America, much bigger than Warsaw—I don't even know how big Warsaw is.

'Maybe someday I will visit you in America, Ruth,' I say, though I don't believe it's possible. My father is in Laish, not in faraway New York. We talk a lot about America and try to imagine what it looks like.

A few days later, my other shoe falls apart, and I have to be carried back and forth to the dining room under the arm of one of the boys. It's kind of fun when I can get on the back of the boy rather than under his arm like a bag of flour. The boys carry us once a day for the cooked meal. In the morning when we get a piece of bread, they bring it to us in the sleeping room.

Having no shoes while I am indoors is not a problem— I was given socks made out of a blanket and they keep me warm—but going to the outhouse is very painful. The ground is covered with snow, or with cold, wet mud. The first time I went out in my socks, I had to wash them afterwards and wait a few days until they dried. My feet were freezing all the time. Now I take my socks off and go barefoot to the outhouse. I try delaying going out for as long as I can. Oh, it hurts so badly placing my feet on the snow. It burns, it burns. Running back into the house, I cry, 'Halina, Halina!' My sister dries my feet with a corner of my blanket.

'Careful, Halina, they hurt badly.'

'Don't cry. They'll warm up fast,' she encourages me, and continues vigorously rubbing my feet with both hands. My sister too will soon be shoeless; hers are barely holding together. The strap over her instep is intact, but the sides are flapping when she walks.

A few days ago I met our director, Pan Blum, and Masha, a nurse. Blum is a handsome man about forty years old and Masha, thirty-two, is a pretty woman with a sweet smile. Her blonde hair is pulled back with a big pin. All Blum said to me was, 'Hi, you are our new girl, what is your name?' Some kids, however, have a tough time with him, particularly my new friend Chune. Pan Blum is constantly after Chune, he makes him feel ignorant: 'Speak Polish, no Yiddish, hear me? Yiddish will get you nowhere. You want to be a civilized man? Learn good Polish.' Chune speaks Polish poorly, and with a distinct Yiddish accent, but Chune is not stupid, he just doesn't know much Polish because in his home, they spoke only Yiddish. Chune, five years my senior, not much taller than I am, is a shy boy. His shyness doesn't prevent him from finding out about the lives of all adults in the orphanage—where they are from, what they did before the war. You want to hear any gossip, go to Chune. I have no idea where he gets his information, but he has stories about everyone.

'Blum has a wife and children in Poland and lives here with Masha and her five-year-old son. She knows that if his wife survives the war, he will return to her,' Chune tells me.

'Are you sure?'

'Of course I am sure, just ask anyone.'

I find the set-up a little puzzling, though I had met a number of families who were separated by the war.

Adults are expressing their opinions:

'He's a young man, and who knows how long the war will last.'

'He harms no one.'

'An understanding wife will forgive.'

'Who knows why she didn't come with him.'

'It is lonely for a woman in these tough times.'

'Not easy to raise a child alone.'

'Rules change during a war; the world turns upside down.'

Such comments from adults help me to accept the situation without criticism. Never having seen Mrs. Blum, I feel sorry for Masha, and I almost wish Mrs. Blum won't survive the war. Masha is a gentle woman who listens to us patiently, and Oleg, her little boy, is a smart, sweet kid.

The only one loudly critical of Blum and Masha is Pani Rubinsteinowa, a woman complaining about everything, particularly about her missing husband, who is somewhere in the Soviet Union but not looking for her. The older kids are making fun of her. 'Who would want to look for her? The husband is probably glad to get rid of her,' Moshe comments.

We all dislike Pani Rubinsteinowa. She is supposed to be our caregiver, but she is a mean and bitter woman

If one of us girls gets hurt and cries, Pani Rubinsteinowa always makes the same comment, 'You think this hurts, wait until you are in childbirth. This is nothing compared, just wait and see.'

I don't know where our director has gone, but after a few days' absence, he returns with notebooks and pencils. We will have classes, and I'm excited. The dining room is our classroom, and Pan Fogel is the teacher. We have no books, no blackboard, just notebooks and pencils. Kids ages nine to seventeen are all in the same class, listening to Polish history and trying to solve the math problems Fogel dictates to us.

The older boys get bored and restless in no time; they leave with excuses of errands they have to run for the orphanage. Indeed, they do all the physical work—any hauling, digging, and whatever else needs to be done. Some display great skills in persuading a communal farm to contribute a bag of wheat or a bushel of pumpkins to the orphanage. No wonder the older boys have been outfitted with shoes; they are the workers and enjoy a privileged status that brings an extra piece of bread, a second bowl of soup, and whatever else they can scrounge for themselves in the village.

Sitting on the sleeping platform and chatting with girls, or playing some word games becomes fun. I like the game where I have to find out what person or object the other girl has selected. I'm good at this game, no matter how difficult the names or objects. I begin: 'Is it a human? Is the person alive? Was he a scientist? Did he live in the time of our parents? Was he Polish?' And so on. To all these questions I get only a 'Yes' or 'No.'

By now I know about every girl, where she is from, how old she is. What our parents did for a living before the war is unimportant, but we do talk about where they are, their ages, or when they died. Most of the children are orphans, but some, like Halina and me, have one or both parents. I wonder whether the orphans are sad; they speak about the death of their parents as though they're simply acknowledging a fact.

We have been making fun of Sonia. She is eleven and her sister Lucia is thirteen.

'How old are your parents?' I ask Sonia.

'Mama is thirty-eight and Tata thirty-four, but Tata will soon catch up with Mama, only now he is younger.'

From then on, we periodically ask Sonia whether Tata has already caught up with her Mama.

'I don't know, I haven't seen them for a long time,' is Sonia's answer. The poor girl becomes the butt of our jokes. We no longer refer to her as Sonia, but as the 'Tata will catch up with Mama' girl.

The weather is getting warmer. We spend more time outdoors. Everything is better in the warm weather: we don't have to sit on the platforms and can be outside, and my feet aren't freezing any more. Even the soup—pieces of potatoes floating in a bowl of water—seems more filling.

Now the great irritants are mosquitoes and lice; I itch all over. All the kids have lice and compare methods of finding and getting rid of them. The lice get not only into my very short hair but make their home in the seams of my clothing. 'Take a sharp stick and scrape your seams. That's where they deposit their eggs,' some kids advise. Halina is good at finding lice in my hair; she sounds like a hunter getting excited over her prey. We have no place to shower or wash our clothing other than the river quite a distance from the house. In the winter, it's too cold to bathe in the river. Having lice becomes a normal part of life.

All the chores in the children's home are done by the children. Some help in the kitchen, some clean the house; the older boys do the physically heavy work, while others have special outside jobs. For a period of time, the younger girls are assigned to work in a silkworm farm. The silk-producing larvae are really caterpillars, but we call them worms, and they're just as slimy, wiggly, and disgusting. I hate to touch them, but this is my job for a while; the orphanage will get money or food for our labor.

We work in a long, low-ceilinged hut with racks and racks of mulberry leaves and twigs. It's terribly hot, stuffy, and smelly in the hut. Sometimes I pretend to be going to the outhouse just to get away from the stink for a few minutes. Our first task is to place the newly hatched larvae on mulberry leaves. The farmer told us that adult females deposit about 300 to 400 eggs at a time, but not all hatch. Strangely, the female dies soon after depositing the eggs. I am almost eleven and know very little about childbirth—I heard that some women die giving birth, but I didn't think that dropping eggs was such a dangerous job. I want to know more why the larvae die, but the man we work for does not seem very patient or willing to answer questions. Often when I am eager to know something that no other child seems to care about, I remember my mother commenting to friends about me in Yiddish, '*Zee mist shtending visn ve dee fees vaksen.*' By now I know what it means, 'She always has to know everything.' It sounded like my mother was complaining, but I continued asking.

After working a few days and full of questions no one wanted to listen to, I start bugging Pan Fogel, a nice, patient man.

'Pan Fogel, why do they die, why do they eat so much, where do they get the material for thread making?'

'I don't know much about silk worms, but I will try to find out and we both can learn.'

To my excitement, Pan Fogel got a book on silkworms from the Russian school.

Now I can better understand what I see.

Once the larvae are placed on the mulberry leaves, they start eating like crazy. You can almost watch them getting fatter and bigger by the minute—they're ferocious eaters. The loud chomping and chewing of the leaves sound like a choir. When the larvae get very fat—having eaten about fifty thousand times their original weight—they stop eating and begin making silk threads. The salivary glands produce a clear fluid that comes out through two openings in the mouth of the larva. I can see the fluid oozing out and hardening as it comes in contact with air, spinning a silk thread that doesn't seem to end. Over and over, about three hundred times, the worm moves in a figure eight, forming a cocoon in the shape of a peanut. The creature is propelled into a furious dance it can't stop until the work is done. The worm encases itself into a cocoon, unaware that this will become its tomb. If it weren't for the terrible heat, it would be fun watching the worms labor according to a strange plan. I find it fascinating.

'Why are you staring at them?' Dorka asks, 'they are just dirty worms.'

'Look how fast they are moving, they are dancing.'

'You are silly.' I ignore Dorka's comment.

We spread the cocoons on sheets in the scorching sun. The poor things are boiled to death in the heat. 'The worms are asleep,' the farmer tells us, but I know what kind of sleep he's talking about, the kind of sleep from which they'll never wake up. We keep stirring the batch so that all cocoons get exposed to the sun, killing the worms inside. If alive, the silk-worm will eventually break its way out of the cocoon, damaging the thread. A few hearty worms survive the heat and break out. I don't know what they do with the damaged cocoons, but the farmer instructs us to save them in a bucket.

At times I feel like I'm also getting boiled in the heat of the sun. When possible, I like to rest my whole body, flat on top of the cocoons and just let my hands roll in the piles—they are soft and fuzzy. I imagine how wonderful it must be wearing clothing made of silk. I remember the garments I discovered in a suitcase under my parents' bed, before the war; they must have been made of silk. I have never seen Mama wearing these things, and they remain a mystery.

The nice part of this job is that we get to ride in a horse-drawn wagon that holds all fourteen of us. A farmer comes to fetch us and brings us back.

Today we have a marvelous surprise for dinner. It looks like brownish putty, but moist and shiny, and it smells delicious. We each get a teaspoonful on a piece of paper. I don't know what it is, but I have never eaten something so good. It's something fit for a king and queen. This must be much better than *anansy* and *marcepany*. I don't want to finish my treat fast, I want it to last and last. First I sniff it for a while, and then I lick it with the tip of my tongue. It feels a little sticky and marvelous, but what is it? None of the children knows, but everyone thinks it's a special delicacy. Masha, who is helping in the kitchen today, comes out holding a big jar with a label depicting a funny-looking giant, a smiling peanut who's wearing a hat.

'This stuff is made from peanuts,' some of the older boys are shouting in unison. 'It's peanut putty.'

'Do you think they have this in America?' I ask Ruth.

'They have everything in America.' Ruth looks at me proudly. I guess she considers it her America. Though a year my senior, she is smaller than I, giving me a momentary satisfaction.

The taste and memory of this peanut putty stays with me for a long time, and I fantasize that, after the war, I will eat as much of it as I want.

'Irka, a man is looking for you and your sister,' Chune tells me as soon as I get off the wagon.

'For me? Who is he?'

'Go and find out.'

I run in the direction Chune points, and scream, 'Tata, Tata, you've come to visit!'

My father stands tall, holding the reins of a brown horse. His blue shirt unbuttoned at the neck, sleeves rolled up above his elbows, he looks dressed for a special occasion. The brown wool slacks must be intolerably hot, but Tata doesn't have clothing for the summers in Uzbekistan. In Laish, he wears undershorts around the house, but I'm glad he came appropriately dressed.

'Mama couldn't come, but she sends her hugs. Next time she will visit.'

I have never seen my father on a horse, he looks so tall and important. I want all the children to see him. My anger towards my parents for having dumped me into an orphanage evaporates.

'Do you and Mama have food to eat?' I ask, concerned.

'We are doing okay.'

'Where did you get the horse, Tata?'

'I did some work for a farmer and instead of paying me money, he agreed to lend me his horse to come and visit you girls.' Tata has brought us each a *lepioshka* with a piece of *brinza*.

In the past, Tata rarely spent time talking with Halina and me; that was Mama's job, but I'm overjoyed to see him, even if he says little. Halina and I spend the afternoon with our father, showing him around our new home, telling him what we do and the names of the adults and some children.

'Give me a ride on the horse, Tata,' I beg.

Lifting me up in the air as though I am light as a bird, Tata puts me on the bareback horse. Holding the reins, Tata leads the horse around the building, bringing me back to the spot we started from.

'I want to ride him myself.'

'No, no. This can be dangerous,' Tata declares in a voice that tells me this isn't negotiable. I am very happy that Tata came to see Halina and me. When I see him climb on the horse to leave, I feel proud of him, but very sad. A few feet away from the building Tata turns back to wave at Halina and me. His shirt is wet with sweat, and his blond hair stuck to his forehead, but he smiles at us. Watching him grow smaller and smaller, I struggle not to cry. 'I'll come to see you again soon. You're a big girl already, Irka,' Tata told me before getting on the horse, as though he had forgotten what I looked like when he saw me last, six month ago.

The rest of the day I mope around, unable to find what to do with myself. I locate a spot in the corridor away from the other children and pretend to be writing, but I can do nothing.

That evening a group of new kids arrives, led by an eighteen-year-old boy named Wolek. They are covered with dust, and some are limping as though they've walked for days. Before they put down the small bundles each carries, Wolek asks for Halina and me.

'I passed your father on a horse, and he asked me to say hello to you,' Wolek tells us. 'I didn't know how to get to the orphanage and was glad to see a man on the road. The man was blond and tall and didn't look like a Jew, but I took a chance and asked him in Yiddish the directions to the Jewish orphanage. He said to go straight ahead for about two kilometers, and at the fork in the road, turn left, go about another three or four kilometers, and I'd find the orphanage. He said he had two daughters there, Halina and Irka.' Wolek and the six children with him were all orphans.

The most exciting event in our lives is the move to a new building. Pan Blum informs us that we'll be moving to a bigger building and going to a real school. All the children are happy and eager to see our new home. 'It has to be fixed up a little, we can't see it yet,' Pan Fogel tells us. The older boys are doing the fixing up. On moving day, we are all full of anticipation. It's very hot outside, and we have to walk about five miles carrying our belongings, but I don't care how long we'll have to walk. I want to see the new home. We sing Polish songs — someone starts a song and others join in. By now I also know how to sing in Yiddish, but we are not allowed to do so in the presence of Blum and Fogel. My Yiddish is getting quite fluent.

Our new home is an L-shaped building that used to house a school. The boys and the girls are in two separate rooms. We expect to get more children in the near future and will have space for them as well. We can reach the dining room through the inside walkway and no longer need rides under the arms of a boy. The walkway is wide enough to stand in and talk with other kids, or even to sit on the floor without getting trampled. We are promised beds or cots, but in the meantime we sleep on the floor. Sleeping on the floor is fine as long as the outdoor bugs don't get under your blanket. With the advent of hot weather, big insects and other crawling creatures have popped up out of nowhere. The mosquitoes are huge and ferocious, particularly in the evening which seems to be their mealtime. We are the meal.

From our new location, I can see houses and people in the distance. It doesn't feel isolated from the whole world as it did in the old place. The land around the building is packed dirt, with only a few tufts of grass here and there. To my surprise, a horse and a donkey are roaming freely in front of our building, grazing on the sparse patches of coarse grass. I don't know if they'll be ours, but they seem to feel very much at home. In the front of the building, a few yards away from the entrance, is a mulberry tree. The strong V between the branches will make it easy to climb this tree—I can't wait. I've been writing poetry for some time; it will be wonderfully quiet and private writing poetry in the tree. Before, I'd had to wander off to find a quiet spot.

The other children seldom climb the mulberry tree, and it becomes my own tree, my personal space. In the tree, my world enlarges. I can see far away, observe people, and yet remain invisible to them. Whenever someone wants to find me and I'm not in the building, they look for me in the tree, the only place I can be alone. I like being with the children, they are my friends, but at times I want to be alone and quiet. My best poetry I write perched in the tree. I think and write a lot about my wonderful country, Poland, and what it will be like returning there after the war. Will my cousin Ślamek and Ciocia Fela recognize me? I am no longer a little girl, and definitely not pudgy 'Dumpling' as Ślamek used to call me. My legs and arms are thin, but I have a little protruding belly filled with water or some other fluid. When I jump, I hear the sound of gurgling water. I entertain myself by twisting and jumping at various rhythms to hear the different sounds of gurgling water my movements create. As a little girl in Poland, I tried making music by filling a row of bottles with water at different levels and running a stick across them. Now I carry the musical instrument within me; all I have to do is to jump one way or the other, and the music comes.

My mulberry tree now has big white berries, yet rarely does anyone climb it. The berries are sweet and delicious. We are eating much better now, and most of the time we aren't hungry. Besides potatoes, the soup has burned flour, sometimes turnips, and occasionally carrots in it. Pan Blum and the older boys periodically visit the local Party director who is supposed to allocate food for us. The director sends them to one *kolchos* (communal farm) or another with instructions for what to ask. When the head of the *kolchos* refuses, the boys threaten to report him to the Party, 'Disobeying your Party leader is sabotage. You know what that means?' Their threats usually work. Wolek is among the boys who do all the errands, and sometimes I overhear stories he tells Halina about how the expedition went. He likes my sister and sometimes brings her a piece of fruit or a sticky cookie, and possibly other things I don't know about. She is getting fat. The older boys must like fat girls—I see them hover around Halina when she stands outdoors, in her slacks, with one hand on her hip. Halina does have pretty blue eyes. Since my sister got interested in boys and they in her, she no longer tells me things, or cares what goes on with me, but that's okay. I don't need her. Let her giggle like a silly goat.

The first day in school, in a real school, wearing my brown laced shoes and a short-sleeved, blue sweater, I feel a new world is opening, as though there is no war anymore. All girls have the same shoes and sweaters, which we received from an international relief organization. My feet are a little too warm in the shoes, but in winter they will feel great. No longer will

I have to run barefoot to the outhouse . This school has many rooms, some for the local children and some for us, the Polish kids. I have my own desk with room for books, but there are no books. A portrait of Stalin hangs in each room, but this time Stalin is smiling at us. Pan Blum and Fogel divide us into three classes. I am assigned to the group with the oldest kids, including Chune and some other children his age. Chune is five years my senior. No one questions why I am placed in this group, and neither do I. Halina is not assigned to any group, nor is Wolek. She tells me that she will study on her own, but I don't know how she will be able to do this.

We start the school day with a Russian patriotic song, 'My beautiful motherland for whom I will give my life, if called to do so.' We learn all the songs from our Russian teacher, Natalja Gregorevna. Blum teaches us math and geography without a book or a map; the blackboard serves as both. Fogel is our history teacher; and Fogel's wife, Pani Lucia, a woman with some title and a do-nothing job in the orphanage, will teach us Polish literature. None of our instructors has a teacher's degree, but no one seems to care. Except for the Russian textbooks we have no books; our teachers teach from memory. I like solving story math problems, and Blum makes them up for us. Chune and I work on them together. We can sit for hours solving the problems: The train left for Tashkent at 7:00. The distance to Tashkent is 85 kilometers, but the train did not go straight there; it had to make two side trips, one 12 kilometers away and the other 8 kilometers out of the way. At the first stop it took 20 minutes to get the cargo, and at the second stop only 10 minutes. At one crossing, tracks had to be repaired, causing a delay. The train arrived in Tashkent at 22:00. How long did it take to repair the tracks and how fast did the train travel? This one is easy and simple, I want something more difficult, and sometimes Pan Blum comes up with real challenging ones. Pani Lusia teaches us Polish poetry. I like the poem by Mickiewicz: '*Ojczyzna moja*

Ty jesteś jak zdrowie Ile Cię cenić trzeba ten tylko się dowie kto Cię stracił.' My motherland, you are like health; how much to appreciate you only those know who lost you.

For Soviet Union national holidays and for visits of big Party leaders, the school does singing and dancing. My friend Doba and I are known as the dancing team. We make up our dances to the music of some song we've learned. The school principal and the teachers ask us to dance for all special occasions. I love to sing and dance. When Doba and I dance in the yard of the orphanage, other girls join us. At times we get into the exuberant *kozak* dance, kicking up our heels, dancing up a storm. My skinny legs are pretty strong. For the May First celebration, Doba and I dance to gypsy music. With the help of a scarf, and her natural dark complexion, she looks authentic, like a gypsy. We have no instruments, but a choir sings while we dance. I don't plan the movements, just do what I feel at the moment, and the dance is never the same twice.

Sala, five years my senior, is also a good dancer and improviser. She is Halina's age and chums around with the older boys and girls, but she's always ready to join the dancing crowd. Sala and I sleep in the same metal bed that looks more like a crib; we curl up at opposite ends, and somehow manage.

Toward the end of the summer, the man who brought Halina and me to the orphanage shows up and is talking to Pan Blum. Later in the day Blum asks Halina and me to meet him in the dining room—he has no office. This is strange; he has never before done such a thing. I wonder why he wants to meet just with the two of us.

'Sit down girls,' Pan Blum points to the bench across from him. Sitting, he is my height, and for the first time I could meet his eyes, but he averts them, looking at the wall.

'Halina and Irka, I have bad news.' He pauses. Puzzled and worried, we both look at Pan Blum.

'Sorry to tell you girls, but your father has died.'

I look straight at Pan Blum, but his face is a blur now. All I can see are his lips repeating over and over, 'Your father is dead; your father is dead.'

I can't believe it. It must be a mistake! Tata was strong and tall when he was here, with one hop he was on his horse. How could he be dead? No, no, not our Tata! It couldn't be our Tata, it must be a mistake. I turn to Halina for assurances that it is a mistake, but she sits looking at the walls, as startled as I am. A few minutes go by in silence.

'How do you know?' Halina asks Pan Blum.

'The man who was here talked to your mother in Laish. Your mother will try to come see you soon.'

I don't know how long I sit, unable to move, unable to talk, looking at Blum who seems not to see me as he just gazes into the distance. Tears are stuck in my throat. Halina tugs my sleeve and we leave the dining room. I turn away from Halina, climb into my tree, and sit there staring over the neighboring houses and the fields in the distance for a long time until Ruth calls me down for supper. I don't respond, just wave her away.

I'm not hungry, but strangely, the taste of almond-covered pastries is fresh in my mouth. Yes, these are the triangular pastries filled with cream that Tata would bring when he visited us in the country where, before the war, Mama would take Halina and me for the summer. Tata would arrive with a boxful of pastries and butter for me from Warsaw—the butter in the country smelled of cows, I claimed.

My Tata is so strong, how could he die? He carried me in one arm when we walked in the forest to meet Ślamek. His hands must've been very cold, but he gave me his mittens.

By now, all the children have learned that my father has died, but I don't want to talk about my father. I don't want to talk at all. I want to hide and be left alone. I, who am always full of words, have now nothing to say. My throat feels tight, my chest heavy, I cling to the branch on my right and close my eyes tightly. No longer am I the fake orphan with two parents — maybe even Mama will die and I will be a genuine orphan. I will have no one, only Halina. Suddenly tears pour down my face, flow down my neck, wetting my shirt, but I don't bother wiping them. I sit in the tree until darkness falls.

Halina and I talk about Mama coming to visit, but not about our father's death; we deny his death by our silence. From my perch I watch for my father to show up on a horse. What color horse will it be? My poems are sad, and they include Tata. Sometimes my father is a prince on a white horse, but more often I see him with carpentry tools making beautiful furniture fit for kings. In one poem, Tata and I walk to the rich farmer who treated me to a feast in his home. Because it is a long walk, Tata carries me on his back.

A few weeks later, the Jew brings Mama with all her belongings to the orphanage. She has lost even more weight since I last saw her. Her striped cotton dress, mended below the belt, now hangs loosely. Mama's black shiny hair either hasn't been washed for a long time or has turned a dusty color. She looks tired; it must've been a long, hot journey. I am very glad to see Mama, but when we hug, I burst out crying. Mama is dry-eyed, while Halina and I cry.

The man who brought her has arranged a job for my mother in a brewery that makes alcohol from beets. She will live with a Jewish family in Chelek.

The work turns out to be physically exhausting, the hours long. Mama lives at some distance from the orphanage, but she comes to see Halina and me at least once a week. She tells us about the people who work with her and the Russian neighbors she met. The family she lives with is a nice old couple. When Mama returns from work, they are usually already asleep. I find out a lot about white beets and red beets and how they crush them and then mix them with other ingredients to make beer.

Yesterday Mama was very upset, a woman who worked with her didn't show up in the morning. Mama learned that in the middle of the night, she and her husband had been hauled away by the NKVD, the secret police. No one wanted to talk about it, but somehow everyone knew what had happened. The Russians who have lived in the area for a long time, have grown accustomed to people disappearing in the middle of the night. No one speaks of it, but everyone knows this happens and that those who disappear are never heard from again.

'Such a decent woman,' Mama keeps repeating.

'Why did they take her away, Mama?' I ask, though I already know that there is no good reason. The Soviets shipped us out from Ignatki in the middle of the night for no obvious reason.

'No one knows and everyone knows. It doesn't take much to be accused of something, of sabotage or hell knows what. Irka, don't talk to anyone about it.'

'Mama, I know not to talk about such a thing.'

My parents' disillusionment with the communist system, the anguish and pain caused by the loss of their ideals, and the tarnished heroes, have long ceased to be a Yiddish secret.

After working a few months in the brewery, Mama loses her job without explanation. The orphanage gives her work as a night supervisor, one of those do-nothing jobs. We are all asleep at night and so is Mama. The compensation for this job is a big crib in the boys' room and the same food that the kids eat. A number of people here have do-nothing jobs. They get a title, but do very little or nothing at all. We also have a few hang-around Polish Jews: a former judge sitting in the sun scratching his head or picking lice off his shirt, an old woman searching for her husband who left Poland for the Soviet Union before the war. Occasionally these people get a bowl of soup, but always plenty of company and conversation. Mama and the judge sometimes sit on the ground, leaning against the building, talking and talking. People tease Mama that the lice-covered judge is in love with her.

Now that Mama is with us daily, I feel special, particularly when she is making shirts for Halina and me from an army blanket. Our shirts become the envy of many children.

It takes many months before Mama tells Halina and me that Tata died of dysentery, in an epidemic that wiped out many of the Polish Jews in the area. Mama rushed Tata to the regional clinic, but they had no medications.

'We have no drugs, we have nothing; they may have some in the bigger regional clinic,' the medic told her. That clinic was thirty kilometers away. Mama sold the last of her night-gowns, which a Russian woman bought, thinking it was an evening dress, and went on foot to that clinic. She walked the whole night, and when she returned the following evening, Tata was already dead and buried in one of the mass graves. Mama could not find out in which of the graves Tata was laid.

My father was forty-two years old when he died.

I try not to think about the mass graves, but the image keeps haunting me, popping up out of nowhere. For a while I dream about mountains of dead people, but my father isn't among them. Having been apart from Tata for about a year, I don't miss him constantly, but in my tree, away from all the kids, I remember with sorrow that I do not have a father any-more, that I will never again see my Tata.

Living with older girls in the same room, and being in the same classroom, I see the changes of their bodies and hear when they talk about menstruation. I am twelve, but don't yet menstruate, and I am flat-chested. Big tits look gross. I would rather be flat than look like a cow, but I would like to have breasts, small elegant breasts. I am concerned that I might never look like a woman, but I have no one to talk to about it. Though Mama lives with me in the orphanage, I never talk to her about personal matters, or ask her any questions. Most of the adult women have ceased menstruating, but Mama can't stop bleeding. She is often lying in bed in the daytime, her mattress soaked in blood, embarrassed before the older boys, who make fun of her, though not to her face. There are no sanitary napkins, no cotton, nothing to absorb the blood flow. Mama tore up the few pillowcases she still had and uses the pieces as rags between her legs.

'Irka, wash the bucket of my rags in the river,' Mama tells me.

Looking at the smelly bloody rags, I think I will vomit, but I can't refuse her. I feel bad for my mother, but also angry at her for asking me to do this disgusting job. It's a long walk to the river. I try not to look at the contents of the bucket and not to think about it, but swarming flies don't let me forget what I carry, and the smell is with me constantly. Very sensitive to smells, I sense them long before people around me notice them; this suffocating stench hits me right in the nostrils.

I walk fast, hoping that no one I know will meet me on the way. What would I say should one of the Russian girls see me carrying this smelly mess? I don't even want to imagine meeting a boy; I'd just die from embarrassment.

At the riverbank, my dilemma is how to wash the rags without looking at them, but there's no way. The rags create a red river around me as I swish them around, two at a time, one in each hand. It takes a long time before the rags even start looking grayish. They won't become white no matter how long I rub them on stones with the harsh soap that feels like sandpaper in my hand.

I have to find a place to dry the rags, away from all the kids who would ask me what these ugly things are. Luckily the sun is so hot now that it doesn't take long for the rags to dry. Mama doesn't bleed continuously, but when she starts, the flow lasts sometimes for over two weeks, and it is my job to wash the rags. I say nothing, but looking at my face, Mama apologizes, 'Sorry, Irka, that you have to wash these for me, but I can't walk to the river in this state, and Halina is already a young lady, I can't ask her to do it.'

'It's okay, Mama,' I tell her, though I hate washing the bloody rags and wonder why Halina, the young lady, can't do it as well, but feeling bad for Mama, I say nothing.

'Why don't you go to the river with the bucket?' I angrily ask Halina.

'Mama asked you to do it, not me; I'm busy working in the kitchen.'

'I don't know what big job you have in the kitchen, you just hang around with the boys.'

'You're being nasty because Mama asked you, not me.'

'She can't depend on you to do anything,' I growl, and storm off.

There is a lot of talk among the adults and the children about the Nazi killings of Jews in Poland. Whatever the adults talk about, we kids know about it right away. There are no secrets in this place. I heard something about burning people, but can't believe it. How can even the most horrible person do such a thing? It couldn't happen to my cousins, not to Šlamek. He wouldn't allow anyone to do a thing like that to him, or to anyone else. I have nightmares about people burning, and at times I wake up startled, thinking that I am aflame.

The Nazis perform horrible experiments on women in the camps, using them like guinea pigs, I hear. They train dogs to rape women to see what comes of it. They tie the women and observe how the dogs rape them. I have seen horses, donkeys, cats, and other animals mate, even two people facing each other, leaning against the wall of the building, and in rapid rhythmic motion moving together, but human intercourse is still a little vague to me. Hearing these stories, I create an image of a theater stage with bright lights and the women tied with chains, screaming as the Nazis look on and laugh.

I always visualize stories I hear and become part of them, but seeing this picture is extremely disturbing. Worse yet, I become the woman on the stage, frightened, helpless, wanting to scream. I would rather the Nazis kill me than be raped by dogs, I decide.

I feel as if I walk in a nightmare, but can't wake up. To escape from these thoughts and images, I go into the mulberry tree to write poetry about returning home to Poland. It helps when we hear success stories from the battlefield. Each allied victory gives us greater cause for anticipating our return home, but most victories also bring with them new horror stories about what the Nazis do in the occupied territories. The war will not last much longer; the Germans are losing and running in defeat. Some people in the village have radios, and the news spreads fast. With each new allied victory, we sing and dance and I write new poems about Poland, my motherland. By now I have several notebooks with poems, and I permit a few of my friends to read some of them. Pani Fogelowa, our Polish teacher, wants me to send some of my poems to a Polish newspaper, but I don't want total strangers to read what I've written. Maybe someday, but not now.

I write a poem to the rhythm of a marching song we all know, and sing it to my friend Doba, 'The sun will shine, the crowds will cheer as we enter Poland, our homeland we longed for.' Doba is excited that she is the first one to hear it, and we hum it together, tara, lalaal lalallla. We learn to sing it well before we let others hear us. Little by little, we teach a few more children to sing it as they march.

'This can be our marching song into Poland,' Doba declares, rubbing her palms, which she does when excited.

'I hope we aren't going to walk back to Poland from Uzbekistan,' someone in the group comments, laughing.

'Don't be a smart aleck,' Doba retorts

In the midst of all this churning of news, the big event in our lives is that Halina and Wolek are getting married. I've noticed them hanging around together, but I often have seen Halina with Moniek, another of the orphanage boys. Whomever she tells us she is marrying will seem natural and not a big deal to me. Halina doesn't appear especially excited about the marriage, but I have never been around people who are getting married and don't know how excited they should be. I do enjoy the commotion of Mama trying to make wine from the grapes Wolek managed to find, from who knows where. Mama also plans to make a cake. I haven't eaten cake since the war broke out.

I don't know how Halina and Wolek arrange to get a place of their own, but they do have a one-room house, and this is where a dozen friends come to celebrate the union of two orphanage children, now adults. Halina is eighteen and Wolek twenty-one. I have to get used to the idea that my sister is an adult. Yesterday, she was a kid in the orphanage, but today she suddenly is an adult. The last few years Halina and I have lived separate lives, though under the same roof. She has been with the older kids and has shared whatever interests they had, while I've had my own friends and various activities that did not involve my sister. Halina and I haven't even spoken much, so her moving out as a married woman doesn't significantly affect my life.

'THE WAR IS OVER, THE WAR IS OVER!' people are shouting, running all over the village. We jump, scream, hug. The orphanage bubbles with talk and excitement. It feels as if something special needs to happen, a surprising storm and a rainbow, white horses galloping in the sky, or at least in the fields, some little miracle to mark the monumental event, the end of war, but nothing does. At supper Pan Blum announces that the war is over, but by then we all know it.

'When are we going back home?' many children call out.

'We don't know yet, but we will leave as soon as things are arranged.' None of us knows what has to be arranged, but these are just details, we decide.

For the last few years I've talked, I've dreamed, and I've written about how glorious it will be to go back to Poland, to go home. Now that the reality is almost before me, I can't translate my dream into an image of a home. The memories of my childhood before the war are blurred, and I know that what I left behind no longer exists. I try to envision the physical destruction of buildings and parks, and what I remember of my Warsaw neighborhood, but I never consider the loss of my relatives possible.

The war ends in 1945, but we do not return to Poland until 1946. We are told that preparations have to be made before we return. Who pays for our passage to Poland, where we will live in Poland, and other decisions keep us waiting, decisions that have to be made by other people, officials, not the adults in the orphanage.

Finally the day of departure arrives. We kids are elated. This time we travel on passenger trains. Spontaneously, children break out in song, my marching song about how wonderful it is to go home to Poland, our motherland. We are all in high spirits, singing and joking, not even troubled that we still don't know where in Poland we are headed. A representative of some agency meets us in a Polish border town to dispatch us to our various destinations in Poland, our new homes.

Polski Dom Dziecka number 23, the children who made up my home, who were my companions and my friends for almost four years, are now being scattered in all directions. It happens so fast, so unexpectedly, that we can only say quick good-byes to one another. In a sudden POOF, the orphanage disintegrates. Fogel, Blum, Masha are gone, and some strangers take over. Sala and I are the only kids sent to Krakow; she is eighteen, but still living in the orphanage. Halina, Wolek, and Mama also come to Krakow."

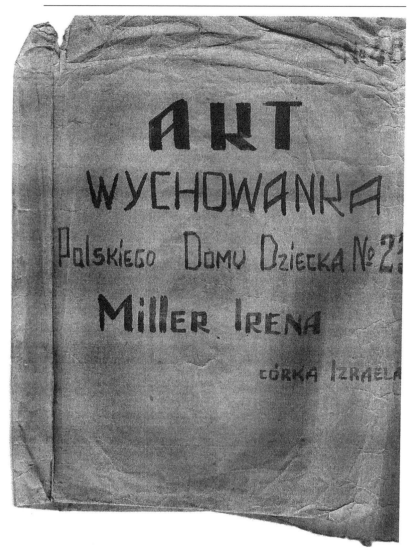

The cover of the folder from the orphanage,
containing personal information about me.

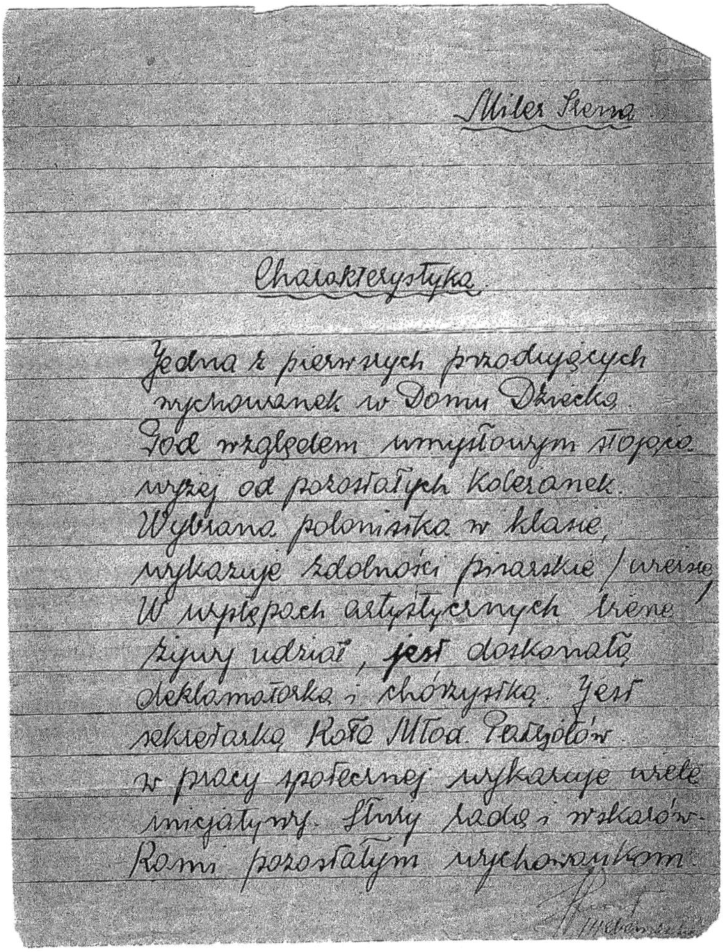

Miler Irena

Charakterystyka

[handwritten Polish text]

Miller Irena

Characteristics

One of the most advanced girls in the Children's Home.
Intellectually above all the others. An outstanding **polonistka** (expert user
of the Polish language). She has literary gifts and writes poetry.
A top **deklamatorka** (reciter of poetry) and chorister.
Is secretary of the Youth Organization and shows a lot of initiative in
social and communal work.
She provides advice, guidance and counsel to the rest of the girls.

245

11

Krakow

"Mom, weren't you disappointed you weren't returning to Warsaw, to your childhood home?"

"Home became an idea, an emotion, a hope for normality, and a return to what I remembered as a happy childhood, rather than a specific house or even city. By the time the war ended, I knew that Warsaw had been destroyed and the ghetto leveled. I was sure our Niska Street, being in the center of the Jewish neighborhood in Warsaw, and within the ghetto, had long since been obliterated. Since I had nothing to return to in Poland, I was not surprised to be put in an orphanage."

"The children in the Krakow's *Dom Dziecka*, the Children's Home, have come from many areas of Poland, but they know one another; some have been in this home for almost a year. Sala and I are the only newcomers—outsiders. She plans to leave the children's home as soon as she can make other arrangements, but at thirteen, there is no other place I can go. My mother is ill, she has no housing, and no way of supporting herself. She shares a room with a few other people in a house in Krakow, all supported by an agency in Israel. Halina and Wolek are in a similar situation. I am not the only child in the orphanage who has a parent.

I have been assigned to a room with five girls, all about my age, who seem a bit cliquish and exude an air of superiority. Deciding not to try to gain their favor, I ignore their uppityness and go about exploring this new home of mine.

Walking through the long, wide hallway of the third floor where most of the bedrooms are, I wonder why all this space was wasted on hallways that are many times the width of our hallway in Chelek. My bedroom is big enough for six beds, three against opposite walls, and a tiny table with two stools under the window, leaving enough room to squeeze between the furniture. A small alcove at one end of the room has a rack with hangers and a shelf above for our clothes. I have only two cotton skirts to hang, one navy and the other gray. The rest of my belongings—two shirts, a sweater, and underpants—I store in my suitcase under the bed. I own no bra, though I'm budding little breasts. The rope around the suitcase kept it from falling apart all the way from Uzbekistan to Krakow.

The second floor has a few rooms for the older kids, small individual rooms for staff who live on the premises, a big meeting and study room for all the children, and a storage room with used clothing sent by charitable organizations in the United States. On the first floor is the apartment of the director, along with a big room that serves as a day care center for kids who come only in the daytime. The dining room is in the basement, next to the kitchen.

The orphanage is housed in a gray three-story building on Augustiańska Street along the Wisła River. The building is set back from the street, leaving a front yard big enough for a football game. A chain-link fence provides some privacy but allows a clear view of the street, whose only traffic is pedestrian.

Seeing the big oak in the front yard, I feel homesick. The oak reminds me of my mulberry tree in Chelek. I have no home now, no friends. This is a big house with lots of strangers, but it is not my home—Chelek became my home.

There is no one I can talk with. Halina and Mama are also in Krakow, but I have no idea where. They were to be placed in some communal home, but as yet I don't know where it is.

Not knowing what to do with myself, I cross the street, lean against the railing along the riverbank, and take in my new reality, feeling lonely and lost among all these strangers who look and talk differently from my friends in Siberia and Uzbekistan.

Watching the calm Wisła waters flowing, I wonder what other cities the river visits and what they look like. I know so little of the Poland that I dreamed about, the Poland I talked and wrote poetry about, its literature, history, and geography. I know so little about the world in general, and there is so much to be known. How much knowledge will I have time to garner before I become an adult, I wonder. I don't want to grow up an ignoramus. My friends in the Soviet Union considered me smart, even my teachers thought I was very bright, but my education up to now has been like Swiss cheese with vast holes; I don't even understand the extent of my ignorance. Yes, I am not stupid, but knowing so little, I will appear dumb.

I must have spent a long time gazing into the river; it is getting cool though it's June. I turn back. Some kids are playing a game that calls for running fast and catching a ball. If you can't catch the ball or avoid getting hit by it, out of the game you go. When the next game begins, I join in and no one objects. I am a fast runner, but have no experience catching balls—we had no balls in Siberia or in Uzbekistan. I succeed in catching the ball twice and evading quite a number of hits, but eventually someone smacks my hip with a ball, and I am out of the game.

'You're a good runner, but need practice catching balls,' a boy tells me. His blond hair falling all over his forehead, he looks kind of cute.

'Do you want to throw balls to me so I can get some experience?' I ask.

'Okay.'

Zygmund, my ball-catching instructor, is fourteen, a year older than I, and he's liked by a lot of girls, which lends me, the newcomer, a little status.

With the ringing of a bell, all children head downstairs for dinner. Rows and rows of tables and benches beside them form the well-lit, freshly painted dining room. The brightness of the room and the lively chatter of the kids cheer me up a bit; maybe this will become my home.

For dinner we have dumplings made with farmer's cheese, sprinkled with sugar; you can eat as much as you want. The cook, her white apron tied around a black cotton dress, her gray hair cut short as though chopped off with scissors without any concern for style, comes into the dining room to see if we have enough food. She looks old, but energetic—moving briskly from table to table.

'Are you the new girl? What is your name?' she asks, resting her hand on my shoulder.

'Irka.'

'Let me know, Irka, if you're still hungry.'

'Thank you, the *kluski* are delicious, but I've had enough.'

Later I learn that our cook's two grown daughters had been killed in a concentration camp, and that she is working long hours in the children's home without accepting any pay. To cook for nearly a hundred children, all hearty eaters, must be a lot of work.

All the children are Jews, each of us with different war experiences. We don't discuss our lives during the war either among ourselves or with the staff, or our teachers. Now and then, I hear a comment about one of the children who lost parents in Auschwitz, or witnessed the shooting of his or her parents, but this information is stated flatly as a fact, and we turn our minds to the business of the moment. Hanka, age twelve, the youngest girl in the room, yells out 'Jesus!' when frustrated, and when she's scared, she crosses herself. 'It's just a habit. I don't even know I'm doing it,' she tells me when I ask. Hanka survived the war in a convent, unaware that she was a Jew. She has no recollection of her parents. Hanka's only relative is an aunt, a journalist before the war.

My roommates and I talk late into the night, and in the morning, I feel lonely no more. They tell me which boy likes which girl, who is smart and who is stupid, and that our director is romancing Pani Lusia, one of the staff. I don't know any of these people yet, but I feel good that my roommates confide in me.

Frida, one of the girls in my room, offers to lend me a dress—she has two of them. Zahava, a tall, broad-shouldered woman in her late twenties with a big warm smile, is one of our live-in *wychowawczynie*, or educators. She specializes in physical education. I didn't know that anyone did such things—physical education, whatever that is, but I like Zahava as soon as I see her. Zahava is taking a group of us girls for a walk into town, and I am extremely eager to see Krakow.

Krakow is a big city with many historical buildings, cathedrals, churches, theaters, concert halls, cafés, stores, and busy streets full of pedestrians. The city shows no signs of the war—all the buildings are intact. Aleje Krakowskie, a park around the old city, is busy with mothers pushing baby buggies or sitting on benches, rocking the strollers and socializing with one another. Old men are reading newspapers, and some just sit observing the people passing by. Across the street stands the famous Jagiellonian University, but we have no time to look any farther. All these sights and sounds are so new to me, everything feels like such a dream that I wonder when I will wake up.

It has been two weeks since I moved to the children's home, and I haven't heard yet from my mother or sister. Here and there I think about them and wonder where they are and what they are doing, but most days I'm so busy and involved in my new life that their absence is not very disturbing.

'Your sister was here looking for you,' Hanka tells me one day.

'What did she say?'

'She left you this note with their address and directions how to get there.'

Unfamiliar yet with the city, I have no idea how far away it is, but I'll find out when I'm ready to go there, maybe on Saturday.

School will start in three weeks, but in the meantime I get books from a public library, a half hour walk from the orphanage—the same distance as my school will be, but in a different direction. Knowing the names of Russian writers better than any others, I start with the *Brothers Karamazov* in Polish translation.

'Dostoyevsky will be too difficult for you,' the librarian tells me.

'I don't think so.'

'How old are you, girl?'

'Thirteen.'

'If it turns out that you don't like the book, you can exchange it.'

'Thank you.' I leave knowing I would not have any trouble reading the book, and certainly would not exchange it for some silly reading material.

Life now is at a fast pace and full of wonder. I sign up for a ballet class and also for piano lessons. The Jewish Community of Krakow keeps us under its wings; we children who survived the war are a treasure of sorts, and those with no family or home get special attention. Jewish Community leaders visit to see how we are doing. Some people volunteer their skills in the Children's Home, giving music lessons, while others come to take a few of us for special outings. Between the Jewish Children's Home, the Jewish school, and the Jewish Community Center, I live in a Jewish world, in a city that is probably 99 percent Roman Catholic. Riding the streetcar, I face a church on almost every corner, and I'm the only person who doesn't cross herself. At times, many eyes turn to me when I leave my hands in my pockets. I feel somewhat self-conscious, but look straight into the faces of those who stare at me.

Though my immediate world is made up of Jews, neither Jewish religion nor traditions are a part of my life. We learn Yiddish songs in school and our curriculum includes a class in Yiddish, but that is it. Because my Yiddish is fluent, I can get away reading a hidden Polish novel and just occasionally volunteering an answer. The children who survived the war in Poland don't know Yiddish. If the language had been spoken in their homes before the war, they had forgotten it.

Soon I discover that the education of all eighteen students in my class has big holes and gaps. Many of my classmates know much less math, geography, and composition than I do. To catch up for our lost school years, we proceed at a rapid pace. It feels like swallowing without having time to chew, but I'm eager to swallow as much as possible. I'm in a race with time and have a ferocious appetite for experiences. Everything I hear about I want to study. Esperanto, for instance, seems like a great idea. Imagine if in every country in the world, in addition to having their own language, people also knew and used Esperanto. People could communicate with one another with great ease, it would make the whole world a much friendlier and safer place. I sign up for an Esperanto evening class at the Palace of Culture, formerly a private mansion of a wealthy family. Many of these buildings have been confiscated by the communist government.

All my classes are free of charge, and my time is pretty much my own to use as I wish once my homework and my household chores at the orphanage are done. After a few months of piano lessons, I conclude they are a waste of time, I have no musical talent. But I love dancing and continue with ballet classes offered in the orphanage by a dancer who volunteers her time. Weaving also catches my attention, and I learn how to use a small loom. My first project is a black, gray, and burgundy plaid scarf for Wolek's birthday.

Mama, Halina, and Wolek share a very small room in a building they call a kibbutz. Mama continues to hemorrhage intermittently, Halina is pregnant, and Wolek is studying to be an electrician. They live about a forty-five-minute walk from me, but I am so busy that I visit infrequently.

Out in the evening, on my way back to the orphanage, when the streets are lit and life in the apartments is visible through the windows, I pause at times and stare, wondering what life is like inside. Behind the glass and behind the walls are families, a mother, a father, and children living in the same house, in an apartment all to themselves. It must be wonderful to live in such a place. How does it feel to live in a home with your family? I don't remember, but it must be very special. I feel envious. At times I envision myself in one of the windows—the daughter in the family. Would I have such a family life were my father alive, I wonder. I grow sad and feel pangs of loneliness and longing. Thousands and thousands of brightly illuminated windows in which life goes on, people sitting around dining tables, children giggling, here and there a couple embracing. I can see the people, I can hear them, yet they are so remote from my reality. It almost feels like I am watching a movie, they are the actors and I can only be the spectator. None of those windows are mine.

It's too late to go visit Mama and Halina—maybe tomorrow after school—but visiting Mama doesn't feel warm and loving. My mother has never been affectionate, but now when she is ill and unhappy, she is even more distant. Not finding any of our Polish relatives alive has been extremely painful for her. She searched through the Red Cross, through Jewish organizations, and in every other way she knew, but found no one alive. Two of her brothers in France and one in Belgium survived the war, but to me these uncles are just names; I never have seen them or heard much about them.

Although I am considered an outgoing, accomplished girl and am asked to appear at various functions to represent the Jewish youth of Krakow, and although I have friends, am known by many in the city, and am told by some that I'm pretty, there's no one in my life who puts his or her arms around me and tells me he or she loves me. I feel a hunger of the heart and soul when I see a parent hugging a child. I am fifteen now and consider myself almost an adult, but in such moments I want to be a little girl again, though I don't even remember Mama ever hugging me, or ever telling me she loved me when I was little. This longing intensifies when twice a week I visit the home of eleven-year-old Zosia, whom I tutor in math, Polish, and other subjects. A streetcar brings me to the elegant apartment, a home with rugs and chandeliers. I like sitting on an upholstered chair behind a mahogany table and am pleased to earn money, which I use mostly for theater tickets. Often I leave the apartment longing to be a girl in such a family and in such a house. But these are just fleeting moments of loneliness and longing; otherwise I am content, and so busy that I find little time to be lonely.

After waiting many months, my mother is admitted to a city hospital for removal of the tumor that has kept her hemorrhaging all these years. On my second visit to the hospital, I find my mother hooked up to feeding tubes, the blood transfusion bag suspended on a pole, and she is the color of clean snow.

'How are you feeling, Mama?'

'Well, what can you expect when they've removed a tumor the size of a child's head? They showed it to me.'

'Now that you won't bleed so much, you won't be anemic any longer.'

'Maybe.'

'I'm sure you'll feel much better in no time.'

'I can't move, tied up with all those tubes; I haven't had any food since the surgery four days ago; and I need peace and quiet, but this miserable anti-Semite in my room keeps screaming, 'Take this Jewess out of my room! She smells of onions and garlic, like all of them Jews do."

'Did you tell the nurse?'

'The nurse is no better than my roommate.'

I leave the room to look for a nurse or physician.

'Who is in charge now?' I ask the woman behind a desk.

'I am,' the woman answers.

'Do you know that my mother's roommate is verbally abusing her?'

'What do you mean?'

I repeat what my mother told me and wait for the nurse's response.

'Maybe Pani Millerowa does smell of garlic—I don't know.'

'That's ridiculous! You know she is fed by tube, and I assume you didn't put in garlic or onions. Either move my mother to another room or make sure the roommate behaves in a civilized way.'

'We will try.'

My mother stays in the hospital for three weeks, and the situation with her roommate and the staff's disregard doesn't improve.

My school is going to visit Auschwitz. I had heard stories about the horrors of the concentration camps, though in Krakow we don't talk about them. I don't know what to expect—no one prepares us for the trip, and I try not to think about it.

It is the first time since the war started that I travel in a comfortable passenger car, but my anxiety about the camp keeps me from enjoying the ride.

It's a gray October morning, the air feels heavy and still. The brown leaves on the trees I see from the train window hardly move—they look brittle, fragile, and motionless. I try to block out every thought that comes to mind and to forget where the train is headed. Yet again and again I see my cousin Ślamek and can almost hear his voice teasing me, '*Telca bez widelca.*' He wouldn't recognize me now. I don't look like a dumpling. I don't know why he used to call me a dumpling, I was never fat, but that did not matter. I knew Ślamek loved me. I think of Ciocia Fela and see their house.

Suddenly I am startled by this huge black metal gate with a big sign in German: "*Arbeit Macht Frei.*" Work makes you free. This massive gate was the entrance to the death camp where maybe some of my relatives died. The wire fence enclosing the compound is there, but the current that electrocuted those trying to escape has been shut off. The watchtowers, though empty of German soldiers, still stand ominous and threatening. Inside the gates, emptiness and silence surround us, with neither a person nor a sound coming out of the long barracks that used to house the prisoners, Jews destined to die in the gas chambers. My eyes momentarily closed, I can see skinny people in striped uniforms standing in a line-up, some falling to the ground and being beaten by a Nazi in uniform. I don't see any children—had they already been killed? All the concentration camp horrors I've heard and read about come to life, as my mind paints pictures too painful to watch. It is too painful to include my cousins and my other relatives, too many even to list. I am upset that I forgot the names of some of my uncles and aunts. What was the name of the cobbler who lived in a very small basement apartment? He was the poorest in the family.

'These wagons took the individuals from the gas showers to the crematorium,' the guide explains. The words—showers, crematorium, sanatorium, auditorium—sound so innocent and sophisticated. Why doesn't the guide just say, 'This is where they gassed the Jews, and this is where they burned their bodies'?

My eyes quickly scan the big, dark room where the guide has led us. Before she utters a word, I grow stiff and cold before the pile of human hair as tall as I am. To the right is an immense heap of worn shoes—men's, women's, children's, some no longer than my finger. A pink little bootie with a pompon dangling from it lies on top of the pile. Next to it is a brown shoe with a high heel, a bit worn out but still looking stylish. I wonder how old the woman was who wore the shoe, what she looked like, and whether this was her baby's bootie. Next to the shoes is a pile of eyeglasses, thousands of them. I have never seen a baby wearing glasses, but some are so tiny they would have only fit an infant.

'These shoes, glasses, combs belonged to the people who went to the gas chambers. The pile of hair you see here is women's hair intended for use in wigs and other products. When a woman had good hair, they cut it off and set it aside.' The guide relates the information as though we are looking at rows of materials in a factory manufacturing products for use in daily living. I start coughing, choking. I am in the gas chamber now, and my shoes are somewhere in this pile. I must have turned pale.

'Are you okay?' the teacher asks me.

'Yes, something got into my throat,' I tell her, but I have to lean against the wall or my knees will buckle.

'The shade of the lamp in that corner is made from people's skin, and the soap from human flesh.'

I don't know what else the guide is saying. I hear her voice but the words don't register. The guide shows us the gas chambers, the ovens where the corpses had been incinerated, but I follow all this description like a sleepwalker.

I have heard a lot about Janusz Korczak and his refusal to accept the Germans' offer to go free, leaving the children of his orphanage to be gassed. Instead, he led the hundred children in song, walking with them into the gas chambers. Before me now is a long column of singing children unknowingly walking to their death. Were some of them my age? Were they truly ignorant of what was about to happen to them?

Absolute silence prevails on our trip back to Krakow. Eyes closed, I try but cannot block out the images of what I have just seen. God, oh God, not my cousin Slamek, his shoes could not be in the pile. I remember how he fed and bathed me, soaked my sore feet, how I fell asleep in his lap after leaving the no man's land. Why did he return to Poland, why did he do it?

A heavy burning rock is sitting on my chest, and I can't free myself of it. Maybe if I could cry, it would dissolve, but tears don't flow, though I feel terribly sad. No matter how I choke up, I am unable to cry wet tears. I want my aunts, my uncles, and my cousins back; I want to have a family; I feel terribly alone.

Auschwitz doesn't leave me for a long time; it keeps popping into my thoughts. I always visualize the things I think about, images are constantly floating in my mind.

No one talks to us about the death camp, and we kids keep silent about it as well.

Four weeks after visiting Auschwitz, I am headed to Warsaw for the opening of the memorial monument for the Warsaw Ghetto fighters. I have been sent as a delegate from the Krakow Jewish High School along with Adam Zielinski, a Jewish college student. On the train, Adam and I talk about plays we each had been to, the books we liked to read, the places we'd like to travel to, but nothing about the reason for our journey to Warsaw. I enjoy this tall and handsome man's flirtation and am able to forget Auschwitz and the ghetto for a while.

The overpowering sculpture of the monument stands in what used to be my neighborhood. The Warsaw Ghetto means my family, aunts, uncles, and cousins, all dead now. Listening to the speeches, I see my relatives vividly before me, sitting, talking and laughing in Ciocia Fela's apartment, or in Uncle Hershel's home. The ghetto is also my childhood home, vanished without a trace, leaving no evidence that I was once a child. That night, alone in my hotel room, I weep and cannot stop, but in the morning I am ready to explore with Adam what is left of Warsaw.

More and more individuals and groups of representatives from various organizations come to the Children's Home to ask about our war experiences. Our cook is putting together a book and asks each of us to write a few pages. Hanka's aunt, the journalist, is back at work and wants to interview us for her book. I don't like to talk about my years in the Soviet

Union and don't want to write about it. This was a time I shared with other children; those with me now would not understand what I am talking about. I feel almost that I would be betraying something, I don't know exactly what. I wrote a few pages for our cook, simply because I like her, and I know she is very sad for having lost her two daughters. Some individuals come to take photographs. I stop being curious who they are, it's just another photo for who knows what.

Then there are those interested in how our Home functions, based as it is on the educational principles outlined in the works of Makarenkow, a Russian pedagogue. In the Home, we children form an internal government with branches responsible for the various aspects of our communal life. For example, the Culture and Recreation Committee decides how our funds shall be allocated: theater, ballets, or outings to special points of interest, such as the salt mines near Krakow. The head of Domestic Affairs distributes assignments in housekeeping, and so on. Each area of our life has its committee responsible to the President of the Children's Government. Supposedly, the president and the heads of various divisions are elected by the children, but I have a hunch our teachers make the final decisions so that their choices are implemented. I don't believe that my becoming the President of the Children's Government is purely the children's choice, but I am reelected to my second term, each term being a year. I take my work very seriously and make a point of not asking for any special privileges. I do, however, enjoy being the one to open all the huge cardboard boxes with used clothing that arrive from charities in America. Doba and Frida are helping me today. It's an honor I bestow on girls I like—everyone wants the excitement of seeing what has arrived. When each of us finds an item of clothing we like a lot, we can be the first one to put in a request for it with Pani Lusia, in charge of the storage room. It doesn't mean we will get it—it depends on what we already have. Most of us have only three or four changes.

I like pulling out and inspecting the dresses, the skirts, the shirts—they all look so beautiful. I cannot understand why anyone would give away things that hardly look worn and are so pretty. People in America must be very rich to give away such nice things.

'Look, look at that girls,' I pull out a handful of candy bars. We have never eaten candy bars, but I recognize by the aroma that they are sweets.

'Since we are working so hard, we should compensate ourselves,' I declare, ripping the wrapping off one bar and dividing it into three pieces. As soon as I take a small bite, I recognize the marvelous taste of the special treat we had in the Children's Home in Chelek, the peanut putty. I say nothing to my friends about it, they wouldn't understand. Doba survived the war on a farm with a Catholic family, she didn't starve. Frida lived in a convent, and though food was limited, she didn't starve either. And who wants to talk about the war, anyway? The three of us delight in the candy bar.

'How about opening another one?' Frida asks.

'I'd love another piece too, but I don't think we should,' I declare.

'Look, look Irka,' Doba whispers to me, pulling out a pink sweater. 'Oh, I would like to have it.'

'Ask for it.'

'Pani Lusia doesn't like me, I won't get it.'

'You never know, try, maybe she will give it to you,' I encourage her.

One day a group of Americans arrives with a photographer and translators. They are representatives from New York's "Friends of Krakow" organization, which has been sending us used clothing and providing other assistance. They've come to see how their orphans are doing. We gather in the study room for a group picture. How they can fit us all in one picture, I wonder, but Americans can do anything. They came with sophisticated equipment and look confident in what they are doing. Afterwards, we line up for individual photos. Lately I feel as though I'm on display, with all the visitors inquiring about the children in the Home. As the President of the Children's Government, I am interviewed at length by the American visitors. I describe for them the children's government and how our lives are conducted. Knowing no English, I use my Yiddish and the help of a translator. I am eager to tell the visitors how good our life is, how much freedom we have to initiate and explore interesting activities. Not only do we have functions in school, but in the Home we can take dancing, singing, and other classes.

'I take Esperanto in the Palace of Culture.'

'What is Esperanto?' a visitor asks me.

I am surprised that he doesn't know, but patiently I explain it to him. I must admit that I feel important after this interview, but I don't want to show it.

A few weeks later, I receive the greatest of surprises—a letter from New York. I know no one in New York, or for that matter in the entire United States. I forget about the Carter sisters whom I have not kept in contact with. I'm extremely eager to know who would write to me from New York, yet I hesitate to open the envelope, fearing it is a mistake, a letter intended for someone else. Much to my disappointment, the letter is written in English and I know no English. I bring the letter to school, hoping one of my teachers can read it. Yes, yes, the letter is written to me. A girl named Esther, born in New York, saw my picture in some Jewish periodical. She read a little about me and wants to become my pen pal. I never had a pen pal, and it sounds exciting to correspond with an American girl, but what about the English? I respond with a brief note in Yiddish, 'I would very much like to correspond with you, but I know no English, only Polish, Russian, and Yiddish.' Surprisingly, the New York-born Esther knows Yiddish, and we commence a correspondence that will persist a lifetime. Esther's mother, born in Europe and active in Jewish organizations, made sure her children knew Yiddish and identified strongly with Yiddish culture.

Reading plays and going to the theater when I have money for a standing ticket inflames my desire to act, not just in school plays, but on the legitimate stage. With money I've earned tutoring, I buy Stanislavski's book '*Rabota Aktora Nad Soboi*' (The Actor's Work on the Self). I buy it in Russian—it is unavailable in Polish. I study it page by page. I enroll in an acting class in the Palace of Culture and dream of becoming an actress.

My greatest stage moment occurs when the famous Yiddish actress Ida Kaminska arrives in Krakow with her theater group and needs a young actress for a very small role that includes singing a Yiddish song. The school recommends me. I am on the stage no more than five minutes, but receive considerable recognition from my friends and teachers. For some time I remain the special girl who had the honor and recognition to appear on the same stage with the great Ida Kaminska. I bask in the glory, embellishing the backstage stories more than a little.

The older kids in the Home, me included, are going to spend a month in a summer camp for Jewish children. Having never been to a summer camp and never to the sea or ocean, I bubble with excitement and anticipation. Though unaware of what to expect, I'm confident the adventure will be lots of fun, and fun it turns out to be. Jewish children from various parts of Poland gather in camps near the Baltic Sea. I like the outdoors and sports—we compete with other camps. Being good at distance jumping and volley ball, I enjoy the attention of boys, even some college boys from a nearby camp.

'We are going to town on Friday, would you like to come with us?' Zbyszek asks me.

'Who are the "we"?'

'Janek, Tosia, and possibly Jurek.'

'I'll come if we walk through the woods, it's no fun to take the train.'

I've met all these people before; their camp is nearby and they had occasionally shown up unexpectedly to visit our camp.

It takes us three hours to get to the resort town of Osielnice. Many before us must have gone this way, leaving a foot-worn pathway.

The morning sun peeking through the leafy branches throws a glare at the birches, making them glow like silver candelabra. It is late June, but the air is brisk, and we walk fast to keep warm. The chirping birds and crunch of leaves under our feet are the only sounds around.

'Where do you live, Irka?' Zbyszek asks.

'In Krakow.'

'Really?'

'Why are you surprised?'

'I live in Krakow too, I'm at the Jagiellonian University.'

'What do you study?'

'Medicine. I finished the first year.'

'So you must be nineteen.'

'How old are you?'

'That's a secret.'

I find Zbyszek very handsome, tall and muscular, though slim. Straight brown hair partially covers his tall forehead. His bright blue eyes have at times a sparkle of excitement. Observing Zbyszek's swaying walk, I wonder why he invited me to town. I don't dare to believe that this nineteen-year-old man is attracted to me. I just turned sixteen; he would think me a kid if he knew my age. Zbyszek tells me confidentially that he is a titled prince, a dubious honor in communist Poland.

'So you are the son of exploiters of the working class, a dirty bourgeois,' I kid him.

'But my mother is Jewish, doesn't this even out the score?' Zbyszek smiles mischievously.

'Not with me, ask the Party leaders.'

I am more and more at ease with Zbyszek and by the time we stop at a patisserie for iced coffee topped with whipped cream and chocolate shavings, I forget about the age difference between me and my companions. On the way back to the camp, sitting next to Zbyszek on the train, apart from Tosia and Janek, I feel as if I am on a date, though I have never been on one before. Even girls older than I seldom date; they go out in groups with boys.

Zbyszek's attention brings both a new excitement and anxiety—a nineteen-year-old man is interested in me. I am considered smart, but am I pretty?

The summer month is one adventure after another.

I am told that when the tide recedes at the Baltic Sea in early morning, it leaves behind a variety of shells and bits of amber. A few kids agree to come with me in the early morning to discover the treasures of the Baltic—assuming we get a ride. We persuade our counselor that it will be an educational experience to watch the tide pull back. It takes a lot of persuasion, but we get a ride to the seashore.

Standing in the back of a truck, squeezed in with my fellow campers, I enjoy the wind blowing in my face as we drive to the seashore, ten miles from our camp. I am a poor swimmer and afraid of deep water, but it doesn't keep me from enjoying the sea. At six in the morning, empty of swimmers and noisy bare-bottomed kids, the beach looks serene, though the waves mount high and foaming. You can see far into the distance without boundaries, making it difficult for me to think of the earth as round. A tiny speck moving on the horizon must be a ship, but I lose sight of it after a while when it merges with the cloud overhead. I stretch out on the wet sand. Though it is a little cold, it feels silky-soft, a magic carpet ready to carry me into my dreamland.

'Irka, did you come here to sleep? Get up!' one of my friends shouts.

'Coming!'

Looking for amber and interesting shells tossed out of the Baltic feels almost like picking mushrooms in the Taiga, though the surroundings are very different. Walking on the beach, my eyes glued to the ground, here and there digging my toe in the sand when something protrudes, feels like a treasure hunt. I like it.

I return to the camp with a bagful of shells and bits of amber. My next project is gluing them into a design on the top of a small wooden box. Pleased with the outcome, I keep this box for many years.

At the end of the month, I leave the camp not just with my shells-and-amber box, but also with my first awakening as a young woman to whom men can be attracted.

My friends in the orphanage are very impressed when one day Zbyszek comes asking for me. 'He is so handsome and so dignified looking,' Frida tells me. He came unannounced, we have no telephone. I am very sorry that I wasn't home and hope he comes again soon.

Thinking of meeting Zbyszek again, I am both excited and scared. I know nothing of what is expected, what is appropriate between a boy and a girl. How should a young lady act? No one ever talked to me about it. It must be very unladylike to want to kiss a boy, but I want Zbyszek to kiss me.

When I do meet Zbyszek and we go for a walk, I try to act very sophisticated and nonchalant. When he puts his hand on my shoulder, I act is if unaware of it, even though the arm burns on my skin.

Children seventeen and over will have to leave the Home. A new group of young kids has to be accommodated, and space is limited.

Once more my home and my temporary family are abruptly severed from my life. All that I had known for the last four years, the people who had been part of my daily life, my family and my friends, have all vanished, scattered into different parts of the city, country, and world. Some of the children have relatives with whom they can make a home, a few are moving to Israel. Marta, one of my roommates, is going to France where a relative agreed to sponsor her. I am moving into a residence for needy college students quite a distance from the orphanage.

My new home is a tiny room I share with two medical students in a house owned by the Jewish community. The four-story dingy old gray building houses the offices of community agencies, with the third floor reserved for students. A room with two tables and a few chairs is our dining room where I eat mostly cold food, as the cooked meals are not very palatable. I am the only high school girl on the floor and feel out of place when all the others show off their university caps in a variety of colors, depending on what they study: blue represents medicine, green is for languages, red means engineering, and so on. Ignoring me, my roommates study aloud, the room was theirs—I'm just an interloper. Young men constantly flow in and out, as the door stands ajar all day. My roommates turn even more hostile when the visiting male students start paying attention to me. I try to stay out of the room as much as I can. When the dining room is quiet, I study there; otherwise I have a tough time finding a peaceful corner to do homework. I watch amazed as two students across the hallway rub their still clean caps on the floor to make them look worn—no one wants to admit being a freshman.

Moving out of the Home also means changing schools. I was in a school just for Jewish children and now, as far as I know, I am the only Jewish kid in my public high school class of forty-five students. I interpret all student eyes as being hostile to me. The comradery of fellow students and the respect of teachers that I was used to is gone. I am a stranger. The school is quite a distance from my new residence, so I have to take the streetcar. As we pass a church, everyone in the streetcar but me crosses themselves. All passengers' eyes turn to me. Krakow is full of churches and each time we pass one, the scene is repeated.

My stipend provides for not much more than transportation to school, but lately I have a little money from an unexpected source. Periodically, I get a package of used clothing from the United States, from Esther's mother. Most of these things I give to a store on consignment and use the money for my other expenses. Though it's not a reliable source of income, I am delighted and grateful to have the money for necessities—and for theater tickets, when some of it is left over. My correspondence with Esther is a source of pleasure. I like knowing how a girl in America lives and try to envision her home and her city that she identifies as Brooklyn, rather than New York. I realize that the used clothes I receive are not Esther's, but assume that she too must be as wealthy as the people who give away dresses that are scarcely worn. Esther's mother sounds like a warm and loving woman. In one of her letters, Esther has written that her parents would like to adopt me. I'm extremely moved but reply that I have a mother, but because she is unable to provide for me, I am in the Home.

For some time, Mama, Halina, and Wolek have been talking about immigrating to Israel, a place I know little about. Establishing a life in Poland on the ruins of a devastated family and Jewish community is particularly hard for my mother. It is not the Poland she knew and remembered. 'I live here on the graves of my brothers and sisters, I can't breathe this air,' my mother declares.

I am very conflicted. Initially I am unwilling to join them. A Zionist I surely am not, nor do I know how strong my Jewish identity is. What does it mean to be a Zionist, how should it feel to be a Jew? I question myself periodically and come up with no answer.

I want to study medicine and also theater. Zbyszek and I talked numerous times about psychodrama as a means of helping the mentally ill. I want to study so many things.

'A seventeen-year-old girl has to be with her family,' Mama tells me, forgetting that I am not with my family now nor have I been with them for many years.

I am torn by the many aspects of my life I would be leaving behind: studies, Zbyszek, a language I know so well. My report cards state "*Doskonała Polonistka*"—an expert of the Polish language. I don't know a word of Hebrew, the language of Israel. Now, out of the Home, I again feel homeless and lonely, and a little scared to forge my way alone. Seeing a new country, the exotic Israel, I tell myself, will be exciting, and I decide to go.

Knowing I will have to support myself in Israel without the knowledge of Hebrew, I take evening courses in therapeutic massage. We all apply for exit visas. Halina, Wolek, their baby, and my mother get their visas, but not I. There is no way to find out why I was refused the visa, so we apply again. This time Mama and I get visas, but not my sister and brother-in-law. We conclude that we might never be able to leave together, so the family decides that Mama and I should go to Israel while Halina and Wolek continue applying. We hope they will join us soon.

There is a limited list of things we are allowed to take out of Poland. This list even specifies how many dresses, skirts, etc. No valuables of any kind, but we have none. All our belongings fit into one small suitcase, including two pounds of dried salami we will sell for money to meet our basic needs. We were told that salami is very expensive in Israel and difficult to buy. Mom's brother in Paris sent us money to buy the salami and some other small items. We each have basically three changes of clothing.

I am seventeen when I leave Poland, a few months before graduating from high school. Zbyszek, saddened by my departure, comes to see me off at the train station. I too am aching and torn but try not to think about it. I stay by the window and see how my friend runs after my train until he fades into a small doll-like figure."

"Mom, looking at you, one would never know you went through so much hardship. Do you often think about your childhood and the war years?"

"Occasionally, some event or thought brings back a flash of memory of my childhood, but I don't dwell on it. My life is full and I appreciate all my blessings. And you, my daughter, are one of them."

Naomi puts her arms around me and lingers for a minute.

"What about this Zbyszek, did he become your boyfriend?"

"Not what you would call a boyfriend, but we became romantic friends."

"You mean no sex?"

"No sex, but he told me if I married him, my hands would never touch dirty water, I would be his princess. Well, my girl, I wouldn't know how to be a princess, nor would I want to be one."

"Mom, you are a princess in many ways, and a very special woman. I want to write a movie about your life. I will, Mom."

"Thank you, Naomi, I'll be honored."

My son Avner
High school graduation,
1976.
(Photo courtesy of
Winship Studio.)

My son Dan 2012.

My daughter Naomi,
in 1994, shortly before
she was killed in a traffic
accident.

Lisa, Dan's wife.

My grandchildren Josh, Carly, Adam.

12

Israel

"Mom, coming to Israel must have been another tough step. Not knowing anyone, not having any money, not knowing the language, how did you do it?"

"Just a day at a time, or sometimes only a meal at a time. I did what it took to survive. Though the Holocaust ended, the turmoil in my life did not. I had to fight for my existence and do it all alone."

"I arrived in Israel from Poland on a slow-moving ship, a ship that sailed to the shores of Haifa at the speed of a breast-stroke. It carried passengers whose crossing, like my mother's and mine, was paid for by some organization in Israel. We embarked in Haifa almost four weeks from the day we boarded the ship in Italy; it had waited for additional passengers to arrive from many corners of the world.

We were housed in the belly of the ship, on wooden platforms one above the other, with just enough space to place our bodies at night. The one small suitcase my mother and I shared we stowed under our sleeping space. We were lucky to get the lower bunk and could use the space below it.

I awoke the first night to find a heavy, limp arm, wrapped in fur, hanging over my face. For a moment, I wasn't sure whether I was dreaming or if I was awake. Jumping off the bunk, I stood a moment, rubbing my eyes, looking around, hardly able to see, but soon realized that a human hand was sticking out of that fur. On the bunk above me slept a man who resembled a gorilla. Never before and never since have I seen a man with that much hair on his body. The thick, black growth covered his torso like a fur coat with three-quarter-length sleeves, with a line on his arm where the hair abruptly ended, as though the furrier had run out of fur.

Our quarters were extremely hot, and we had to sleep in a minimum of clothing. During the days, I spent my time where the light and sun could be found.

The ship was packed, and to move on the deck, you had to elbow your way and walk gingerly to not step on anyone's feet. When the bell rang for lunch or dinner, it looked like a stampede of wildebeest in Africa.

A few first-class passengers had private cabins. In Krakow, I would buy a cheap standing-room ticket to the theater or opera and nonchalantly walk into a balcony or box seat area. Frequently some young gentleman would give me his seat and stand behind me during the entire performance. I didn't think I could try this method to get a private cabin, but I fantasized about it.

One such private-cabin passenger was Jamal, a young Arab who was traveling with his pregnant wife. He often tried to get my attention by offering me chocolate or his chair on the deck. He asked me a lot of questions in a broken German, but since my knowledge of German wasn't much better, our conversations were limited. I was glad to have company; it was boring doing nothing all day long.

I found Jamal extremely handsome, in an exotic way. With his dark eyes, olive complexion, and well-trimmed mustache, he looked so different from all the other boys and men I knew. He wore crisp white slacks and silk tunics, looking to me like a character from "A Thousand and One Nights." I was pleased and flattered that this handsome, elegant man paid so much attention to me. As his wife was very obviously pregnant and often seasick, I didn't see much of her.

One morning my mother came looking for me; she was flushed, out of breath, and appeared as though trying to hide from someone. This man from "A Thousand and One Nights" had asked her for my hand in marriage! He wanted me to be his second wife and had offered to take care not just of me but also of my mother. I thought it was a joke and said, 'See Mama, you just found someone who wants to support you, and you can be a lady of leisure and stay in bed eating bonbons.'

'Irka, he is serious.'

'How could he be serious? He has a wife.'

'I don't know, he said he likes you very much and wants you for his second wife.'

'Mama, the man is crazy.'

Jamal spoke to me himself and declared that our meeting was destiny. He'd met his first wife on a ship, and I was destined to be his other wife. I told him I had no intention of becoming anyone's wife yet, and surely not his. Out of curiosity, I asked how many wives he planned to have, and how many at one time. He answered that he was rich and could afford more than one bride. This situation was so bizarre that I did everything possible to avoid him for the rest of our voyage. Jamal, however, was very persistent and would show up out of nowhere, even following me after we'd landed in Israel. Mama feared that he might kidnap me, but eventually he lost track of us after we relocated.

Upon our arrival in Israel, we were placed in *Shaar Alya*, a transition/quarantine camp for immigrants, about twenty miles from Haifa. The camp housed thousands of newcomers in army barracks surrounded by yellow earth that turned into clouds of dust with each step. It was too hot and dusty to stay outdoors under the scorching sun, but too muggy to be under a roof. A wire fence surrounded the compound; it felt like imprisonment. Eager to see the outside world, I wasn't going to wait for official permission to leave the camp. A young Israeli soldier enlarged an existing gap in the fence and helped me get out. I was to keep this escape route a secret.

We came to Israel without a penny to our name, only the kilo of dried salami that could be converted into cash. Money for the bus ride to Haifa came from the salami my mother sold. Without Hebrew, or knowing a soul in the city, I ventured out to discover what that new world, Israel, was like. Though my mother came with me to Israel, I did not view her as my caregiver; she hadn't been that since I was a young child. I knew I had to take care of myself, and I was eager to start looking for work.

On my second visit to Haifa, I headed straight to the major hospital to inquire about work. The employment office waiting room was full of people sitting on chairs against the wall. It seemed like nothing was happening; no one was coming out of the office and no one was walking in, we were all just sitting, waiting and waiting. After what seemed like hours, a woman showed up in the waiting room and announced, 'No more interviews today, come tomorrow.'

My bus money was running out fast, and I knew I didn't have money left for many "tomorrows."

'What is your name, girl?' a woman standing in front of me asked in Yiddish.

I raised my eyes to this gentle-looking, soft-spoken middle-aged woman. 'Irena Miller,' I answered. The woman lowered herself into an empty chair next to me.

'Where are you from Irena?'

'I came from Poland a few days ago.'

'Where are you staying now?'

'In *Shaar Aliya.*'

The woman sat quietly for a while, looking at me intensely. She dug into her handbag and pulled out a business card. 'Irena, if you don't find work, come see me,' and she handed me the card which read "Dr. Shoshana Altman, Dentist." I thanked Dr. Altman and put the card in my pocket, not thinking that I would ever go to see her.

When the money ran out, I hitchhiked to Haifa. Watching how soldiers stood on the road with their thumbs up, I did the same, and it worked. For the next few days, I made the rounds of Kupat Cholim clinics in the city. When a clinic had no need for me, I asked for the addresses of others. Eventually I found a job in a physical therapy clinic, but I had no place to stay. My mother was being relocated to a tent camp about two hours from Haifa and away from any established community. I was determined to stay in Haifa; I hadn't come to Israel to be shoved away into a tent who knows where.

Though I didn't think I would ask Shoshana Altman to find work for me, I kept her card.

But when I found out I had only a few days left before the people in my barrack had to vacate the camp to make room for the next group of refugees, I hitched a ride to Haifa and showed up at the home and office of Dr. Altman.

'I am sorry, girl, but she isn't home now,' a man told me at the door.

'I would like to wait for her, may I?' Without asking me who I was or what I wanted, the man led me into the small living room. 'You can wait here, but I don't know when Shoshana will be back.'

'Thank you, I will wait.'

I waited for an hour, for two hours, sitting on a chair, looking at the blank walls. I was getting very hungry, but I was determined to see Dr. Altman, the only person I knew in all of Israel. Finally the door opened and Shoshana walked in.

'I wondered what happened to you, Irena,' she said, standing in the door.

'I found work.'

'Good.'

'Yes, but I don't have anywhere to stay.'

Shoshana stood silently for a minute, a heavy canvas bag in her hand, a cabbage and a bunch of carrots visible on top.

'What kind of work?'

'In *Cupat Cholim*, on Jaffo Street.'

'What about your mother, where is she?'

'They will relocate her next week to a tent camp north of Haifa—I don't know the name of it.'

For the first time I noticed how tall Dr. Altman was. Dressed in a brown cotton skirt, a white blouse, and sandals, she looked older and thinner than I remembered.

'Are you hungry, Irena?'

'No, thank you,' I lied, embarrassed to admit I was.

Dr. Altman walked into the kitchen and came back with a bowl of oranges. 'To eat our wonderful oranges, you don't have to be hungry. When I came to *Eretz*, Israel, we didn't have much more than oranges, but they kept us alive.' She pulled up a chair next to me.

The orange was wonderful, sweet and juicy. I had to use a lot of willpower to eat only one, as I hadn't eaten anything the whole day. Oranges were a novelty for me; before coming to Israel, I had never eaten one—it fell into the category of exotic food for the very rich.

'My daughter is at the University in Jerusalem, but my niece is sleeping in her bed and,' Shoshana paused as if searching for words to finish the sentence.

'Take the job,' she said resolutely. 'I will put up a cot for you in the living room right next to the piano.'

'Thank you, but I will not have any money to pay you until the end of the month.'

'Pay me for what?'

'Staying in your home.'

'You are in Israel, we take care of one another. You will stay and eat with us until you find a better place.'

The next day I packed my few belongings in a paper bag and hitchhiked to Haifa, ready to start my new life. I didn't know exactly where they were relocating my mother, but I assured her that I would find out and visit her after I received my first pay.

The first day at work, I learned that my job was temporary, filling in for a woman on maternity leave. I didn't tell Shoshana about it, not wanting her to feel sorry for me. I was sure I would find another job when this one was over.

A few days into my work, I learned from a woman in the clinic about *Baith Hachalucot,* a house for immigrant girls, and I went to inquire about admission.

'*Bachurah* (girl), there is a long waiting list; I can add your name to it, but don't know when your turn will come.'

'Please put me on the waiting list.'

'Come every few days to check with us.'

'*Toda* (thanks), I will.'

My job was to help the physical therapists in whatever way needed, but I didn't know any Hebrew and could communicate only with patients who spoke Polish, Russian, or

Yiddish. Still, it felt good to work, particularly getting my first paycheck!

On my way back from work, I stopped at the outdoor market and bought fruits and vegetables the Altmans had been using: lots of grapes, bananas, oranges. Meat, butter, and many other food items had been rationed. I gave my ration coupons to Shoshana. On rare occasions, when we would receive a half pound of beef per person on our ration coupons, she would make a stew, which was quite a treat for us.

The following Saturday I went to visit my mother, taking two buses to get there. I waited under the scorching sun for what seemed a very long time until my second bus arrived.

I had to ask numerous local people how to get to the immigrants' tent camp.

It turned out to be a long walk from the bus stop to the camp. There were no streets, or any other organized way of finding a tenant among the 200 tents. I moved from tent to tent asking, 'Do you know where I could find Bella Miller?'

'Sorry, girl, I don't know,' was the answer over and over.

My shirt was getting wet with sweat and I was very thirsty. I looked in all directions but could find no water in sight.

I moved to the next row of tents. 'Do you know where Bella Miller lives?'

'Three tents down this way,' a woman answered. But my mother was not in the tent. I walked around in the area until I heard her voice.

'What a surprise, Irka!' She was happy to see me. Of course it was a surprise, we had no telephones.

'I told you, Mama, I would come to see you after I got my first paycheck.'

'Yes, you did.'

It took my eyes a few seconds to adjust to the darkness in the tent, even though there was a big opening for the door. The only things in the tent were a cot, the suitcase we brought from Poland, a cooking pot, and some metal utensils sitting on a heavy cardboard box.

'How do you cook, how do you eat, Mama?'

My mother turned the cardboard box around and pulled out a single-flame kerosene burner. Seeing me observe the object, she said, 'This is a *ptiliah*, you can cook anything you want on it, you just have to watch the flame and adjust it periodically.' Mama dug into her box to see what more she could find in it.

'You must be hungry, Irka, all I have are green peppers and bread; I can buy only the amount of cottage cheese or margarine that I can eat in a day. It's so hot, I can't keep it overnight.'

'Mama, bread and peppers will be fine, but I am very thirsty, where do you get your water?'

'There's a water hose next to the latrine, but I have some in a bottle.' The water was almost hot, but I was so thirsty that it didn't matter; I gulped down the whole bottle.

My mother was getting a temporary subsidy from the Israeli government until she found employment. Not knowing the language, not having a profession, and having physical limitations made her employment possibilities very limited. With the influx of immigrants from Europe, even professional people had difficulty finding work. After a few visits to my mother, I learned that one of the bus drivers was actually a physician. Initially, I thought it was a nickname when I heard the locals greet the driver, 'Shalom, Dr. Blum.'

When a young woman was very selective in choosing a mate, there was a saying, 'My, my, she's so picky, a doctor isn't good enough for her—she thinks she deserves a bus driver?'

There was a surplus of physicians and other professionals, but drivers were organized in a cooperative and earning very well.

As advised, I stopped at the immigrant girls' house every two days to inquire whether there was a bed for me. 'Wait until two more girls get married, and you will have a bed.' The only time a girl would leave the house was when she got married, or decided to go back to her country of origin. Renting an apartment was impossible, none was available, and the cost would have been prohibitive, even if one was. Housing was extremely scarce. My co-workers found it unbelievable that a stranger took me into her home. 'People don't want to take in family members; they will never get them out, no place to go,' one co-worker commented.

'Why did she pick you out of all the people in that room at that hospital?' another asked.

'I don't know, maybe just luck,' I answered.

The week I was told a bed had finally become available and I could move in, I was informed that my job had ended; the worker returned from her maternity leave.

I thanked Shoshana for all she had done for me and moved out the next day, without telling her I had lost my job.

The four young women I shared a room with were strangers, from different countries, without a common language. Circumstances had thrown the five of us together into a room in a house for immigrant girls. The two-story gray stone building had sixteen rooms and housed young women from many parts of the world. Being a Jew seemed to be the only commonality among us.

The year was 1951; the country was swelling with immigrants. I'd waited several months for the privilege of living in the house and felt fortunate to get even one fifth of a room, without a closet, a shower, or any other conveniences. It was a bed of my own I didn't have to pay for—who could've asked for more?

I had some money saved from my job and decided to enroll in an *Ulpan*, an intensive course of Hebrew, a language so different from the ones I knew; even knowing Yiddish didn't help me. Though I was very cautious about my expenditures, I treated myself to a Polish-Hebrew dictionary and a pair of cheap sandals. In the scorching heat of 100 degrees F, my heavy shoes from Poland felt like torture tools, burning my feet and causing me blisters. Both of my investments I put to heavy use. I walked everywhere, taking buses only to visit my mother. The dictionary helped me read books when I understood only a fraction of the words. 'You are a brave girl,' the librarian told me when I had difficulty telling her in Hebrew what I wanted.

'Read, read, it's good for you.' She encouraged me.

Five weeks into my Hebrew course I had to drop out, my money ran out.

Again I set out on job-hunting rounds, but nothing was available. I left my name in every outpatient clinic I found, and revisited them often to inquire whether a job opening became available. At the same time I was looking for interim work wherever possible so I could eat. I noticed a posting in the hall of my residence, 'A girl wanted to clean the floor in a wedding hall.' I ran to the nearby office that placed the notice to ensure that no one beat me to the job. I needed the work; I had only two green peppers and a piece of bread left and not a penny to my name. 'I will take it. Where is the place?'

The next morning I got up at five, took the green pepper I had left, and went looking for the wedding hall. At 6:30 I found myself in front of the long brown building, searching for a doorway. There were many small windows, all high up, but no door. Do they expect me to climb through a window?

I thought. Looking in the back of the building, I noticed what seemed like a gate to a fortress, with heavy brass knockers hanging at the side. I knocked a few times before a man showed up at the gate.

'Are you the girl to scrub the floor?' he asked.

'Yes, I am.'

The man handed me a big bucket, a scrub brush, and a container filled with soap paste. '*Bachurah*, get on your knees and scrub very hard, the floor is dirty after a big dancing party. Change the water many times.' He handed me a few rags to dry the floor and left the room.

I hiked up my skirt and tucked it around my waist to keep from getting it wet. After a while on my knees, the wooden floor felt like a hot rock burning my skin and grinding my bones. I wished I could use two of the rags to place under my knees, but I needed them to dry the floor. I had been scrubbing for hours, but the room was huge and there was so much left of the floor to be done. I must have carried at least ten buckets of water from the basement. The green pepper I ate on the way to work didn't stop my hunger for very long. I was thinking of what I would buy to eat after I got my payment. Suddenly I heard voices not far from me. I raised my head and saw a young woman and two men with her, headed in my direction. I pulled down my skirt and resumed scrubbing. The group stopped almost at my working hands. They were discussing the wedding arrangements.

'Definitely stuffed fresh figs, I don't care where you have to get them, I want figs,' declared the bride. With her next move, her foot landed on my hand. Biting my lip not to scream, I pushed her off, 'Watch where you are stepping!'

The woman looked down, as if seeing me for the first time, and continued her menu conversation. I felt like pouring the dirty water in my bucket right over her head. If not for my hungry belly, I would have left at once.

It was late afternoon by the time I finished the work, feeling tired, hungry, and full of indignation. This ignorant woman treated me as if I were dirt on the floor, or invisible. What a stupid, empty-headed creature she was, I kept thinking. My skirt still wet and dirty, I walked in the residential area, glad that no one knew me. I stopped at the market, bought two loaves of bread, a small yogurt, and two oranges. Little by little, ripping off tiny pieces, I finished off one loaf before reaching my room.

I responded to another "labor wanted" notice for a tobacco factory worker.

I was placed in a small room with eight girls, all of us sitting on the floor, leaning against the walls. Between us was a tall pile of tobacco leaves we had to sort according to size, color, and condition of the leaves.

'No talking, *bachurot*, just pay attention to the leaves and make sure you put them in the correct piles,' the supervisor reprimanded us. After an hour or two sitting in this room piled with tobacco leaves, I was unable to talk anyway. I kept coughing and coughing, and had difficulty breathing. Toward the end of my day's work, my chest was burning and stiff like a board, and I thought I was suffocating. After one week I had to give up the work, my chest pain and difficulty breathing became totally incapacitating. Unable to eat much during that week left me with some money, which I decided to use on bus fare to visit my mother.

'I wondered what happened to you, Irka, you haven't been here for a long time.'

'I was busy working.'

'You are so thin, aren't you eating enough?'

'I am okay, Mama.'

For the first time in about two months, I ate a cooked meal. On her *ptilia* Mama cooked dumplings with farmer's cheese and sugar; it tasted wonderful. She still was not able to find work, and like most of the residents of the tent camp, continued to be supported by the government.

'Where have you been, Irena? We didn't know how to find you.' I was greeted in one of the *Kupat Cholim* clinics where I kept asking for work. Well, a job was waiting for me as a physical therapist in a clinic that specialized in treatment of polio cases. All I knew was to give a massage, but they promised to teach me how to use the equipment in the clinic. I was elated; I had a bed and a job!

My working hours were until 7 p.m. On the way to my residence I would buy a yogurt and cottage cheese and eat it sitting on my bed. The room had no chairs or table. On rare occasions I treated myself to a vegetarian meal at *"Midbach Poalim,"* The Workers' Kitchen. Meat of any kind, or fish, was too expensive. I felt lonely looking at all the unfamiliar faces. My loneliness was intensified on Saturdays when I joined the crowd of promenading people on the main street of Haifa. Families chatting, couples holding hands, but I didn't know anyone. Mania, one of my co-workers, also from Poland, invited me to her apartment for dinner. A cooked meal was a special treat. I appreciated the invitation and enjoyed the dinner, but left feeling sad. Mania, who had wealthy relatives, owned her apartment, but I wondered if I would ever live in a room of my own. Not a moment of privacy in my surroundings. The door of my shared room had been constantly ajar with strangers coming and going. The only space I could call my own was my bed and the space underneath it where I stored bread and yogurt, my staple foods.

One Saturday, coming down the stairs in my flowery long housecoat from Poland, on my way to the shower stalls in the basement, I bumped into a young man running up two steps at a time, ignoring everyone as if he were late for a train to an important destination. When I returned to my room he was sitting on my bed. Puzzled, I looked at him. He stood up.

'Are you Irena Miller?'

'Yes, I am. And who are you?'

'I am David Saferstein. Your friend Shlomo told me about you.'

'Told you what?'

'That you want to learn English. I can be your teacher,' he said in broken Hebrew.

Before me was a man of 5 feet 8 inches, with blue, penetrating eyes and a beautiful smile that held mystery and mischief. The khaki shorts and snuggly fitting shirt displayed his broad shoulders, strong legs, and flat belly. He was radiating charm and eagerness to please. I was self-conscious about the towel on my head and the housecoat, which I suspected wasn't very flattering. We stood a moment looking at each other; David with an inviting smile, and I, the towel falling in my face, eager to bring this encounter to an end.

'How much do you charge for lessons?'

'Oh, I wouldn't charge you anything—you're a friend of Shlomo.'

'Why so?'

'Well, you could teach me Hebrew; you speak it much better than I.'

'That's a deal.'

Shlomo was an engineer who worked with David. I had gone out with him several times but found him boring and stopped dating him. It turned out that when David had bragged that he could get any woman to bed, Shlomo had challenged him. 'I know one girl you won't get too far with.'

'Give me her address,' David had responded.

Shlomo changed his mind and refused to give David my name and address. David kept bugging him for so long that Shlomo finally gave in. I knew perfectly well that the English lessons were a ploy, but I was willing to go for it.

We didn't have many language lessons, but when David proposed marriage four months later, I accepted. Loneliness strengthened my desire for nesting, and I was in love and eager to play house, even in a Quonset hut without a ceiling, electricity, or toilet. The place did have water; the building used to be the shower hut for the British military.

How could a young woman not fall for a good-looking guy with the courage to leave his country, the United States, to fight in Israel's War of Independence, a man who, at twenty-five, was an engineer with many accomplishments? A man who shouted, 'I love Irena' as we drove through the streets of Haifa on his motorcycle.

We ventured on the motorcycle into the mountains of Galilee, surrounded by hostile Arab villages. Our eyes penetrating the darkness, we felt like fearless conquerors, too young to be afraid. Yet, on still nights, our tension mounted, but the full impact of the danger we'd been in hit us only after we'd arrived back to Haifa, greeted by friendly lights. The motorcycle had a small, meagerly padded backseat. After a few hours of riding, hanging onto David for safety, I was sore and walked gingerly. Neither the hostile surroundings nor the discomfort of the seat, however, restricted our explorations. Most of the time the motorcycle carried us faithfully, but at times we had to carry the motorcycle.

One night when we were riding on a dark mountain with no human in sight and no sign of life, the engine stopped and we couldn't restart it. In the silence I could hear my heart beating. We were hours away from any city and had the choice of spending the night in the open or taking our chances on finding a friendly village. We hid the motorcycle behind bushes and walked through the darkness to the nearest settlement. Luck was with us; we found Jewish settlers who put us up for the night and helped us find a mechanic in the morning.

We were married in the home of a rabbi. The room, scarcely able to hold the dozen guests, had no furniture other than a long narrow table with folding chairs. The sparseness and bare white walls made this reception room look uninhabited. My mother and her friend baked cakes on top of a kerosene burner. David and I bought wine—that was it. Our wedding gifts, which we appreciated, consisted of a colander; a box of tomatoes from David's brother, who lived on a kibbutz; a few potatoes; and the tops of green onions. The potatoes and the onions were a gift from one of my patients. My patient had left the onion bulbs in the ground, so they would regenerate, I assume. David and I got married in December; vegetables in winter were scarce, and onions particularly were considered a treasure.

Many patients in my clinic were young children who had contracted polio; others, however, had a wide range of medical problems. One, a twenty-five-year-old man, had been coming twice a week to have his legs massaged. A towel draped over his loins, I massaged and massaged his thighs, hoping to cure whatever ailed him, but he wasn't getting any better. The man continued coming twice a week. Frustrated with my ineffectiveness, I sought advice from the director of the clinic.

'Don't worry; we'll cure him in no time.'

'Yes?'

My patient was reassigned to Wilhelm, a burly, no-nonsense German immigrant. After one massage with Wilhelm, my patient was cured, and I got a little wiser.

For the first time since I was a young child, I had a place to call my own home. During the war, when I was still with my parents in the Soviet Union, we lived with a few families in one room; then came orphanages in Uzbekistan and Poland.

It was a minor inconvenience that our so-called house had no electricity and no ceiling, and that the roof was a curved sheet of corrugated metal. It was a home, and I was content to have four walls; a ceiling would come later, I figured. The building, originally a long barrack for British soldiers, had been subdivided and taken over by a number of families.

As his wedding gift, David's company gave him the use of a truck for one day, the day of our wedding. From early morning we loaded and unloaded bricks and other building materials to improve our portion of the hut. By the time our very small and simple wedding took place in the late afternoon, I was exhausted. Luckily the ceremony was short; otherwise, I might have fallen asleep. All I remember of the ceremony is Mrs. Simon repeating to me in a grave voice, 'One more, one more, don't be afraid, my dear, it will be soon over,' as I was walking in circles under the chupah, the wedding canopy, with my mother at my side. The woman sounded so funny that I had a tough time stifling the giggles. I didn't know what I was supposed to be afraid of. A few days later, Mrs. Simon, the wife of the director of the physical therapy clinic where I worked, tried to educate me about sex.

'Do you know, my dear, about the marital bed? You are so young, a child, eighteen years old. Did your mother talk to you about it?'

'Thank you. I'm fine.'

'Talk to me about it, my dear, anytime you want.'

I was a novice, but I trusted Mother Nature more than old Mrs. Simon's attempts to instruct me in sex.

Well, I was a married woman and had to get used to my new status. When the morning after our wedding, I walked out of our hut and a neighbor greeted me, 'Shalom, Mrs. Engineer,' I turned to see who was behind me. It dawned on me after a moment that the man was greeting me! 'Shalom,' I responded. That was funny, I thought—me, an eighteen-year-old girl, 'Mrs. Engineer.' I didn't know the man, but I was certain he was from Poland. I recognized the Polish etiquette of addressing a married woman by her husband's title or position: 'Mrs. Doctor,' 'Mrs. Lawyer.' Just the same, it sounded strange to hear someone addressing me in such a manner.

David and I had no refrigerator, but it wouldn't have helped to have one, our hut had no electricity. The ice deliveryman came to the neighborhood daily, but we weren't home. After work David and I bought a big block of ice, and sitting on the back of our motorcycle, I held it with giant metal prongs, water dripping at my side. By the time we reached our home, the ice would have melted to less than half its original size. What was left of the block, I slid into the small icebox. With the limited food supply, we had no need for even that big an icebox. Subsidized bread, cottage cheese, and yogurt were our staple foods. In season, we had vegetables and lots of citrus fruit. Fresh figs and guavas had a very short season, but they were wonderful. Occasionally, we found some delicacy in the grocery store, such as herring spread in a tube, like toothpaste. David and I weren't hungry; life seemed good.

A few days after our wedding, we took a train to Jerusalem to file our marriage documents with the U.S. Embassy. David, born in the States, was a U.S. citizen. December was the time of torrential rains; returning late at night, we found our house flooded. The bed, a metal frame and cotton mattress, looked as though it were floating, the water reaching up an inch or two short of the mattress. There was no place else to go, so we elevated the small bed on a few bricks and went to sleep, too tired to worry about ending up in the water. By morning the water was gone; there were advantages to having drainage grooves the size of a dried-out brook!

With the aid of an oil lamp, I read in Polish and in Hebrew the books I borrowed from the Haifa Public Library—Upton Sinclair's *The Jungle*, Victor Hugo's *Les Miserables*, Dostoyevski's *Crime and Punishment* and *The Brothers Karamazov*—and I didn't feel poor or deprived. I felt freedom and power to aspire to and plan a future that would include education, interesting work, and visits to other countries. As I hitchhiked to work, I imagined future travel. One day I startled my neighbors by arriving at my doorstep on a fire engine; I had hailed the fire engine and they picked me up and drove me home. These were still pioneering times, with few rules and little caution. Hitchhiking was a common way of transportation.

In the community where many lived in circumstances like David's and mine—or worse, in tents like my mother's—there was no poverty of spirit. I didn't complain about these conditions or find them difficult to accept, other than the cockroaches, which at night took over our place. Huge and disgusting, they were revolting to coexist with. They came in through the drainage system, an open ditch to the outside. I could think of nothing more abhorrent than a cockroach on the cooking counter. I still shudder when I think about them.

In time David and I installed electricity by ourselves. One connecting box even had my name on it. David encountered a technical problem he couldn't solve and I came up with a solution; he dubbed this electrical joint 'Irka box.' In my underpants, I climbed between the ceiling and roof to stretch and tie electrical wires; summer having come, it was too hot for any more clothing. After three separate inspections, we finally switched on the lights. Oh, what a thrilling moment to light all the three naked, lonely bulbs that hung from the ceiling on wires. David and I celebrated by burning the lights all night.

A friend who knew about plumbing helped us set up a toilet. For some reason the toilet bowl had to be elevated off the floor and resembled a royal throne. After using the outhouse in the winter, getting soaked by the rain and hit by the door when it was windy, this new seat of ours truly did feel regal.

I heard about a free government program, *Seminar L'morim* (teachers college), in which one could study for a year to become a public school teacher. I wasted no time making an appointment with the director. By then I had been about a year in Israel and was told by many that my Hebrew was amazingly good for a newcomer, yet it still was a new language, limiting my ability to express myself. When during the course of the interview I found out the director, Uri Levi, also spoke Polish, I switched to my native language to convince him to accept me into the program.

After a lengthy interview, which seemed to have tired *adon* (Mr.) Levi, he paused, both hands under his chin, just looking at me. 'It's a very demanding course of study, and a great responsibility. Do you think you will be ready in a year's time to be a teacher?'

'Oh, yes, definitely,' I responded.

I was accepted, and the next day submitted my resignation at the clinic.

I was the youngest of the 25 students in the training program. It was indeed a demanding schedule. Six days a week the classes started at eight in the morning and lasted until four or five in the afternoon, with only a short break for lunch. I did not need much time to eat my bread and margarine and an orange, when in season. Fridays we left around three. I had a long walk to the bus stop, and from the last stop home.

Our days had been packed with lectures, and the lectures left very little time for questions and discussions. There seemed to be an enormous amount of material to cover. Though all of the students were Jews, none was born in Israel, and very few of us knew Jewish history, traditions, and other such things expected of the teachers. Public schools did not teach or promote religion, but biblical stories were presented in various grades.

After ten months of training, Uri, as we all began to address our director, called me into his office, 'Orna (the Hebrew name I was given at the school), we have a school for you, you will start teaching next week.' I was very excited, too confident and too naive to be anxious. 'I am sure you will be a very good teacher. You are a bright kid and a gutsy girl.' He paused for a minute, sat looking at the bare walls, the small electric fan blowing in his face. 'Do you know why I accepted you into the program? I thought that if this girl has enough courage to want to be a teacher within a year's time, and cannot even convince me in Hebrew why I should admit her, then I should have enough courage to take a chance on her. I am glad I did.'

Forty-nine boisterous, noisy first-graders from almost as many countries, became my charge. My initial challenge was to remember the strange-sounding names with origins in many cultures and languages. The first day in class I realized that many of my students did not speak Hebrew; they had no idea what I was talking about. I tried to seat each new immigrant child with a Hebrew-speaking one. I found myself facing problems my training did not prepare me for. My teacher's education did not address how to interest students with such diverse backgrounds, how to teach kids who don't understand the spoken language, and how to maintain sufficient discipline to be able to teach. The school had no one with whom to consult; I was on my own and very frustrated. I experimented with special ways and projects to engage the troublemakers and the few hyperactive kids. Having forty-nine pupils in a small classroom with traditional double-seat student desks did not allow for much flexibility. The rule was that when a class reached fifty pupils, it had to be divided. For the two years I taught, I had forty-nine students. I am sure it was by design; there was a great shortage of teachers.

At the parent-teacher conferences, I was able to communicate with European parents using Yiddish, Polish, or Russian. However, these languages did not help with parents who spoke only Arabic. My school was located in an area with a big number of Jewish immigrants from Arab countries.

I had to learn quickly and be innovative with very limited resources. At the end of the first school year, all my students spoke fluent Hebrew and met all required standards, and I felt like a teacher. Teaching became more rewarding.

The following year I moved up with the same students to teach second grade.

My mother was relocated to a tent camp closer to Haifa. She found work in a few households cleaning and cooking. The work was physically demanding and difficult for her, but even more stressful was the injury to her pride. I believe the problem was not how she was treated by her employers but how she perceived her status. According to her Polish-Jewish upbringing, a domestic worker was someone of the lowest class, and never a Jew. My mother had been raised in a home that had a live-in maid, a Polish peasant woman. Listening to my mother make fun of the women she worked for and express how she felt demeaned by her work, I told myself that I would never find myself in such a situation. I will have a profession and feel dignity in the work I do.

David and I continued living in the Quonset hut and co-existing with the cockroaches. On our salaries we could not even fantasize about moving into an apartment—the cost was far beyond our potential. The desire for better living conditions, David's unhappiness with his work, and my eagerness to see the great America drove our decision to go to the United States for two years. The plan was to earn enough money in the U.S. for a down payment on a *shikun*, a government-sponsored condominium in Israel. We had saved enough money for two one-way tickets on an old ship in the cheapest section, and we set a tentative date for departure.

Our plans, however, had to be changed. David received a call from the kibbutz in which his brother Simcha lived. Simcha's behavior became so disruptive that he no longer could function in the community. Apparently David's brother had severe emotional problems before coming to Israel, but I knew nothing about his mental illness until the kibbutz called. Simcha had to be taken to the United States to a psychiatric hospital. We had no money for an additional ticket, and Simcha could not travel by ship. Airline tickets were much more expensive than travel by boat. My mother borrowed money from a number of her friends for two airline tickets. Ships from Haifa to New York sailing infrequently, I boarded one two months before David's and Simcha's departure by air. In New York I met my pen pal Esther and her family. I stayed with them in Brooklyn until David arrived.

For the next two years we lived wherever David's work took us—Detroit, Fresno, Pasadena. I taught in a Hebrew school in Detroit and in California did whatever clerical work I could find with my very minimal English. Pregnant and with enough funds for the *shikun* down payment, we returned to Israel.

We did not enjoy our new condo for very long. David declared that he was unhappy with his work and there was no professional potential for him in Israel. After a lot of soul searching, we decided to make the United States our permanent home. In 1958 we came to the United States with our one-year-old son Avner.

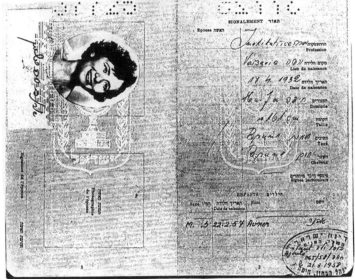

Leaving for the United States

Epilogue

I am frequently asked how my life evolved and what impact the Holocaust had on it. Everything that happened in my life influenced who I became. The Holocaust, having been a crucial part of my childhood, must have affected me in more ways than I recognize.

Like a house without a foundation, I am an adult without a childhood. My childhood ended abruptly with bombings, fire explosions, and corpses in the streets. I have no memory of a childhood friend, a toy, a game, or a shred left of anything that would remind me that I had once been a child. Occasionally I still experience the pain of this loss and have a longing for continuity in my life. I am envious of people who can revisit places where they were born and raised, who have childhood friends with shared experiences, who have extended family members around them for love and support. The Holocaust deprived me of all that and this is what I miss most in my life. I listen with pain to recollections by my women friends of bonding experiences with their mothers. Living eight years in orphanages, I have no such memories.

In times of stress my dreams are still interwoven with war experiences: I am frightened and escaping from something, but I don't remember what it is; I am freezing and have nowhere to go; I am hungry but Mama won't give me bread.

When I dream of running barefoot in the snow and my feet are hurting badly, I wake up touching my cold feet.

Yet, I had never thought of myself as a Holocaust survivor. I had no tattooed numbers on my arms, and my life had not been affected, I thought, by my war experiences. I was a woman content, full of exuberance and the joy of living.

I have lived with a feeling that nothing would ever crush me. Whatever happens to me, I will pick myself up and go on—although the death of my daughter Naomi almost destroyed me.

A single telephone call on an August night shattered my world and changed it all. It erupted like a volcano, cracking, breaking, smashing, and exploding all the particles of my life into the air. It blocked the rays of the sun; all around me turned dark, utterly dark. My Naomi was killed in a traffic accident while vacationing in Jamaica. She was only 28 years old.

The year that followed Naomi's death had been the toughest one in my life. Nothing had ever been as painful and as difficult to accept as the death of my daughter. I died with her and had to be reborn. But how?

I felt extremely lonely and isolated. Wherever I was, alone or with people, I was lonely — a coldness of the soul that nothing could warm. I was from another planet, a Martian who didn't belong on Earth. No one knew or understood all the other worlds in which I had lived in the past. No one knew what it had been for me to be a lonely, often frightened, always hungry child. They were all strangers I didn't share a common language with.

My daughter's death opened the locked drawers in the attic where I had been hiding my painful Holocaust memories. It ripped open the scab of my old wounds I thought had been fully healed, and made them bleed and ooze again.

Nothing seemed to ease my grief and pain. I read and reread some of the letters from Naomi, but that intensified the feeling of loss.

Dear Mom

It's a little after 8:00. A little after I talked to you by phone. It is before I go back to the forward motion of my life. You are still fresh on my thoughts, Irene. I have a sweet potato knish in the oven, the New York Times still spread on my couch. My stomach feels funny, I ate too much fish. I still have that part inside me which --after my Mother's departure feels very small. In my head I don't understand why the sensation of loving someone triggers emotions so deep, why the pleasure always seems mixed with feelings of loss and pain--how reality hits so deeply. The nicest thing about you coming here is that we enter into each other's lives as people. It makes me realize it's hard for me to relate to anyone—relating makes me feel so many, many things. I just wanted to say that beyond all that I'm really glad you came. I'm glad for the things you share with me. The patience and support you have in my mixed-bag way of sharing things with you. I'm glad you read my screenplay. And that you're my friend. This and more.

I love you,

Me

PS. Will you send me a copy of your Detroit Free Press letter, as well the name of the village you stayed in Asia. If you can draw me a rough map. Talk to you soon.

PPS (Later) I reworked the mother-daughter scene of my script based on suggestions you made.

Thanks

Naomi had been asking me over and over to tell her about my childhood, about my war experiences, but I kept postponing it, offering her only little tidbits. The time ran out for us. Naomi's death, though, led me to writing this book, and I want to keep my daughter as an integral part of my memoir. Posthumously, Naomi is the recipient of my Holocaust story, but it is meant for the world to read, hoping that some will find meaningful lessons in it.

I was able to keep Naomi's voice and actions in character. Most of her statements, such as wanting to write a movie about my life, admiring my bravery and courage, are taken directly from her letters I have. But I also wrote things I would have wanted to tell Naomi, and in my head, I heard her reaction. Naomi was an award winning writer and her wish to write about me intensified when she worked in the movie industry. I wonder whether something I fed my children resulted in a love of writing. My son Dan, a psychologist, is also a writer

My friends see me as a survivor, as a strong, determined woman. If being strong means having the courage to make difficult decisions, then I am strong, but I also am vulnerable and take great pains not to disclose that. I prefer to be in situations where I don't always have to be strong, where the soft and gentle part of me can predominate.

A friend observed that my ability to put things in perspective, to separate essence from trivia, must be an outcome of my Holocaust years. Having seen atrocities and survived extreme hardship and deprivation, I can never look at life superficially. I experience everything deeply; my emotions go to the core of my belly and to the tips of my fingers.

Determination and perseverance have been a constant element in my life. Nothing of what I accomplished was handed to me, I had to struggle and fight for it. Education had always been very important to me. Thus between babies, and pots and pans, I earned a bachelor's degree in psychology, a master's in social psychology, and a master's of business administration with a major in hospital management. These degrees helped me when, as a divorced woman, I had to support my three children. I was a healthcare executive with a diverse and interesting career. I ventured out at a time when a hospital could tell me in a letter, 'Our community would not accept a woman in such a position,' the position being that of an assistant administrator of the hospital, and the year 1968.

I had the privilege of serving for a year on an advisory committee in Washington DC, dealing with issues related to women, children, and substance abuse.

I believe that my great compassion for those who suffer and my fight against discrimination and prejudice have their roots in my Holocaust background. Looking at a homeless man wrapped in a blanket on the pavement, I feel the cold hard surface, and I try to understand his desperation. He is someone's son, and my thoughts turn to the mother. When I see on the news a photo of a young man or woman killed in Afghanistan, Iraq, or some other place, I experience a physical pain in my chest, and the face becomes imprinted in my memory. I grieve the loss of young lives and cry for their mothers.

Hunger particularly strikes a deep chord in me. Seeing images of hungry children in Africa, I experience their aching bellies, their feeling of hopelessness, and remember my own years of hunger. Occasionally, when I shop in a supermarket, I experience the overpowering amazement of being surrounded by all that plenty and being able to buy as much food as I want. I like to feed people I love--my family and friends. Since my home cannot hold all those I would like to feed, I contribute to organizations that work to alleviate hunger.

Telling my Holocaust story to a group of youngsters who come from difficult neighborhoods and home situations, I use my background to encourage them, to stress that no matter what life dishes out, they have the power to become the persons they want to be. 'It takes a lot of hard work, but you can do it. You have within you the power to do it,' I tell them. I would like to hold all these children in my arms and pass on to them my compassion, give them courage and strength so they can overcome all obstacles to achieving a productive and healthy life. After one of my talks at the Holocaust Memorial Center, Farmington Hills, a boy of fourteen, tears rolling down his face, told me that his grandfather had been a Nazi. I took the child in my arms, repeating a few times that he is not responsible for the actions of his grandfather, that it took courage for him to tell me this, and courage for his parents to share this information with him.

I try to live by the Jewish principle of *"Tikun Olam,"* repairing the world. In my small way I work to make the world a better place for all. I do so by volunteering my time and skills in various areas of communal life. I serve on the board of directors of the American Jewish Committee, the oldest civil rights organization in United States. This group works tirelessly to create both a nation and a world that promote pluralism and freedom for all religious and cultural groups. Only in a world in which all minorities are respected can we, as Jews, have our rights safeguarded. Though not religious, I am a deeply rooted, spiritual Jew. I take pride in my heritage and in what we Jews contribute in many spheres of life to the enrichment of our country, the United States. I feel fortunate and grateful for the opportunity to call this nation my home.

My life has been filled with pain and with joy. I continue to have a high level of energy, a joy of living, and a desire to learn and grow. Immediately after retirement I entered an arts study program, an endeavor I had no time for while employed. As a docent at the Detroit Institute of Arts, it gives me great pleasure to continue gaining knowledge of the arts, cultures, and history, and sharing it with the public. With each new exhibit I am excited to learn more and to share more. Like a school kid, I feel some apprehension before each exam.

My eagerness to be challenged, to learn new skills, led me to become a volunteer mediator for the courts. I find my psychology and sociology background helpful, particularly in family mediation.

I continue counting my blessings and have many on my list: my family, my friends, and my health that permits me to carry out activities that reward me.

Halina and her family live in Israel and I visit them every year. She and her husband Wolek have been my guests in the United States several times. For many years Halina has been suffering with chronic depression and now is in very poor health altogether.

My mother spent the remainder of her life in Israel. For three years she lived in a tent, until my husband David and I left Israel and gave her our part of a Quonset hut. She died when she was in her fifties, still a young woman. I was writing weekly letters to my mother, and when I was able to afford it, I brought her over to visit me in the United States. She enjoyed the visit, in spite of her poor health. Though I had not lived with my mother since I was a little girl, after her death I felt an intense pain and sadness at being a real orphan.

In spite of all the difficulties, pain, and losses I have experienced, I believe in the potential for goodness in people and in the power of the human spirit.

My life is full. I wake up in the morning and the world looks good.

I am a Holocaust survivor, and still the proverbial cat of nine lives, but they exist in harmony. One of my past lives finds a warm home in the Michigan Holocaust Child Survivors group. I speak at the Holocaust Memorial Center about my experiences and the moral lessons, and will go to almost any school, or group if invited to talk on the Holocaust subject. I hope that hearing the life experiences directly from survivors, others might understand the horrors prejudice and hate cause, and learn to be on guard to prevent future atrocities from happening.

I may be contacted at nomanslandmiller@gmail.com for speaking engagements and group discussions.